MONEY FOR LIFE

The "Money Makeover"
That Will End Your Worries
and Secure Your Dreams

STEVE CROWLEY

SIMON & SCHUSTER
New York ◆ London ◆ Toronto ◆ Sydney ◆ Tokyo ◆ Singapore

SIMON & SCHUSTER
Simon & Schuster Building
Rockefeller Center
1230 Avenue of the Americas
New York, New York 10020

Designed by Irving Perkins Associates
Manufactured in the United States of America

1   3   5   7   9   10   8   6   4   2

First Edition
Library of Congress Cataloging-in-Publication data
is available

ISBN: 0-671-76124-2

Contents

I
THE DREAM

I

THE DREAM

1

The Money Makeover
That Will Change Your Life

THROUGH the miracle of television and radio, I counsel 25 million Americans about money matters every weekday of the year on syndicated Money/Pro reports seen and heard in more than 100 major cities. For four and one-half years I reached another 5 to 10 million people 125 times a year as the money editor of "Good Morning America." Hours of talk radio, seminars, and several live TV programs every month, as well as volumes of mail every week, put me in touch with many thousands more people on a one-to-one basis. To judge by what's on their minds, I can only conclude that there's a great deal of apprehension in our land, and many restless and dissatisfied people. They don't feel well off, they're unhappy in their work, they're displeased about their surroundings, and they're scared about the future. They see themselves more and more vulnerable to inflation, recessions, and the whims of their employers. They sense that they're falling behind financially, feel encumbered by debt, and are incapable of saving for their children's college education or supporting aged parents.

Worst of all, they are beginning to doubt the ability of our democratic institutions to solve our country's problems and to improve their own situations in the process.

It's conceivable, of course, that I'm hearing only from a minority of malcontents, that the overwhelming majority of my audience is so pleased with life it feels no need to complain. But I don't believe that's true because the message I'm getting from my callers and letter-writers is reflected in the concerns of my friends and colleagues.

Problems, of course, are as individual as fingerprints, but virtually every story I'm told contains two basic elements: The first is that the storyteller is not living the life of his or her dreams, or anything close to it; the second is that he or she hasn't the financial wherewithal to effect the kinds of changes that might transform those dreams into reality.

I can't imagine anything worse in life than doing something that makes you unhappy in a place where you don't want to be—and I am speaking from experience. I started my professional life in 1970 as a certified public accountant in Providence, Rhode Island. At the time my net worth was zero. Within three years, at the age of twenty-six, I was a manager at Price Waterhouse & Co., one of the legendary Big Eight accounting firms, making an exceptional living. Then I quit to start my own firm, and before long I was earning more money than I'd ever dreamed of. I owned a spacious colonial house on an acre of land, a Mercedes 450SL, a BMW, and a Cadillac, and a Wellcraft speedboat that in today's dollars would cost $60,000. By 1981 I had more possessions than I needed, all the money I could use, and the ability to do anything I wanted. But I was not a happy man.

Nor were any number of my peers happy—men who, like me, had started with nothing, prospered to the same degree, and used their new wealth, just as I had done, to buy as many expensive possessions as they could. Remember that bumper sticker that said, "The one with the most toys wins"? That was us. One of my ultrasuccessful clients called his possessions "gim-cracks." One day he said to me, "I've been through all the gimcracks, Steve, and I've discovered that gimcracks don't make you happy." At the time, I wasn't convinced. I truly believed that yet another Mercedes, bigger than the one I already owned, would make me happy, or, if that didn't, then a bigger boat would make me happy. And none of it made me happy. I became increasingly miserable—and increasingly aware of the source of my discontent.

I hadn't fulfilled my dreams. I was living in the wrong place and not doing the one thing I had always wanted to do, which was to be a broadcaster. I was as miscast as Eddie Murphy playing Hamlet. I was thirty-four years old, and I hated myself.

Take the word of a man who's been there: If you're not doing what you want to be doing in the place you want to be doing it, the amount of money you're making is absolutely irrelevant.

The paradox, of course, is that without enough money you're immo-bilized, incapable of addressing your discontent. No matter how pure or exalted your dreams may be, they are inevitably intertwined with the reality of your financial condition. Given the hard times that so many Americans seem to be experiencing, it's little wonder that they complain of being incapable of living life according to their dreams.

Lord knows, it's not for lack of trying. At Senate hearings in the 1950s futurists predicted that computers and robotics would make life so easy by the year 1990 that we would all be working six hours a day and three days a week. As we all know, just the opposite has happened. High technology has put more, not fewer, burdens on us, and we all seem to be working harder and faster and longer. As 1991 began, more than 7 million Americans were working at two jobs to try to make ends meet—a higher number than ever before.

Virtually every communication I receive from viewers and listeners contains the same question, whether explicit or implied: *What am I doing wrong?* The circumstances they describe are so similar that nine times out of ten they provoke the same reply. "My friend," I say, "you can learn everything there is to know about how to protect your money or make it grow without learning the most important lesson of all, which is that money is nothing more than a tool to improve your life. Building mountains of money won't help you a bit unless and until you learn how to use your resources to achieve your dreams, reduce your stress, and earn the feeling that you're a vital, useful person. What you need, first and foremost, is a financial strategy that works in both good times and bad, a strategy whose objective is not to produce vast wealth and countless toys but an authentic and gratifying life."

It's when they get into the specifics of money management that so many of the people I hear from demonstrate how truly disoriented they've become. By and large, they are attempting to operate in the nineties with financial concepts they learned in the sixties and seventies. That's just not going to work because the rules we lived by in those days have little if any bearing on the economic realities of today.

REALITY NUMBER ONE: DEFLATION CAN HURT US MORE THAN INFLATION

Most of us are all too familiar with the word "inflation" and its impact on our wallets and assets. We were born into inflationary times, so experiencing inflation became as familiar to us as driving down a freeway, watching TV, or strapping ourselves into the seat of a jet airplane. The knowledge that most objects would be worth more and cost more next year than they do this year, that our dollars would buy fewer goods and services next year than they do today, became part of our sensory input. At first, all we could do was worry about inflation and struggle to cope with it. Then we began to learn how to turn it to our advantage.

In the motion picture *Lost In America*, actor Albert Brooks rejoiced about the wonderful ride he and his wife had taken on the "inflation train." They could cash in their California house for far more than they'd paid for it and retire, at least temporarily, to the good life. The picture rang a bell for many of us because during the seventies and eighties inflation had become our seductive friend. In truth, it was a friend to the "haves" and an enemy to the "have-nots." If you were living paycheck-to-paycheck, with few assets, chances were your standard of living was going down. Everything else, it seemed, was going up: hamburgers, which cost fifteen cents in 1965; new cars, $2,850 when I bought my first, a Chevrolet Impala; even the Beverly Hills minimansion, including servants' quarters and projection room, which I priced for the heck of it in 1969 and could have had for the now paltry sum of $125,000. The way to beat inflation soon became clear: buy real estate, collectibles, stocks, a business, and then you'd be on the inflation gravy train—because each year the value of these properties would rise as a reflection of increasing demand and the diminished value of the dollar. Inflation seemed to be offering "something for nothing," and in a sense it was, but only if you had lots of noncash assets that were going up in value.

Then along came Donald Trump, the man who taught us that inflation couldn't and didn't operate at all times. He would outbid the competition on a building or a business, fully expecting to ride the inflation train yet another time, just as he'd done so consistently and with such spectacular results for so many years. What Donald failed to notice was that the train had stopped, reversed direction, and renamed itself the "Deflation Express."

Deflation starts when supply begins to outweigh demand, when financial promises can't be kept, and when the enormous debt bubble bursts. Unless you're well into your seventies, you probably don't remember the last time the United States experienced a deflationary cycle. It happened back in the 1930s, when the two "D" words, depression and deflation, went hand in hand. Prices plunged, and cash was king because nobody seemed to have any. Dollar bills were valuable; you could paper your wall with stock and bond certificates. Debts went unpaid, people went jobless, houses went empty. Those who did have cash bought up everything in sight at increasingly lower prices. Savvy investors knew the cycle would complete itself and prices would start rising once again. All they had to do was wait. In this manner, a fresh batch of millionaires was made.

Imagine a financial world turned topsy-turvy, a world in which our dollars—if we had any—would buy more stocks, small businesses, real estate, commodities, even cheaper food a year from now than they would today. Can it happen in the nineties? To an extent, it already has. As 1991 began, you could buy a house in many parts of the country for two-thirds of what it would have cost you just two years earlier. In the fall of 1990 you could buy many stocks that make up the Dow-Jones average for 25 percent less than you would have paid for them just six months earlier. As early as mid-November 1990 the major retailers were offering price cuts in anticipation of a sluggish Christmas shopping season. Throughout the recession of 1991 fast-food chains were offering "specials," a code word for price cuts.

Deflation, of course, is the opposite of inflation. Yet it's possible to experience deflation and inflation at the same time—some goods and services becoming less expensive, others continuing to rise in price. Even in those circumstances, however, the inflationary game, which worked so well for so many people during the seventies and eighties, will not work any longer.

Will deflation continue, and, if so, for how long and with what effect? No one, of course, knows the answers, but a lot of economists and market analysts earn a handsome living by making informed predictions.

We all know that prices are based fundamentally on the laws of supply and demand. What is often forgotten, however, is that demand is based in good part on emotion. When times are good and people are euphoric, they tend to overspend and borrow to keep up the buying spree. When times are bad and people are depressed, they stop spending and borrowing. It follows, therefore, that recessions, depressions, and deflation are reflections, to some extent at least, of fear and anguish. Many economists felt that the recessionary fears being exhibited as the nineties began were unwarranted because they did not reflect economic realities. That did not stop employers from tightening their budgets and laying off employees, nor did it stop investors from fleeing the stock market and rushing toward safer, interest-bearing bank accounts. Inflation makes us want to spend more while our dollars are worth more, while deflation encourages us to hold off on the purchase of a house or an investment in common stocks. Such tendencies, of course, are bad for business, and deflationary pressures are further increased. In such an environment, stock prices can go into a free-fall, interest on savings can drop to 3 percent, and—as so many Americans have already learned to their pain and sorrow—the value of houses can plummet.

REALITY NUMBER TWO: A HOUSE IS NO LONGER A GUARANTEED NEST EGG

The bedrock of our financial faith used to be that our principal residence would provide us with the equity we'd trade in on retirement for that condo on the golf course. The faith was so substantial it gave rise to people I call "houseaholics." "Why bother to save?" they said. "I have my house." They counted on big equity bucks to bail them out of bad savings habits. No longer. Deflation has seen to that.

In many parts of the United States today, Americans are living in houses worth less than they paid for them. Phoenix is in a real estate depression reminiscent of the 1930s. A young man I know in Orlando watched the value of his house plummet by $50,000 in two years. In Boston and Providence, prices of houses fell in 1989 by almost as much as they rose in 1988. Even California, whose skyrocketing real estate prices throughout the eighties seemed as though they would never reach orbit, began a downward descent as the nineties began; by the fall of 1990 prices in many neighborhoods of the Golden State were down 5 to 20 percent from the fall of 1989.

In many states, the value of houses has sunk so far that people are simply walking away from mortgages that exceed the value of the property. A number of economists and mortgage bankers have referred to these shaky loans as "neutron bomb" mortgages. After the values drop, the houses are still standing and the people are gone.

REALITY NUMBER THREE: A SOCIETY OF BORROWERS DOES NOT PROSPER

Another article of faith in the sixties and seventies was that borrowing and leveraging would make us rich in the long run. Today we know that control and ownership make us rich in the long run.

Most of us grew up believing that credit was what made this country tick, and that anyone who paid cash was actually losing money because debts could be paid off with ever-cheaper dollars. The government and corporations taught us to live for today and pay tomorrow. We figured that if they were doing it, we could do it ourselves. The big difference is that the government can print money and corporations can raise it through stock issues, but we can't do either.

Today millions of people are "upside down" on their loans, meaning that the loans on their houses and automobiles exceed the value of these properties. Our society is rife with "chargeaholics," people who carry a dozen credit cards, have large balances on most of them, and end up paying twice for everything. So enslaved have we become to the plastic habit that we're even using credit cards in the supermarket. Very few of us could buy a house outright, but why on earth would you want to pay interest on your grocery bill if you don't have to?

This live-for-today, pay-tomorrow mentality has brought our banking system to the edge of ruin. We used to think that if anything was secure, it was the bank in which we kept our money. Almost every deposit was insured by the government up to $100,000. Today, not only are savings and loan banks failing by the hundreds but commercial banks are in danger as well, and although deposits are still insured the system that insures them is virtually tapped out.

The junk bond crisis of recent years was really the ultimate expression of a belief in debt so profound that we stopped caring if it would ever be paid back.

That mind-set is changing. We have come to the realization that the borrower society we've created is not working, and that we must find a smarter, craftier way to live. We have seen a resurgence of people trying to figure out a way to get out of debt. They don't know how, but they are trying—some of them seeing credit counselors, others ripping up their credit cards, still others attempting to end their "chargeaholic" dependency by stopping cold turkey.

REALITY NUMBER FOUR: FAR FEWER TAX BREAKS

In the sixties and seventies one of the most important considerations of any investment or expenditure was its potential tax consequences. Today, that's no longer true. Taxes are important, but not nearly to the extent that they were. Loopholes have been closed. Real estate shelters don't shelter much, if anything. And tycoon and small businessman alike can deduct only so much for their cars, regardless of how much they paid for them.

Remember how we thought when we bought a car ten years ago? Let's say the car cost $10,000, and the sales tax was 4 percent, or $400. Well, gee, that's not so bad, we told ourselves. We can live with that, because the $400 is deductible. And we put $1,500 down and financed $8,500, which meant $2,500 in interest over the life of the loan and we thought, that isn't so bad, the $2,500 is deductible. Today neither sales taxes nor interest payments on anything other than house loans are deductible.

The reason the auto industry has recently been in a slump has far less to do with the state of the economy than it does with the realization on the part of Americans, several years after the fact, that deductions on automobile purchases have gone to zero. Consumers used to buying a new car every three years can't handle the load anymore. Rather than become "upside down" once again on their loans, they have decided to fix up the '87 Olds and drive it another four years.

REALITY NUMBER FIVE: LIVING PATTERNS THAT DO NOT PRODUCE EQUITIES

In the sixties and seventies, we prepared ourselves for the working world on the assumption that we would have but one career. Our models were often our parents. My father, a butcher, worked at the same market for 32 years. When I started my professional life as a certified public accountant, one of my firm's clients was a manufacturer of water heaters that distributed a pamphlet about retirement benefits to every new employee, no matter how young, illustrated with a picture of an elderly man smoking a pipe and seated by a fireplace. That image was designed to encourage the employee to dedicate his or her life to the company, and many people actually did that. That concept is now as outmoded as the image.

Today many Americans get two or more graduate degrees and have two or three careers, sometimes two at once. They can't see themselves spending their working lives at a single job. They seem uninterested in making an investment in a firm and building a relationship with their employer. As an employer, I find that people become bored more easily than they used to, and take less kindly to criticism. On more than one occasion I've sat down with a writer to go over his script, only to have the writer say, "I quit."

Along with the desire for professional change comes a desire to move about. Young people starting out today talk about spending part of their lives in Montana or Seattle or somewhere in the Sunbelt. When I was growing up in New England I lived among people who couldn't conceive of moving away, and couldn't understand anyone who did. Today, New Englanders by the thousands are relocating in Florida, and the average American remains in the same dwelling no more than seven years.

All this change undoubtedly makes for a more exciting life, but there are consequences to career and geographic mobility that require us to rethink our economic game plan. When you change jobs every three or four years you're not going to retire with a pension. When you sell a house every few years, you're not going to build an equity, even during periods when house prices are rising. For most Americans, building an equity in their houses was almost their only savings. When equity buildup is subtracted, they saved less than 2 percent a year during the last fifty years, far less than Europeans or Japanese.

Without pensions or home equities, where will the money come from to finance the golden years? If you think the answer is to settle into that job you've got, after all, even though you're unhappy, you had better think again.

REALITY NUMBER SIX: THE DECLINE OF JOB SECURITY

Another assumption of the working world was that loyalty, talent, and effort translated to guaranteed employment. Today job security is one of our most perishable myths. Across the country corporations are replacing valuable employees with people half their age who will work for half the salary. The even sadder truth is that the older person, after being displaced, may not be able to find employment in his or her chosen profession, let alone at the same salary level. If we don't adapt quickly to the new rules of play, and stay flexible and malleable in our careers, we may experience bitter days without work and sharply decreased income. Once, while covering the failure of Braniff for WPLG TV in Miami, I met an ex-Braniff captain who was selling shoes to make ends meet.

Increasingly, corporations are insisting that employees take a pay cut as the price of keeping their jobs. One Friday in 1990 an American corporation fired all of its executives and managers. The following Monday, it offered all of them their jobs back at half-pay. "We're in a contracting industry," management offered by way of explanation, "one that's already experiencing a depression, with rising costs and smaller revenues each year. If we're to stay in business, we have no other choice but to do what we did. We hope you'll stay with us, but we can't afford you at the salaries you were making."

Those forced to take a cut in pay may find their benefits dwindling too. In the old days Blue Cross benefits cost $35 a month per employee. Today they can run $600 a month, and more. Because the inflation rate for medical services and health insurance is between 15 and 25 percent a year, employers by the thousands are dropping health care plans on the grounds that they can't afford them. Today, one-third of the working population has no health insurance at all, and a federal court ruled recently that corporations may stop delivering health benefits to retirees.

"Downsizing," the act of eliminating jobs, especially on the management level, in order to produce as much or more revenue with fewer employees, is yet another management option especially popular in times of deflation. A recent estimate put the number of jobs lost per month because of downsizing at 30,000. That's 1,400 jobs lost per day. But downsizing isn't merely a phenomenon of deflationary times. During the roaring eighties, some 3 million middle-management positions were lost, an average of 25,000 a month.

Why are corporations cutting back? There are a number of reasons: greater and tougher sales and product competition, both nationally and internationally; more pressure from stockholders to deliver increased profits each year; shortsightedness of management, which focuses on raising profits at whatever cost, with no reference to long-term growth; consolidations; debt-financing and higher interest costs forcing layoffs in order to balance the corporate budget.

Whatever the reason or combination of reasons, the bottom line, if you're employed, is that there's no longer any such thing as guaranteed job security. If your job isn't secure, it follows that your pension isn't either.

REALITY NUMBER SEVEN: THE NEED TO FINANCE A LONGER RETIREMENT

We grew up believing that a working life of forty to forty-five years would be followed by a brief retirement. We thought of seventy as old—and, even more to the point, the seventy-year-old thought of seventy as old. Today seventy-year-olds are playing in tennis tournaments and running gates on the ski slopes. More healthful living habits combined with rapidly advancing medical technology have given us a life expectancy far greater than existed for our parents when we were born. The most recent actuarial tables suggest that most women will live to be ninety-five and most men to eighty-five.

But what will life be like for us during these twenty to thirty years of retirement? Will they be the golden years they are supposed to be, or will they be corroded by want and financial worry?

The greatest fear among older people today is that they will run out of money before they run out of life. Even persons in their forties and fifties, caught in today's economic squeeze, are worried about life past sixty-five because very few persons in that age bracket have saved for retirement. With the value of money cut in half approximately every ten to twelve years, along with the decline of job security and fringe benefits, those who don't prepare could wind up working at McDonald's. What could be worse than to turn sixty-five knowing that you have twenty good years of life left and not enough money to enjoy them?

There's no need for that to happen. We *can* survive deflation, be free of debt, ahead of inflation, and secure for life by the twenty-first century. We *can* live our dreams, in both good times and bad. What's needed, first and foremost, is a complete overhaul of our financial strategies, to accord with the realities of the nineties. I call it a "money makeover."

THE MONEY MAKEOVER: WHAT IT IS, WHY YOU PROBABLY NEED IT, AND HOW IT WILL HELP YOU ACHIEVE YOUR DREAMS

A "money makeover" determines to what degree you're living in ways you neither intended nor desired, and then helps you rebuild your life financially in terms of what you really want. The day you start your makeover those money pressures that have been grinding you down will begin to ease, and you'll know that, while you haven't arrived where you want to be, you're at least on the right track. Within months you'll be a far happier human being, with a greatly enhanced self-image. I guarantee that when you have $25,000 in the bank you'll awaken in the morning with an entirely different feeling about yourself than you do when you're $25,000 in hock.

When I was a teenager, I met an elderly man who had made a great deal of money throughout his lifetime. "Steve," he said, "if you want to be a millionaire, it's really very simple. You make your plan, and you work your plan." Working the plan is the easy part. It's making it that's tough—unless we know what to do, and how and when to do it. That's the purpose of this book.

There are dozens upon dozens of books about personal finance, and most of them offer sound advice. But not one of them, in my opinion, goes far enough. They may instruct you on how to buy your home and automobile right, and how to buy the right insurance, but they don't put these instructions in the context of whether you're living your life right.

Everything you need to know about beating inflation, diminishing debt, and building a fortune is included in this book. But we begin with a far more primary task, helping you to resurrect that spirit of idealism and sense of purpose that motivated you when your working life began.

You'll start by compiling a "Makeover Wish List" that will leave no doubts about what you want to do with your life, where you want to do it and with whom. Is your dream of dreams to quit your job and go into business for yourself? To move to Florida or California or the Pacific Northwest? To gain more free time? The important agenda at this point is to come clean to yourself about what you want to do with your life and what would make you happy, even if it requires you to confront some truths you hadn't wanted to face.

Once you've identified your dream, you'll price it, discovering what kind of lump sum you'll need at the outset, the amount of income you'll require as you proceed, and the amount of effort it's going to take. You'll learn how to calculate the key equation in any change, the expense/reward ratio.

Next, you'll develop a three-step plan for chasing your dream: how to set the stage, how to target your new source of income, and how to gain support for your plan from those it will affect.

Now, with your dream identified, targeted, and in your sights, you're ready to consider personal money matters in the context of the kind of life you really want.

We begin your makeover with the most primary task of all: changing the manner in which you spend your money. You'll learn how to cut your spending a little here and a little there until you've got a sum significant enough to make a difference in your life. More important, you'll replace bad habits with good habits in the process. We'll also teach you how to calculate your Personal Inflation Index.

Next, we'll look at the deceptively easy manner in which debt can turn from ally to foe. We'll distinguish between good and bad debt, and set guidelines for evaluating how much debt makes sense. And we'll teach you how to beat the banks at their own game, extracting yourself from debt years ahead of schedule.

Then we'll turn to savings, establishing how much you should have at a minimum, then describing several different strategies for getting started— the first of which could help you to change your entire perspective on saving. If you're a parent of college-bound children, we'll show you how to start today on a program that *will* guarantee there'll be enough money on hand when the time comes to pony up.

We'll take a close look at your greatest expense, your shelter. Whether you're a renter, a first-time buyer, or a longtime owner, we'll show you how the new rules of the game apply to you. We'll discuss clever tricks for first-time house buyers, talk about the best mortgages, and, if you're one of those lucky enough to have a sizable equity in your house, how to transform that equity to cash.

We'll take a close look, as well, at the second biggest expense in most households, transportation, and tell you why you may want to change your car-buying and -financing habits.

Then we'll look at investing to show you how to pyramid your savings so that you'll be earning at least 12 percent a year, the magic number if you don't want to fall behind inflation. Whole books have been written about mutual funds; but in fact you don't need to know more than a chapter's worth to make an intelligent choice—and we'll show you how to do that.

We'll talk about the new tax game and how to win it, how to protect your family with the right kind of insurance, and how to retire early and rich in the ways that make for a fruitful life.

I repeat: Our objective is a financial strategy that works every bit as soundly in bad times as it does in good times. The objective of this strategy is not to see how much money you can accumulate but how much happiness you can create for yourself and your loved ones as you pursue and achieve your dreams.

2

Identifying Your Dream

WHAT goals did you set for yourself when you were starting out? To be worth a million dollars by a certain age? To own your own business? To do a lot of traveling? To learn to play a sport well? To gain a sense of inner peace?— How many of those goals have you achieved?

What do you consider your greatest accomplishment, and how does that accomplishment measure up to your expectations of yourself? Do you consider yourself today the person you started out to be? If your doctor were to tell you tomorrow that you were suffering from an incurable disease and had only a few months to live, what would you most regret not having done?

If a family member or a friend were to shoot a dozen close-ups of you, would you like what you'd see in those pictures? Would it be the face of a happy and contented person, or one filled with worries and frustration? If it were the face of a stranger, would you get the instinctive feeling that here was someone at peace with himself or herself, someone you'd like and admire?

Where do you want to be five years from now, and what would you like to be doing? How about ten years from now? Twenty years from now?

Who are the people you admire most, and what could you do to be more like them?

What do you least like about your life right now, and how would you like to change it? Are you able to devote enough time right now to the people who mean the most to you?

What would make you happy or, if you already consider yourself happy, happier than you are today?

These may be obvious questions, but the answers are neither obvious nor easy. They require a lot of soul-searching, and probably some fact-gathering, as well, because you may not have the information you require to know specifically what you want. To help you identify your dream, I've broken the quest down into eight specific areas.

WHERE DO I WANT TO LIVE?

Choosing the right place to live is, to my mind, the single most important decision you can make to achieve a happier life. Asked in a 1990 poll how they would have changed their lives, one in five senior citizens said they would have lived in a different place. A majority of the successful people I've interviewed attribute a great measure of their success to a wise choice of place in which to live and work. Conversely, many people have succeeded in conventional terms but don't enjoy the areas in which they live and work.

Recently I met a native of Los Angeles who had moved to Boston because he felt it was the right place to center his business, a not-for-profit organization that finances college educations. If you want to put your child through college but don't have the equity to borrow the money, The Education Resource Institute, with over $50 million in equity, will put up the collateral for your loan and charge you a fee for doing so over and above the interest you'll pay on the loan. Considering that you couldn't have secured the loan without the institute, it is providing a valuable service and has earned the success it enjoys. When I met one of the founders of the company, I immediately noted that he didn't have a Boston accent. "How come?" I asked. He told me that he'd lived in Los Angeles until he was thirty-one, but had located the company in Boston because with so many institutions of higher learning in the area the city was identified in the public mind as the center of education. "I don't like the climate in Boston," he admitted. "It's so cold and dismal."

"What do you do about it?" I asked.

"During the winter, I'm constantly traveling. Our biggest markets are Florida and California, so I just make it a point to be in those states during the coldest months of the year."

What follows seems so self-evident that it probably doesn't need saying, but I've met so many people who have lived their lives in environments they dislike that I'm going to say it anyway. It behooves you, before anything, to ask yourself if you're living where you really want to be.

Of all the factors that go into choosing an enjoyable place to live, climate is undoubtedly the most important. Preferences vary. Some people require days filled with warmth and sunshine virtually around the year. Others prefer environments with four distinctive seasons. Dedicated residents of the Pacific Northwest readily accept the frequent rains that give their region its incomparable beauty. Minneapolis residents don't seem to mind the cold at all; to the contrary, everyone I've ever met from that city looks forward to winter as a time for winter sports.

But if you're living in the Northeast or the Midwest and you don't like to shovel snow or drive on icy streets, you're probably not going to realize the life of your dreams no matter what else you do. Once again, I speak from personal experience. A major factor in my decision to move from Rhode Island to Florida was that I couldn't stand cold weather and the many dark, dismal days that characterize Rhode Island in winter. I mean no offense to the good people of Rhode Island, among whom I count many relatives and friends, and with whom I share many wonderful memories. But I am a person whose disposition is directly affected by the climate. If it's overcast, so am I. If it's sunny, so am I. When October or November rolled around in New England, I would go into a depression that I wouldn't come out of until spring. It was for this reason, more than any other, that I became obsessed with moving to a warmer climate. From the moment I arrived in Florida, I felt a measure of happiness each day no matter how my fortunes were faring. My experience wasn't exceptional; according to medical doctors, many people suffer from "seasonal affective disorder," or SAD as it's aptly known. Prolonged periods without light cause the pineal gland, which is located at the base of the brain, to secrete a hormone called melatonin, which adversely affects not only the emotions but one's mental and physical state. The only known remedies are sunshine and bright lights.

Of all the factors in choosing a *practical* place to live, the economic environment is the most obvious. That's true today in the United States more than it has ever been. In school we learned about the Great Depression, an experience that afflicted Americans everywhere. One of the singular characteristics of the nineties is how regionalized boom-and-bust cycles have become. If you live in the Pacific Northwest these days, the chances are you're relatively well off; if you live in Massachusetts, you could be in trouble. Areas that were up just a few years ago are down today, and vice versa. Seattle today is booming largely because Boeing, its biggest employer, is prospering, and also because so many people from California want to move up there to benefit from the area's extraordinary quality of life. But it seems like only yesterday that Boeing had completed work on its jumbo aircraft and was laying workers off left and right, producing a recession throughout the area. Someone back then erected what may be the best-remembered billboard sign in America. It said, "Will the last person to leave Seattle please turn off the lights?"

Texas was a disaster area just a few years ago. You could buy a mansion in Houston for the price of a modest home in Los Angeles. Today the state is on a strong rebound. Conversely, Arizona, which just five years ago was portrayed in national magazines as Boomtown, USA, was being portrayed in 1990 as Ghost Town, USA, by those same publications.

Just fifteen years ago, Florida was perceived as a sleepy retirement haven. When I moved to Florida from Rhode Island in 1981 my friends told me I was nuts. Only old people move to Florida, they said. Today many of those same friends are trying to figure out how to move to Florida, which each week receives 5,000 new residents.

Real estate is particularly sensitive to regional economic conditions. In midsummer of 1990, Norman Flynn, the head of The National Association of Realtors, declared that the fifty states of the union were equally divided between those that had a down real estate market and those that had an up one. So choosing the right area at the right time can determine, over the long term, whether you will make or lose money on any real estate you acquire.

The right choice of locale can gain you other economic benefits, some of them intangible. If you have the entrepreneurial spirit and want to start a business, you can give yourself at least a psychological edge by starting your venture in a place other than your hometown. At home, you must deal with the fear of failing in front of family and friends. In a new environment you can fail without notoriety. It's not just your ego that's on the line; to the degree that you're worried about failing, you're going to be less enterprising and courageous—the very qualities you may need to make your venture a success.

A second economic benefit of a wise choice of locale is the savings in time. If you're a commuter, you know first hand that few things are more expensive than a long commute. A wisely chosen new locale can give you two extra hours of productive time a day and save you the cost of commuting, as well. Between the two, you could be ahead thousands of dollars. The psychological benefits are incalculable.

Given the importance of finding a locale you enjoy, it astounds me how little effort most people put into doing that. I know Bostonians who have never been west of Chicago and Californians who have never been east of Las Vegas. If they don't know what's out there, how can they be certain they're living in the best possible environment?

Where you think you want to live may prove, on inspection, to be unsuitable. A place far down on your list may turn out to be exactly what you're looking for. The only way you'll know is through a great deal of exploring and testing. Years ago, when airplane travel was relatively slow and expensive, travelers learned about the United States through the window of an automobile or the observation platform of a train. If you're not living your dream life and you sense it's because you're in the wrong place, I recommend that on your next vacation you emulate your ancestors and use your car or a train to visit regions of the United States where you sense you might want to live. That's exactly what I'd done in the five years prior to my move to Florida. By the time I made my decision, I'd sampled every region of the country that met my requirement for a year-round sunny climate. For years I'd been conducting a love affair with Los Angeles, which, despite its problems, is one of the most enjoyable cities in the country, and had spent every minute of my free time there, but I chose Fort Lauderdale over Los Angeles because the cost of living was so much lower and also because I would be nearer to my two children from my first marriage.

WHAT KIND OF WORK DO I WANT TO DO?

There are thousands of options out there; unless special circumstances tie you down, there is no more need to be working at a job you hate than there is to continue living where you don't want to be. Here are just a few stories from a bulging file of people who decided to live their dreams:

• A New England housewife who at forty-six announced to her family that she'd decided to become a pediatrician. Against the strenuous objections of her husband and children, she enrolled in medical school. Today she has one of the biggest pediatric practices in the Northeast.

• A successful but unhappy businessman who wanted to be a golf pro. Today, he's teaching golf, earning far less money but enjoying life far more.

• A couple who lived in California and elected to cash in on the tremendous equity in their house and move to a less expensive locale. They chose South Carolina, where the temperature was similar to California, they could sail year-round, and the price of their new house was one-tenth the price of their old one. They're not earning as much in their jobs, but the income from the money they freed up has bought them tranquility and freedom.

Living one's dream often requires economic sacrifice at the outset, and occasionally there's no economic return at all, just the satisfaction of doing what you want. I once heard from a successful financier who had dreamed all his life of playing the piano. One day he walked out of his office, never to return, hired a teacher, and began to practice four hours a day. Two years later, he was an accomplished pianist.

In the summer of 1990 I received a newsletter from the committee working on a twenty-fifth reunion of my high-school class. A paragraph in the newsletter was devoted to a member of the class who at age forty-three, with a wife and children, was quitting his job to go to law school. He has tough years ahead of him, but he's decided that he didn't want to die without being able to say that he'd been a lawyer.

People who discover that they studied for the wrong career, or spent years in the wrong profession, are not unique to this era. The difference today is that there is a propensity among those who make such discoveries to acknowledge their mistakes and endeavor to rectify them. Perhaps you've listened to Dr. Dean Edell, who dispenses advice on radio and TV. To judge by his range of knowledge and assuredness, I assumed that he'd been a practicing physician for years. But one day, he admitted that he'd never enjoyed medical practice and had only done enough of it to get his license. Once he had it, however, he quit medical practice to do a variety of other things, one of which was broadcasting. What he really enjoyed, he told his listeners, was dispensing advice on radio and TV.

When it comes to being a misfit, I suppose I'm my own best example. In 1981 I was that successful but miserable CPA I described in chapter 1. I'd become a CPA because of family pressure. I was good at it, but I eventually started to hate it. I realized I should have gone off in a totally different direction. But by 1981 I was making so much money that relinquishing the work seemed like an exercise in self-destruction. As much as I detested what I was doing, I was very proud of being a CPA. Those three letters after my name were very important to me. Without them I didn't feel like a professional. Giving them up would be like a doctor relinquishing the letters MD after his name.

By this point, however, I'd been working in television and radio part-time, mostly without pay, for seven years, partly because I loved doing it and partly to receive training against the day when I might have the chance to live my dream. On a morning in August 1981 my ambivalence came to an end. When I arrived at work, I found two lawyers, both good friends of mine, in my office. "What are you doing here?" I said.

"We don't know," one of them replied. "Carl told us to be here. He said he wanted to say something to you in our presence."

When my partner Carl Weinberg arrived, he came right to the point. "I want a partner who's fully committed to our partnership and our clients, and you're not that man," he said.

Carl proposed that we split everything in half, the building, the employees, the clients.

"I'm not going to do that," I said. "That's too disruptive. But you're right, I do want to pursue a career in television. I'll make the decision right now. I'm out of the CPA business. I'm going to go into the next office and I'll put a number down on a piece of paper and that's what I want. I'll give it to the lawyers. If the price and the terms are acceptable, I'm out of here today."

So I went into the next room and wrote down a figure that was about half of what I knew my share of the firm was worth. But this was a bargain-basement sellout, and I knew I couldn't get any more. I also knew that Carl would say yes to my offer because he was so upset, and I suddenly wanted out more than anything I'd ever wanted in my life. So I asked for half right away, and another half over two years. The lawyers took my proposal to Carl, and came back minutes later with an agreement. "The only stipulation," one of them said, "is that Carl does want you out today."

"Fine," I said. I was a free man. I had the day off, the week off, the rest of my life off.

Nine out of ten people are said to be as unhappy in their jobs as I was. The dream of most of them is to quit their jobs and strike out on their own, exactly as I did. I could not be more supportive. It's widely believed in our society that owning and controlling your own business, no matter how small, is the key to independence and freedom. I not only subscribe to that belief, I've gambled my whole life on it.

In recent years, the concept of self-employment has undergone a reevaluation, and is today much more broadly applied. The current thinking by career strategists and small-business advisers is that, because you are your own best asset, you are a self-employed person whether you have an employer or not. They argue that when you accept employment, you are really leasing yourself out to an employer. In effect, you are a small business. In an age when more and more people are taking jobs for three, four, or five years, and then moving on, the concept makes a lot of sense. The more frequently you change jobs, the more the concept applies.

The entrepreneurial label is also conferred on those who remain with large companies for many years and through ability and effort rise to significant positions. They may end up being the president of a much bigger company than they could have wound up with by starting from scratch with a bank loan.

But to my mind, the true entrepreneur is the one who strikes out on his or her own.

How do you know whether you've got it in you to be an entrepreneur and live the self-employed life?

The beginnings of the answer are probably in your past; you're far more likely to have a taste for the entrepreneurial life if you were around it in your formative years and liked what you saw.

I had the rare opportunity of growing up in an extended family in which both self-employed and employed people lived under one roof. My father was (and is) an extremely intelligent, well-read man with a vast library filled with books on philosophy and the Civil War. Early on, he had decided that he didn't want to be shackled in any way by the corporate world or to be anybody's boss. He wanted to live an unstressed life so that he could come home at night and read his books. His father had been a steamfitter who believed his union would look after him; he became a meatcutter, with the same faith in his union that his father had held. When management attempted to promote him to a supervisory position, he said, "No, I don't want to manage people. I just want to cut meat." His decision, of course, meant an extremely modest life economically, and so he, my mother, my brother Jeff, and I lived upstairs from my maternal grandparents and one of my mother's brothers.

In contrast to my father, both my grandfather and my uncle were always self-employed. I doubt that they ever considered working for anybody else. My grandfather had been self-employed since his teens, when he quit school to study cello at the New England Conservatory of Music. After his graduation, he played in the Providence Philharmonic and in string quartets that performed in many a Newport mansion. One day, in our attic, I found a diary of his and discovered that as far back as 1908 he was earning as much as $100 a night—during a period when $100 a month was considered a decent salary. There came a time when he felt the need to have something to fall back on, so he opened up a greenhouse and, with my grandmother's help, began to grow plants and flowers. During the day he would be up to his wrists in soil potting plants and at night he would put on his tuxedo, take the train to Boston and play in theater orchestras. My Uncle Bob was exactly like his father in key respects. He quit school at sixteen, just as his father had, bought a piece of land, and built a greenhouse of his own. By the time he was nineteen, he owned several greenhouses and employed a considerable staff.

So, growing up, I had a vivid, daily comparison between being your own boss and working for someone else. For me, in those days, the difference boiled down to a single word: freedom. My father rose very early each morning in order to get to work on time. My grandfather and uncle both got up when they wanted to, had a leisurely breakfast, and went to work at their pleasure. My father took a lunch to work, which he consumed on his break. Both my grandfather and my uncle could take their lunch at home whenever they pleased.

I loved and admired my father, but it was my grandfather and my uncle to whom I gravitated, spending far more time downstairs with them than I did upstairs with my father. They struck me as living a far more exciting life, more on the edge, to be sure, but filled with the highs of success.

There's an undeniable excitement to being an entrepreneur. Each assignment, each contract, each deal becomes a form of conquest, producing its own adrenaline rush. The other side of that, however, is a phenomenally high-anxiety quotient that can ruin your life if you're the kind of person who can't stand uncertainty. I would never characterize the entrepreneurial life as eternally pleasant, and yet it's the life I've chosen to lead. A few years ago, when my fledgling company was still on wobbly legs, I visited with the man who'd been my biggest client when I was a CPA in Rhode Island. He, of course, wanted to know how the company was doing. At the time, I wasn't all that certain it would make it. And I said, "Well, if this doesn't work out, I'll go work for somebody." And he said, "Steve, I sometimes wonder if you know yourself at all. You could never work for anybody. You're much too independent and headstrong." And I said, "You may be right. That's probably why I left Price Waterhouse."

I'm reasonably certain I know what would have happened had I remained at Price Waterhouse, because promises were made to me when I announced my intention to leave. I would be sent to London for a tour of duty, I was told, and in five years I'd be a partner. As a partner, I would have eventually tapped into the Fortune 500 wealth, because Price Waterhouse draws down millions and millions of dollars in audit fees from its major clients. At the time, as an example, Exxon's audit fee was something like $2 million a year. But while my prospective partners were all very rich and successful, they were also extremely regimented. They all seemed to say the same things and act the same way and live by the manual and work far too hard for their own good or, ironically, the good of the families in whose behalf they were presumably working so hard. As far as I was concerned, it was life in the Navy, but without the uniform. That dedication to work and regimentation, which characterizes so many of the Big Six accounting firms, may be one reason why they're having so much trouble these days holding onto their young people.

The entrepreneurial life is definitely not for everyone. When I left Price Waterhouse to start my own firm, one of the managers said, "I could never do that. I need that paycheck every other Friday." In my first year on my own, my income dropped precipitously. But within two years, I was earning twice as much as the people I'd left behind. And in four years, I was earning four times as much. To me, the excitement had meant more than the money.

WHAT INTERESTS DO I WANT TO EXPLORE?

The right locale sets the stage, the right career gives you the wherewithal, but the end purpose of both is—or should be—to enable you to pursue your passions.

We all have passions inside us, those five or six objectives we'll get to, we tell ourselves, when we get the chance or, failing that, when we retire. No. Both your locale and your career must be chosen so that the pursuit of your passions coincides with your pursuit of a living. If those passions aren't integrated into your daily life, you've made the wrong choice of locale or career or both.

Suppose you knew that you had only five years to live. How would you live those years? What experiences would you like to have? What interests would you like to pursue? In answering such questions for myself, I find that making a list is a great cathartic, and to encourage you to do that, I'm going to set out my own:

• Knowing the happiness that reading has brought my father, I have a list of books I intend to read over the next five years.

• Although I studied trombone and guitar and played both instruments in bands, my first love today is piano, in which I have no formal training. I intend to remedy that.

• Almost everyone I meet in my travels abroad speaks a second language. I studied French in school, once spoke it reasonably well, and am in the process of reviving it.

• I love tennis. I know I could play better than I do. I also know from my reading that any quantum improvement in athletic skills can be achieved only if you take time out to relearn the basics and then practice them until they have completely replaced your old skills. Only then do you return to competition. A project like that requires time. In my mind, that time is already reserved.

• I've always envied my scuba diving friends. I'm sure there's a measure of danger attached to the sport, and I confess it scares me a bit, but I know it's something I'm going to get to at some point in my life.

Now that's admittedly a big agenda, but my past experience persuades me that I can fulfill it. I may be an incorrigible dream chaser, but I'm also a systematic one.

I'm at a point in my own life where I know that if I don't systematically plan what I want to achieve I'm not going to achieve it. One of my wishes is to visit the countries of Europe, and so I have started a program of seeing at least two countries a year with my wife, if only for short visits, so that we'll know several years down the line which ones we want to return to for more extended travels. One of those countries, I'm certain, will be France, which we visited briefly in the fall of 1990—a trip, incidentally, that inspired me to revive my French.

But the great passion of my life, aside from my family and my work, is flying. I've loved airplanes from the time I was a little child; when I was three years old I used to ask my mother to drive me to the airport so I could watch the airplanes landing and taking off. One of my first acts after turning twenty-one was to sign up for flying lessons. It turned out that I had hooked up with the wrong flight instructor, because I had such a bad experience that I developed a fear of small airplanes. But ten years later I tried again, and this time I discovered that flying was easily learned, safe, and as enjoyable as anything I'd ever done. From that time on, I was determined to become a proficient pilot. Over the past six years, I've spent more than 400 hours in formal flight training, which adds up to more than 1,000 hours in total flight time, and I have a single engine, multiengine, and an instrument rating. I can't exaggerate the pride I feel in knowing that I can jump into almost any airplane, start it up, and fly away. There's a special camaraderie among pilots—a feeling that "we are" and "they're not"—that I profit from as well.

Gratifications of a similar kind are available to anyone who develops proficiency in anything. Do yourself the favor of not excusing yourself on the grounds that you don't have the time. I run a corporation, do one or two television segments each day, write several scripts and stories, and care for my family, and I find time for my interests. They add immeasurably to my sense of purpose at work. I know that I'm not just working to support my own and my family's existence.

DID I MARRY THE RIGHT SPOUSE?

In that same USA Today survey of senior citizens in which they cited their regret that they hadn't lived in a different place, another of their top five regrets was that they had lived their life with the wrong spouse.

You can be living in the land of your fantasies, holding down your dream job, and enriching your life with the pursuit of your interests, but if you're not sharing all this with the right person, your life will be as sour as month-old milk. Part of the makeover process is to take a hard look at your personal life. If you're not happy, and you've tried marriage counseling and it hasn't helped, the time to change things is now. That's exactly what I did.

I'd met Diane when I was nineteen, and married her when I was twenty-two. We had many good times together, but from the outset of our marriage we began to grow apart. I'm not the kind of man who just gets married and divorced; I really worked at the marriage, but it deteriorated year by year. We had two children, Jessica in 1976 and Scott in 1980, with the hope that they might save the marriage, but our situation only worsened. We'd been married for twelve years by the time I finally gave up. I'd like to think that both of us are good people; we just weren't good together.

Some people need to be married. They're not happy if they're not. I had always suspected that I was one of those people. After my divorce I had an opportunity to test that proposition, and I found it to be absolutely true. It was my great good fortune that I discovered Fran soon after my divorce. We were married in 1984 and now have two children, Sean, born in 1985, and Brent, born in 1989.

The day that I sold my business to my partner and decided to leave Rhode Island was also the day that I decided to divorce my first wife. I told myself that it would be best to change everything at once because, even though it was abrupt, over time it would be the least painful way to proceed for everyone concerned.

WHAT DO I WANT TO GIVE BACK TO SOCIETY?

When you're just beginning a career and embarking on a marriage, the question of what you want to contribute to society during your lifetime, if not exactly irrelevant, is probably premature, unless you're one of those people so well-organized and clearheaded in your thoughts that you've got your entire life worked out by the time you finish college. But there comes a time for most of us when our lives have been defined in the professional and personal realms, and we begin to ask, in the words of that great Peggy Lee song, "Is that all there is?" That time usually begins in our forties, develops strongly in our fifties, and can dominate our thoughts in our sixties and beyond.

Giving something back to society is, at its base, a profoundly selfish act, because no one who leads a totally self-absorbed life can be truly fulfilled. Our religions teach us that the more you give to society, the more you get back, and while I suppose that qualifies as a cliché, like most clichés it's true. The reward available to those who help others can't be bought with money. It's a feeling that there's a streak of decency within you, after all, no matter what you've had to do to survive.

In most metropolitan areas, charitable work is the entry into a city's social life. If you aspire to climb a city's social ladder, you have to volunteer your time and skills to the major charities. A lot of good gets done that way that wouldn't otherwise get done, and I'm all for it, but the kind of "give back" I find most rewarding is when I can offer direct help to individuals.

A few years ago we produced a story for television about "single moms" who didn't have any money to buy Christmas presents for their children, and what that did to their lives. The story was meant to illustrate one of the major credit problems we confront every year: that millions of consumers get into such financial trouble during the holidays they often have to spend the rest of the year extricating themselves from debt. For reasons not fully understood, many people become extremely depressed around the holidays, and they make up for that depression by spending. Credit card debt, in particular, increases phenomenally during the thirty days before Christmas. Families with no money at all and no prospects of earning extra money will charge thousands of dollars of purchases at Christmas time. It was in this context that my producer asked me to have a look at a tape that he'd shot of a single mother who didn't have any money to buy Christmas presents for her children. As I watched the woman, I could see her struggling to contain her emotions. She really didn't want to cry on camera, but suddenly she couldn't restrain herself any longer and the tears began to flow. As I watched her, I could feel the tears forming in my own eyes. When the tape was finished, I walked straight back to my desk and wrote out a sizable check along with a note to the mother telling her that the money was for presents for her children. I can't exaggerate the joy that contribution to the happiness of another person gave me, even though we had never met. When I received a beautiful letter from the woman a few days later, that was icing on the cake.

Giving back to society doesn't always require you to write out a check. Actually, doing that is often a good deal easier than giving the most valuable possession you have: time. Volunteer work through existing organizations is one way of contributing time. But perhaps you have it within you to make a more singular contribution, one whose rewards will be far more intense for you.

Surely your experience has taught you lessons that you could profitably pass along to young people on the verge of entering the business or professional world. Pick up the telephone, call your local high school and ask if there's some sort of counseling program that could use your skills. Perhaps they'll ask you if you'd be willing to meet with a group of students who are interested in your field. One hour with those students, telling them what it takes to make it in that field, what the pitfalls and trade-offs are, and what kind of life it'll produce, could literally change their lives, and make you feel good about yourself every time you think about the experience.

Given the problems in our society today, problems that government alone can't seem to solve, let alone pay for, the need for volunteer help has probably never been greater. Happily, there are signs that the more fortunate among us are beginning to pay more attention to these problems than they have in the recent past. As the nineties began, people were giving more of their time and money to charity than ever before—in spite of tight money and budget cuts. In mid-1990 we began to receive letters from our viewers and listeners suggesting that the period of self-absorption that had characterized the eighties was coming to an end. They were letters of a kind we'd never seen before, letters so vitriolic they almost qualified as hate mail. What had incensed the letter-writers in particular was a series of programs we'd done on "DINKs." DINK stands for "double income, no kids," young men and women who have opted not to have children so that they can use their two salaries to enhance their own lives. They admit they're selfish. They say frankly that without children they'll have more money and more free time in which to enjoy it. "We both work hard, we want to be free to take a cruise whenever we want, and we just don't need kids around." By the thousands, our listeners and viewers denounced this view. Their message was: Tell those people on your show to stop worrying so much about how they're going to get enough money together to buy fancy foreign cars and second homes; tell them to wake up and smell the coffee and start giving a little bit of themselves back to society.

I have to agree. I have never met a happy selfish person. Self-absorption is important up to a point; you need to hone your skills in order to make yourself a valuable member of society, one who can earn the kind of money that will enable you to live your dreams. But you can be living where you most want to be, doing what you most want to do, pursuing the interests closest to your heart, and sharing it all with a partner who seems heaven-sent, and still not feel fulfilled. If that description sounds familiar, the restlessness you feel could be eliminated by a gift of time and talent from you to society.

HOW MANY YEARS DO I HAVE IN WHICH TO ACCOMPLISH MY DREAMS?

A lot longer than you might think.

Most of us have been accustomed to accepting what the conservative life insurance longevity tables tell us. Today those tables say that men at birth will live, on average, to seventy, and women to seventy-six, a slight improvement over the tables of thirty years ago, when the life expectancy for men was sixty-eight and women seventy-two. But it's even better than that. What those tables don't tell you is the most important fact of all: The longer you live, the better your chances for extending life well beyond normal expectations. If you're a sixty-one-year-old male today, the conservative tables say you're going to live another seventeen years, to seventy-eight. Actually the life expectancy at sixty-one, mathematically and medically, is eighty-four, an additional six years. For women sixty-one, the life expectancy is not eighty-one, as shown on the tables, but eighty-eight.

Life-expectancy tables are weighted by childhood deaths, as well as all the diseases that affect people up to age fifty. Once you reach fifty, you've already survived many of the hazards to which those who died prematurely succumbed. From that point on, your life expectancy keeps on going up, even into your eighties. If you've survived to eighty-two, you're expected to live to be ninety. Obviously, you could die in an accident or be killed by a criminal, but the overwhelming odds are that you won't. To the contrary, as a survivor you not only have those periods of exposure behind you, you are now in a position to benefit greatly from advances in medical technology that are rewriting the actuarial tables. And children born in the nineties will benefit from medical breakthroughs that are unimaginable today.

In the old days life was divided into three decidedly unequal compartments. Grow up from birth until leaving school, a period of seventeen to twenty-five years. Work until retirement, a period of forty to forty-five years. Retire and die, a period of five to ten years. Today? Consider Vic Mills, who got his college degree when Calvin Coolidge was president and went on to become one of the greatest inventors of consumer products in history. His patents, which fill a notebook, include Pampers disposable diapers, Pringle's potato chips, Duncan Hines cake mixes, and even Ivory soap. Vic, ninety-three in 1991 and retired for nearly thirty years, lives an active life with his second wife Ruth on the northern outskirts of Tucson.

Today, there are 62,000 Americans one hundred years old or older. By the end of the century, there will be 100,000. Nearly 1.5 million American children will have celebrated their one hundredth birthday by the year 2080.

Even those not in perfect health are benefitting from the advances in medical technology. I had a client in Rhode Island who at sixty looked like eighty. He smoked and drank and carried around more stress than any man I've ever known. Every time I saw him I had the feeling that I was looking at a dead man. Then he had bypass surgery and today, fifteen years later, at the age of seventy-five, he looks and acts like a man of sixty.

The improvement in prospects for longer life in the last several decades has caused a few scientists to predict human immortality by the year 2100, or sooner. They look upon aging as a disease; like any disease, they say, it can be cured. In due time, they believe, a way will be found to stop the body's clock. Most scientists would disagree with that entirely, but no one disagrees that prospects for a longer life advance with each year. Even afflictions that are not generally life-threatening appear to diminish with time. "Older may be healthier," says a note in the Wellness Engagement Calendar, which is based on articles from the University of California, Berkeley, Wellness Newsletter. "People over 65 have 50 percent fewer colds and flus than the general population."

HOW MUCH RISK CAN I STAND?

In books dealing with finance, risk is a word associated with investing. We'll get to that eventually, but in this book we're going to look at risk in its larger context: How much is required if you're to realize your dreams.

If fear and greed are the two forces that motivate investors, they are also prevalent in all other choices. If you're fearful of risking your money, you will probably be fearful of taking the kinds of risks that will enable you to reach out for your dreams. As we'll see later on, the safest form of investing produces a return that eventually leads to the poorhouse. That, obviously, won't do. If you're even to survive financially, you have to tweak your level of risk up slightly. So with life. "Nothing ventured, nothing gained" is another one of those clichés whose overuse doesn't dim its truth. Or, as professional investors are fond of saying, "You can't get to the fruit without going out on a limb."

I don't believe in risk for risk's sake. If you're not using a seat belt in your car, you're not only breaking the law, you're taking a chance that proves nothing and could cost you your life. I do believe, however, that in order to live an exciting and rewarding life, you've got to confront your fears of change. Only by doing so will you ever discover that moving to a new locale or changing jobs or even professions isn't all that big a deal. When you awaken in the morning and take the step whose anticipation kept you tossing during the night, you wonder why you fretted.

In investing, we speak of the risk-reward ratio. What that means, simply, is that the more you risk, the more you potentially gain. It works the other way, of course. Your chances of loss are correspondingly greater. But without risk of any kind you end up living a life devoid of color and excitement—a fate devoutly to be avoided in my book and, I have to believe, in yours.

So how much risk *is* involved in chasing your dreams? How great a price must you pay? Which brings us to the final element of your dream, how much money you'd like to have—an element so critical it warrants a chapter of its own.

3

Pricing Your Dream

MONEY is the make-or-break component of every dream because without it nothing happens. If your dream is to return to school, or to become an artist, or even to reward yourself with a sabbatical, you can't do it without money.

But wanting money for its own sake, without reference to how that money will be used, can compromise every other component of your dream.

Herewith Crowley's Theorem: Happiness and success result most often when the amount of money you *want* and the amount you *need* are an identical sum. It's when the desire for money exceeds the need for money that unhappiness and failure result.

Let me repeat: Money is nothing more than a tool to help you achieve your dreams. You need only so much money to do that. Time spent earning more than you need to finance your dream is wasted.

Someone supposedly once asked John D. Rockefeller how much was enough. And the man whose name has been synonymous with great wealth for generations of Americans replied, reportedly with a twinkle in his eye, "Just a little more."

The story—true or not—cuts to the central impulse of American life, an impulse that has probably never been more dominant than during the decade just concluded. In reviewing a movie called *Pacific Heights* in the *Los Angeles Times* last September, critic Peter Rainer suggested that, according to the yuppie ethos, "you are what you acquire" and that materialism had been "the true sex appeal" of the eighties. But it wasn't just the yuppies, and it wasn't just the eighties, because I was a product of the sixties and the seventies, and I've already attested to the hold that the values of those days had on me, and how I learned only after considerable effort and expense that possessions weren't going to make me happy.

To judge once again by that massive volume of correspondence I receive, it's been as painful a lesson for tens of thousands of Americans as it was for me, and one a long time in coming. Perhaps out of frustration with what was happening in the world and their own inability to change it, they had placed more and more emphasis on something they could do something about— their own level of material gratification. In their efforts, they were encouraged by an expansive increase of permissiveness in the economic realm, as demonstrated by government and corporate borrowing, an often wild stock market, and the proliferation of personal credit. I well remember being courted by two young loan officers in the bank below the offices of Price Waterhouse. Did I want to buy a boat, a bigger car, a bigger home? My wish was their command.

Historian Arthur M. Schlesinger, Jr., believes that the United States populace goes through cycles in which its concerns shift between society and self. According to Schlesinger, these cycles repeat themselves approximately every thirty years. In John F. Kennedy's presidential inaugural address on January 20, 1961, he set the theme of his administration with perhaps his best-remembered statement: "Ask not what your country can do for you. Ask what you can do for your country." There is no knowing how American society would have evolved had that theme dominated our nation's life for eight years instead of being abruptly and tragically curtailed in less than three. What we do know is that before another two decades had passed, self-interest had been institutionalized by tax cuts, American business had turned its attention from long-term growth to short-term profit, and corporations were investing their assets in leveraged buyouts rather than the capital improvements that might have enabled them to remain among the leaders in an increasingly competitive race for world markets. The consequence of these and other choices is the dismal state of affairs that confronts us: a horrendous national debt caused primarily by our inability to produce to our potential and to generate thereby the tax revenues to run our government; a government compelled to shut down periodically for lack of funds; a declining standard of living; a neglect of the needy among us; and a degree of personal debt for millions of Americans that spoils their lives.

There comes a point when sensible people recoil—and that time, I believe, is here.

In the summer of 1990 a friend of mine spent several days at The Coeur d'Alene, a splendid new hotel on the shores of Lake Coeur d'Alene, Idaho. While there, he came to know two young executives of the hotel, William Reagan, the manager, and Steve Wilson, the director of sales. Both men were in their thirties, and both worked, they calculated, sixty hours a week. It put a lot of stress in their lives, they said, but they had learned to live with it and considered it an acceptable trade-off for the satisfaction they got from their jobs and the quality of life they enjoyed. Neither man mentioned money as a motivating factor. When asked about this, both expressed certainty that they could be earning significantly more money in larger, more mainstream communities; both agreed that money alone could never have been enough of an incentive to make them work as hard as they did.

The surveys and subjective evidence are telling us that Bill Reagan and Steve Wilson are examples of a major shift in priorities taking hold in the United States. Millions of Americans may still be obsessed with piling up wealth, but other millions today are reevaluating how important money is in their lives, and readjusting their sights. They say they want more free time as much as they want more money, time to be with their families and pursue sports and hobbies, and they are unwilling to work extra hours just to gain extra money. At the same time, they seem less and less drawn to expensive consumer items and much more interested in security. One small but telling marker of such change is the behavior of contestants on the television show, "Wheel of Fortune." Just a few years ago, when given a choice of automobiles and speedboats versus annuities or gold, most of the contestants opted for the automobile or the speedboat. Today, it seems, more people go for the gold and annuities.

During the eighties I watched young secretaries in their first year at work loading themselves with debt just so they could drive a BMW to work. If those 200,000 letters and 15,000 phone calls I get each year are any indication, the mood of Americans in the nineties is that peace of mind is more important than a status statement in the driveway.

To anyone dissatisfied with his or her present life and eager to make a change, the significance of this development can scarcely be exaggerated. We are all social beings; we are all influenced by the prevailing morality. When pressures for material fulfillment diminish in society, they diminish in us as well. Once that happens, the cost of fulfilling one's dream diminishes proportionately—and anything becomes possible.

THE CASE OF THE UNHAPPY BANKER

Some years ago a man I know, sitting at a big desk in an important bank in Philadelphia, made a decision that went completely counter to the prevailing values of his peers. An avid sailor in his early thirties, he determined to remake his life in such a way that he could do what he loved every day instead of just on weekends. He would set up a charter sailboat operation. Summers he would work out of Newport, Rhode Island. Winters he would move his operation to West Palm Beach and the Bahamas. At the time he made his decision, he was a highly respected vice president of his bank, and very good at what he did, but he knew in his heart that he was living in the wrong place and doing the wrong thing. Being a banker, he didn't just put on his coat, pick up his umbrella, and walk out the door. He began a meticulous inquiry into what it would take to achieve his dream.

Each week, using the bank's time and telephone, he reached out to people who could supply answers, in full or in part, to the following questions:

In what country of the world could he buy or build at the most advantageous price the kind of boat that customers would want to charter?

How much capital would be required, and how much would a loan for the balance cost him?

What kinds of operating expenses would he incur, and in what amount?

How much of a reserve would he need for unanticipated contingencies?

How much would he have to charge his clients in order to cover all his costs and retain a profit?

How much would he have to net from his business in order to finance his new life?

How much of his own time and energy would he have to expend to make his new life work?

Once he had his answers, and all of his financing was in place, he quit his job, bought his boat, and set up his operation. By the time he recounted his story to me four years later, he was as prosperous as he would have been had he remained at the bank *and* he was doing exactly what he wanted—living on his dream boat, cruising friendly waters, and meeting fascinating people.

Of the many instructive lessons available from the above example, the primary one is that every dream has a price tag and each price tag has three components:

- The nest egg required at the outset
- The income required to sustain the dream
- The amount of energy you must expend

Let's consider them in that order.

HOW BIG A NEST EGG DO YOU NEED?

Very early on, my friend the banker came to the conclusion that he couldn't take that leap away from his occupation and profession without a chunk of money, over and above what he would borrow, that would pay the expenses of his transition and provide for emergencies, should they arise. So he began to put aside a certain amount of money every month. Only when he'd accumulated his nest egg did he make his move.

A lump sum of cash is an absolute necessity when you step from one life to another. We're not talking here about a down payment on a business, a subject we'll address in chapter 4. We're talking about an amount you need to pay the costs of your transition, as well as a form of financial protection that keeps the wolf from the door, gives you peace of mind and enables you to think clearly as you try to make your dream come true. Without a lump sum of money stashed away, you won't be able to purchase your space in time, and you'll be too scared to make your move.

During the settling of the American west, those inveterate dreamers—pioneers, cowboys, and gold miners—all kept a "grubstake," as they called it, consisting of coins or gold dust, as protection against starvation between jobs or gold strikes. It's a tradition as old as the country but, sad to say, honored by very few today. People in cyclical businesses like farming and tourism understand the need to stash money away, but one of the most fundamental problems of our society today is that most of us get out of bed each morning without three to six months worth of income in the bank to tide us over if something should go radically wrong.

From an emotional point of view, we all need to have a certain amount of money stashed away to make us feel secure. How much that is depends on how much we normally spend and, if we're about to make a change, the ambitiousness of our plan.

If you're a young person who wants to backpack through Europe for a year, it may be enough to settle your debts and put $5,000 away. If you're middle-aged, with a family, and you want to change careers, you could be talking about $50,000 or more.

The size of a nest egg is also governed by our psychological needs. The first goal of my closest friend, Ernie Baptista, on leaving college, was to amass $100,000 in a bank account. "No matter what else I do, or what happens to me, I know that I'm going to feel totally different about myself if I have $100,000 in the bank," he told me. And that, at considerable sacrifice, is exactly what he did. Actually, he'd already started his program before leaving college, and being a man of great confidence as well as determination, he was able to reach his goal in just a few years.

The absolute minimum you should have in the bank, whether you're in transition or not, is the equivalent of three months income. How much more of a lump sum you need depends on the cost of your dream.

The size of a dream and its price tag are not necessarily commensurate. Some of the smallest dreams have the biggest price tags, and some of the biggest the smallest price tags. Here are some examples:

• A happily married housewife and mother wants to become an accomplished pianist, and gives herself three years in which to do it. Big dream, little price tag.

• A bored accounting clerk dreams of becoming an airline pilot, and wants to move to the Sunbelt. Big dream, big price tag.

• A husband and wife, both in their midfifties, decide that they want to be living on a golf course in Florida by the time they're sixty. Small dream, medium price tag.

• A dentist in Manhattan, unhappy with his life, wants to move to the Sunbelt and become a golf pro. Big dream, small to medium price tag.

• A thirty-year-old high school English teacher wants to move to Maine and become a published author. Big dream, small price tag.

In calculating how much of a lump sum you'll need, you must identify four basic components:

1. *The cost of closing your old life down in an orderly way.* This cost is readily identifiable. It consists of any expenses involved in preparing your home for resale, plus the cost of the physical move to your new location.

2. *The cost of bridging the gap.* If you're planning not to work for a certain period during the start-up phase of your new life, you must set aside a specific amount of money, depending on your spending patterns, as well as the known costs of living in your new environment.

3. *The cost of training for your new life.* If you're returning to school to get an advanced degree, you must figure tuition, books, and incidentals. Suppose your dream is to become an airline pilot. There's a flight school in the Southeast that guarantees to do that for $19,950, including tuition, books, flight time, FAA check rides, and a room.

4. *Buffer money.* This is a sum of money over and above what you believe it's going to cost you to shed your old skin and take up your new life, at least $5,000 and preferably $10,000 buried in a bank, to be used in the event your dream doesn't materialize fast enough or if it's not what you thought it would be and you want to return to your old life.

HOW MUCH INCOME DO YOU NEED?

I took a lot of abuse when I identified my dream to my colleagues, family, and friends. Virtually everyone around me told me that I couldn't do it. My partner, Carl Weinberg, said, "Look, Steve, you're dreaming, you're a Warwick, Rhode Island, CPA. You're never going to be on national television. It's just not in the cards." But my lack of experience and exposure weren't the major factor cited by the skeptics; even those who thought I might have a chance professionally kept telling me that I'd never let my accounting practice go because the financial sacrifice would be too great. They were wrong about what I'd do, but right about the cost. It *was* a great financial sacrifice, from $150,000 a year to $25,000 a year, and it was extremely painful.

If you want to change careers totally, you're going to take a severe cut in income. It's not the end of the world. I went broke several times in the process of achieving my dream, but my life didn't end. Franklin D. Roosevelt's great rallying cry during the Great Depression applies to anyone who wants to change careers or start a business. "There is nothing to fear but fear itself." Regardless of how great a drop in income you experience, you'll be far more at peace with yourself because you'll know that you're moving in the right direction at last.

The key to this transition is to make up your mind that the gratification available to you when you follow your heart is worth whatever it costs, and to arrange your life accordingly. This means, above all, crunching your expenses down and avoiding any capital commitments.

Those matters will be taken up extensively in Parts II and III. For now, let me highlight some of the ways in which you can prepare for your new life.

Debt. The moment you even think you might want to make a change, you'll do yourself a great favor, as well as protect your credit rating, by prepaying your mortgage, automobile, and any other installment loans by at least one or two months (more if you can), and then sticking to your payments from then on. That will give you a buffer zone if you run into trouble further on.

This is also the time to eliminate all credit card debt or reduce it to a minimum and to charge only as much as you're positive you can pay for at months' end.

Housing. When you're moving from one area to another, I strongly urge you not to buy a house at the outset. Always make the transition with a rented apartment. In most areas of the United States, you can find apartments to rent for three to six months or, at worst, a year. In the current real estate environment, it's usually very easy to rent a house, and in many cases the rental will be less than you'd be paying per month if you were to buy a house. A house on which a mortgage would typically run $1,200 might cost $750 a month to rent.

Very often people on the move will ask me whether it wouldn't be a good idea to lease their house instead of selling it. I don't recommend that. I've never seen it work out so well that it's worth the trouble and possible problems. You don't want to be worrying about repairs or burglaries or your tenant falling behind on the rent at a time when you need peace of mind above all else. If you're moving on, I strongly recommend that you sell your house. With one act, you get rid of a potential headache, you get rid of debt and, if you bought right and have sold right, you wind up with a nest egg to help you in your new life.

Transportation. If you can possibly do so, this is the time to pay off the debt on your car. One simple way to do that is to send in double payments once you've decided to make your move, sending your extra payment in a separate check, with a note asking that the amount be applied to your principal. Making extra payments in this manner, you can pay off a car loan in half the time or less. If it's not possible for you to make an extra payment, I advise you to dump the car you have and buy a clean used car once you get to your new area. Og Mandino, the super salesman and inspirational author, tells the story, perhaps autobiographical, of the salesman whose great ambition in life was to write a book about how to be successful in business, but who was constantly being tempted with better and better offers by his employer, who didn't want to lose him. Finally, he quit and began to write his book. As his money dwindled, he found the money he needed to finish his book by selling his dream car and buying an old pickup truck.

Above all, resist the temptation to buy a new car. This is not a time to load yourself up with installment debt. If you're determined to keep your present car and you're concerned about the size of the monthly payments, you may want to consider refinancing the loan.

Insurance. If you're moving from one job to another, your new employer will almost certainly have some kind of health and life insurance program, although not as good a one as he might have offered just a few years ago. It behooves you to make certain that you and your family are adequately covered, most importantly against catastrophic illness, and to make provisions for supplementary coverage if the new benefits are inadequate. If you're leaving your job to become self-employed, it's even more imperative that you arrange for an adequate insurance program. Frequently, your employer's carrier will offer a conversion program for employees leaving a company. That may be the best deal you'll get, because it continues your coverage without questions about previous illnesses. An alternative is to shop for a health maintenance organization, or HMO, in your new community. These organizations provide comprehensive medical care, including hospitalization, at prices not available to individuals, requiring only that you use their doctors and their facilities.

If you're young and have a family, and are striking out on your own, you'll want to buy at least $200,000 of the cheapest term life insurance. A term insurance policy for a young, nonsmoking male should cost about $125 a year for each $100,000, a bargain given the peace of mind it offers. Your insurance agent will probably try to sell you a more expensive whole life or universal life policy. At this point in your life, it probably doesn't make a lot of sense, no matter what your life insurance salesman tells you. It almost always makes sense to separate your insurance coverage from your investments.

If the career or business you're entering has even minimal physical risk attached to it—any of the construction and automobile repair trades would qualify—it would be a good idea to arrange for some disability insurance as well. In 1990 I did a story for "Good Morning America" about a man who wrote out a check for a disability policy the moment he went independent, because he felt that he could not take the chance of jeopardizing his own and his family's welfare if he were suddenly unable to work. In order to keep the cost of the insurance to a minimum, he took out a policy that didn't pay him until ninety days after his disability began. That period he covered with a cash buffer he stashed away equal to three months' expenses.

Monthly Expenses. Most of us have a number in our head about what it costs to maintain our lives, and the lives of our families. One of your primary considerations in contemplating a move designed to bring you closer to your dream is the cost of living in the area to which you're moving. Ideally, the cost will be lower. If you know your income is going to be curtailed for a period, the cost of living certainly shouldn't be higher. To move from Joplin, Missouri, to Los Angeles, where the cost of housing may be as much as ten times greater, would bust almost any dream.

CALCULATING YOUR CURRENT COSTS

If you don't know what it's costing you to live, now is the time to find out. You can pay your accountant to do it, or you can do it yourself in a few hours. If you do it yourself, you'll not only save several hundred dollars, you'll get a more accurate breakdown of your expenses, because only you know what each outlay went for.

All you need are your canceled checks and charge account statements, including credit cards, from January through December of the previous year. As you proceed through your records, enter each disbursement under one, and only one, of the following categories:

   Rent, mortgage, and loan payments
   Utilities and telephone
   Property and all other taxes, excluding income taxes
   Income taxes
   Insurance premiums
   Clothing
   Tuition and child care
   Food and toiletries
   Medical and dental expenses
   Transportation and travel
   Entertainment, including vacations
   Charitable contributions
   Miscellaneous spending

When all the disbursements have been entered and totaled, you'll know exactly where your money is going, as useful—and often as shocking—a lesson in personal finance as you can provide yourself. And when you add all the categories together, you'll know exactly what your old life has been costing you.

To find out what it costs you per month to live, simply divide the grand total by 12. To find out what it costs per week, divide by 52. If you calculate your needs on a monthly basis, remember that all months except February are longer than four weeks, and even February is longer than four weeks once every four years. It's for this reason that I like to calculate my needs on both a weekly and a monthly basis, because I feel it gives me more specific and useful numbers. When I convert amounts from monthly to weekly, I divide the monthly number by 4.3, rather than 4, just to be more accurate.

Once you know your expenses, two tasks confront you:

• The first task is to figure out how you can squeeze those numbers down as low as possible during your transition, bearing in mind that you're postponing present for future gratification.

• The second task is to determine where the money is going to come from to sustain you during the transition. If you've managed to set aside an adequate lump sum, well and good. If not, someone—either you or your spouse—is going to have to work part- or full-time. If the amount of time you'll need to devote to part-time work keeps you from studying or training for your new life, you're defeating your purpose; the only answer in that event is to crunch those expenses down still further. Remember that any money not spent on maintenance buys time to prepare for your new life.

THE AMOUNT OF ENERGY YOU MUST EXPEND

The fulfillment of any dream, no matter how small, requires an expense of mental, physical, and emotional energy. If your dream is to operate a lobster boat off the coast of Maine, you're in for a physically punishing life, standing on a pitching deck at night hauling up lobster pots. But the emotional and mental costs won't be as great. If your dream is to return to school for an advanced degree, you'll spend a lot of energy, but on mental rather than physical labor. Finding a new spouse or partner or breaking off with an old one may require virtually no physical and little mental energy, but the emotional expense will be tremendous.

Before pursuing any dream, it will pay you to calculate what kind of energy you'll need and in what amounts you think you might expend it. I've nearly been laid to rest by miscalculating the volume of energy required to accomplish specific goals in my life, such as getting my instrument and multiengine pilot ratings. Those experiences taught me not only to calculate the amount of energy I'd need to commit to a dream *before* attempting to fulfill it, but whether I had sufficient reserves of energy to expend. Would I lose sleep, and if so, could I withstand that? If the effort would be stressful, how would I alleviate the pressure? When was my last physical checkup, and would I be well advised to have a new one?

Before I agreed to write this book, I had to inventory my reserves and calculate how much time it would require and where I would find that time. Would it compromise my other business obligations? Would it prevent me from spending time with my wife and children?

One of the best ways to assess how much energy you'll require is to pick the brains of those who have already been down the trail you intend to take. How difficult was the journey? How long did it take? What were the joys, rewards, and setbacks? Would they do it again? Would they do it differently? Because they might not try it again doesn't mean you shouldn't make the effort, but what they tell you could save you a lot of energy expense.

THE KEY: YOUR EXPENSE/REWARD RATIO

There is no correlation between the absolute dollar volume of an expense and the personal reward you may get from it. For example, if the most thrilling thing in your life is to play a good game of tennis, then the cost of a tennis racket and tennis balls and your time on the court is minuscule compared to the enjoyment you're going to get from it. If playing piano gives you more pleasure than anything else in life, it's important to own a good instrument. You can probably buy an excellent used piano for $2,000 and sell it five years later for that much or slightly less, particularly if you're trading up to an even better piano.

Living in a two- or three-room apartment, you may find that life has become exquisitely simplified compared to what it was in that ten-room house you just sold, and that your reward relative to your expense is far greater than the reward you got in maintaining your costly home. Yes, you had more space and comfort, but you paid for it with time and money. One of the reasons that condominiums and town houses have become so popular is precisely because they free you of worries about crabgrass and leaking roofs, in addition to eliminating the cost of attending to them.

Now is the time to look back at that calculation you made in determining how much you were spending, and on what, and identify those outlays that aren't giving you an amount of pleasure commensurate with what they're costing. Don't be surprised to discover, as so many others have, that the expense/reward ratio most out of whack is the one involving your car. Most of us love our cars when we buy them, but then tire of them after a year or two. Yet we're still paying as much to support them as we did on day one. When we're pricing our dreams, it's time to ask ourselves whether we really need a car costing $40,000 when we can get to the same place in the same amount of time in a car costing $12,000.

This is the time in life to identify those pursuits that give you tremendous pleasure but are very inexpensive. Is there a better example than reading? Books these days can cost $20 or more, but they reward you with knowledge and understanding as well as pleasure. I love films, but when my wife, Fran, and I go to a movie, it's $10 for the tickets, $4 for refreshments, and $20 for the baby-sitter. That's $34 for four hours of entertainment—two for Fran, two for myself—or nearly $10 an hour. If we each spend five hours reading a $20 book, that's $2 an hour.

As I indicated earlier, one of my current dreams is to master French. I studied French for four years in high school, one of those intense suit and tie schools where two languages were required. When I graduated, I could read, understand, and speak French reasonably well, but eventually lost the ability to speak it. When I got the bug to master French in the spring of 1990, I bought tapes and training books for $110; when I actually spoke French in Paris six months later, the payoff was incalculable.

In many cases, the expense involved in pursuing a dream involves far more energy than money. The best example I can think of in this regard is my old friend and colleague Dave Ricchiute. Dave and I started work together at Price Waterhouse and Company twenty years ago. During the busy season, we worked well into the evenings, and on many weekends. At the time, neither of us could imagine working any harder. Before a year passed, Dave had decided that working in an accounting firm with excruciating deadline pressures, and trying to study for his CPA exam as well, was not the life for him. What he wanted was to become an educator and teach accounting at the university level. That meant getting a doctorate, a tremendous expense of energy.

After making a meticulous study of the options, Dave enrolled in a graduate program at the University of Kentucky, which has one of the finest accounting schools in the country. Back in Rhode Island, Dave's wife Jean had worked as well, and their combined incomes had enabled them to live an extremely comfortable life. The first night they moved into their small, empty apartment in Lexington, Kentucky, they had terrible misgivings. For the next three years, Dave had no life of his own. He studied five to eight hours a day, seven days a week, taught undergraduate courses and prepared his lesson plans. On more than one occasion, he would fall asleep and wake up on the floor with an open book. During this period, Jean became the primary breadwinner. Many times during that three-year period they were so exhausted mentally and physically that they didn't think they could continue. But Dave wanted that doctorate more than anything in the world, and Jean wanted him to have it, and there was absolutely no argument between them about the expense of energy they were making.

Today, Dave is a professor of accounting at Notre Dame, the author and coauthor of many articles and textbooks, and one of the most respected men in his field. What he treasures most is teaching; that, he believes, is what he was born to do.

If you want to change your life badly enough, no price you pay or sacrifice you make will be too great. Not only will you wind up with a better life, you'll experience the excitement of getting there. Some people call it the thrill of the chase.

4

Chasing Your Dream

THERE is no satisfaction quite like the one you get from knowing, as you go through the paces of your present job, that two or three years hence you're going to be doing something more rewarding. No matter where I am in my own work, I always try to look forward to something even more gratifying than what I'm currently doing. It gives me energy, happiness, and peace of mind.

For most people unhappy in their work, the remedy is a newer and better job within the same profession. But regardless of the dream involved, be it a change of jobs or career, or a stab at becoming your own boss, there are three steps to its realization.

STEP ONE: SETTING THE STAGE

Time is the most important element in any transition. You never want to make a change abruptly. If you've decided that your current life isn't what you want, don't figure on being profitably settled into an entirely new life twelve months from now. Figure on two years, perhaps three, conceivably five or more.

I spent seven years, from 1974 to 1981, preparing for my transition from accounting to television reporting. I might have made the transition more quickly, but I'm glad that I took the time I did. The last three or four years of that transition qualified as serious work and gave me a solid base of experience to draw from when my opportunity finally came. By that point, I was already half out of one profession and half into the next, so the transition was as natural as a caterpillar becoming a butterfly.

The longer you take for the transition, the smoother it's going to be—and the less costly as well. But at some point, you have to say goodbye to your previous life. The caterpillar must become a butterfly.

Whether you are changing a job, changing careers, or starting a business, it's imperative that you do all your looking from your present job. Do everything you can do to avoid being fired while you're looking.

Don't quit a job until you have another job. You want to quit on your terms, not theirs. The trick is to do it to them before they do it to you. Consequently, it's very important to know how you fit into the operation and to network constantly while you are in your present position.

In chapter 1, we reviewed the principal ways in which corporate America is making a myth of job security in the United States: replacing older workers with younger ones; firing older workers, then offering them their jobs back at half pay; and "downsizing"—attempting to do the same work with fewer employees. To determine whether you might be vulnerable to any of these practices, here are some questions to ask yourself:

Is your employer being merged or consolidated?
Has your employer cut back on positions before?
Is your corporation losing its market share?
Can you be replaced by someone at a lower salary?
Do three or fewer employees report to you?
Is your industry stagnant or contracting?
Is your industry being squeezed by inflation?
Are you fifty years old, or older?
Do you live in the Northeast or Midwest?
Are you middle management or below?

The more questions you answer "yes," the greater the chance you'll be a victim in the next year. Five or more "yes" responses, and you may want to start looking over your shoulder, especially if your employer has a reputation for being cold-blooded.

If you think it's going to happen, don't despair. You've got that much more incentive to make a change. Relocation costs are all or partially tax-deductible, providing you're not changing your career or profession. And remember the old adage that when you're fired, you often end up with a better job, higher pay, or both.

❖   ❖   ❖

A change of jobs won't solve your problems if the work itself no longer pleases you. In that event, your transition will be more complex, but ultimately more rewarding.

Changing careers takes longer, costs a great deal more and doesn't offer any tax benefits. But once you've done it, you feel like you've been reborn, and if your new career gives you gratifications that your old one didn't, the amount of money involved is irrelevant.

In my work I come into contact with a great many television stars. Frequently, they will ask me for advice about their finances. On a number of occasions, some of them have confided to me that they'd be delighted to give up their glamorous and lucrative but unstable careers for less rewarding but more secure work.

I know a lawyer earning $200,000 a year who hates what he does. For his $4,000 a week, he's working twelve- and fourteen-hour days, six or seven days a week. It's not the long hours that disturb him so much as the almost certain knowledge that he's in a job that will define him for the rest of his life. "I'll be making $225,000 next year, and $250,000 three years from now," he told me, "but this is it, this is who I am and what my life is, and I'm not happy because I've always dreamed of doing other things."

As long as he only dreams about what he wants to do and doesn't act on those dreams, he will continue to be miserable. Compare his approach to that of Alan Novich of New York City. Alan's father had been a dentist. Alan had been encouraged to study dentistry, and once he began his practice he distinguished himself as a specialist in dental surgery. For years, he was extremely successful, but he was never happy. "People hate their dentists," he told me. "I didn't want to be hated." One day, Alan abruptly chucked his practice and enrolled in law school. Today he's working on his third career, investment banking. Alan knew enough not to remain in a career that no longer made him happy, no matter how much time and effort he'd expended to qualify.

One man I know has solved his restlessness with one career by simultaneously taking on a second. During the week he's a pilot for US AIR, and on weekends he's a television weatherman in West Palm Beach, Florida. The common thread of the two careers is weather. He loves being a pilot, and he loves being on TV, and the two jobs give him a tremendous income. Because he's a pilot, he has ample time off to be with his family; the television work moors him to his home base. Having two jobs gives him a marvelous feeling of stability, but the talents they require are easily transportable to other markets should the need or the occasion arise. If he loses either job, he still has his other job automatically to tide him through, and because they are both unstable professions, combining the two of them gives him a degree of stability one alone never could.

If you're in a profession that you don't like and you want to be in another profession, expect to train for several years. Start hounding your local library and your bookstore, and read all the right books. Getting yourself to night school or a university extension will give you a head start, as well.

If you're self-employed to begin with, your options are considerably enhanced. Rather than making a clean break, you can diminish the work you're doing, spending mornings or three days a week, and ease into your new career with the time you've freed up. Or if you're young and energetic, you can double up as I did. Let me detail my own transition for you now, not just because it's the story I know best but because it illustrates a number of the points we've discussed above.

The Metamorphosis of Steve Crowley

In 1974, rich and miserable, I wrote a five-page proposal for a half-hour talk show to be called "Money Talks," and sent it to the public television station in Providence. My query wasn't answered. Two months later, I sent a second query, but that wasn't answered either. Six months later, when I'd virtually forgotten the matter, I received a call from a man who introduced himself as a member of a new team that had just taken over the station. "We went through the files and found a proposal for a show called 'Money Talks,'" he said. "Could we have lunch and talk about this show?" At the end of our luncheon several days later he said, "Well, my advice to you is to go buy a lot of blue shirts, because we want you to do the show. We start in two weeks." Two weeks later, I was a regular on television out of Providence. I did that show for three years without pay, but it was my college classroom for learning the TV business.

When I began my transition, I knew it was a long way from doing a pro bono talk show about money on a local public television station to a job on network television. I knew that I would have to get into journalism, about which I knew practically nothing. I'd been interviewed several times by WJAR, Channel 10 in Providence, an NBC affiliate, and had performed reasonably well. So, brimming with confidence, I called the news director of the station, Steve Caminis, and invited him to lunch at an exclusive club. "Steve," I began, "I want to do your money reporting for you. I'll do three reports a week." And he just stopped me cold. "You're dreaming," he said. "You don't have a journalism degree, you don't know anything about TV reporting, and as much as I like you as a person, and as great a job as you do as a guest, you're not going to use my TV station to experiment with your career. I hope this doesn't affect our relationship, but the answer is no."

I was depressed but not defeated. "Steve," I said, "just do me one favor, when you need expert commentary, just keep me in mind." And when we said goodbye, I repeated that request twice.

"Okay," he said, "I'll keep you in mind."

Two weeks later, one of Steve's assistants called to ask if I could come to a taping of a local "Meet the Press"—style show. The guest was to be Royal Little, the multi-millionaire founder of Textron. There were to be four panelists on the show, and I was to represent Channel 10 news.

"I'm going to represent Channel 10 news on TV?" I said, scarcely able to believe what I'd just heard. Sure enough, I was introduced on the shows as Steve Crowley, representing "WJAR TV News." At the time, I wasn't even on the news team.

The show went very well, well enough so that I could call Steve Caminis. "You know tax time is coming up," I said. "Why don't you let me go out with a camera crew and do a few tax reports? If you like them you can air them and if you don't you can throw them away. That's your investment."

"All right," Steve said. "Try three. I'll assign someone to it."

So I did the three reports and he looked at them and said, "How many of these can you do every week? I'll pay you $25 a report."

At the time, I was earning in the neighborhood of $300,000 in today's money as a CPA, but I accepted the offer in a flash.

For the next three years, I worked sixty hours a week as a CPA and twenty to twenty-five hours a week as a television reporter. The schedule nearly broke me, but it brought me into the broadcasting business.

In mid-1981, Steve was appointed news director at WPLG, the ABC affiliate in Miami. Two months later, on a morning in August, I had my showdown with my partner. As I listened to him tell me that he wanted to dissolve our partnership, I told myself that if I was ever going to jump into television full time, now was the time to do it. My first call after we'd reached agreement was to Miami. "Steve," I said, "do you need a good financial reporter down at WPLG?"

"The day you get here is the day you go on the air," he said.

"Are you serious?"

"Dead serious. Could you have dinner with me tomorrow night on Key Biscayne?"

"I'll be there," I said.

The following night, he said, "Look, I have no money in the budget for you, but here's my deal, and it's a pretty good deal. I'm gonna pay you $150 per report, freelance. You won't be an employee, and you won't be under the gun of the assignment desk. When you feel like taking a walk on the beach that day, just don't answer the phone. At your age and having been your own boss, you're not going to want to be told what to do by a twenty-three-year-old kid. Right?"

"Right."

"Now, the way we'll write the contract is that when you do the report once and then recut it twice for later shows, that'll be $450. You do that three or four days a week and you've got a helluva nice little income while you're building your business."

Suddenly, there I was, living my dream at last, gaining big market experience and often making $1,000 or more a week. The reception to my work couldn't have been more positive; within a very short time, my segments were being promoted throughout the Miami area. And I was able to devote myself to setting up my corporation, Money/Pro News Inc.

At this point you may be saying, that's all swell, Steve, but you had a lot of money behind you. I really didn't, considering that I had a wife and two children in Rhode Island to support and a separate life to maintain in

Florida. I had to move to a new location, build a business, and start over. Within six months, my money was gone. But I didn't panic, because I'd had excellent response to my product. My problem was merely cash flow—an eminently soluble problem, as we'll see shortly.

There are three lessons in my story that I want to imprint on you.

1. Don't jump off bridges.
2. Opportunity knocks once. When it does, you have to respond quickly and positively—provided you're prepared.
3. Find yourself at least one mentor, and more if you can.

Finding a Mentor

A mentor is a wise and trusted counselor who's experienced in the field you're attempting to enter and can put some perspective on it. He or she functions as a sounding board for your ideas, and can provide you with contacts when you're ready to make a move. Most often, your mentor will be someone older than yourself, but Steve Caminis, my first mentor in television, was my age.

Today, a good mentor for me would be Dick Clark, whom I know and respect. Dick owns his own television production company, and is engaged in the development of a number of different shows—exactly what I now aspire to do. As successful as he's been, he's an eminently approachable man, generous with advice. When I'm pitching a TV product to the networks, it's good for me to know that when Dick Clark pitches a TV product he has the same or similar difficulties that I do. He gets turned down and frustrated, just as I do. But he succeeds far more often than he fails, principally because he's trained himself to maintain a perpetually youthful outlook, the key to his ability to program successfully for young people after all these years.

How do you find a mentor?

The best mentors are successful people from your own field. Although it's helpful if you know them before you approach them, it's not essential. Very few successful men or women can resist a well-written and well-reasoned letter asking for advice. Calling cold without having written first is generally a waste of time, but telling your prospective mentor in the last paragraph of your letter that you will call in several days in the hope of getting an appointment is very much in order.

Mentors don't necessarily have to be in the same business in which your interests lie. The Small Business Administration has a cadre of mentors called the Service Corps of Retired Executives, popularly known as SCORE, who are available on a volunteer basis. In New England, there is a special organization called SBANE, which stands for Smaller Business Association of New England. Its members are top regional small-business owners and entrepreneurs running the gamut from multimillionaires all the way down to Mom and Pop operations. If you're starting a small business, SBANE will put you together with three or more successful businessmen or business-women once every two months to help solve your particular problems. The theory is that experience is the best teacher. It's like small-business group therapy. A few people I know who have availed themselves of such resources have been disappointed by some of the advice they received, but most say that ultimately they were helped.

STEP TWO: TARGETING YOUR NEW SOURCE OF INCOME

Whether you're moving to a new job, a new career, or a new business, the rules are the same:

Rule One: Gather as Much Data as You Can

If you saw the movie *Wall Street*, you may remember a statement made by Gordon Gecko, the unscrupulous investment banker, to the effect that infor-mation is the most valuable commodity of all. The statement was absolutely right. Information is power. Information makes money. Information is what impresses potential investors when you're looking for backers.

Whenever I need information, I start with Matthew Lesko. Matthew is a gatherer of information beloved by the small-business community. He di-vides his time between Washington, D.C., and Orlando, Florida. In both places, he spends most of the working day at the public library, poring over thousands of documents printed and distributed each year by the U.S. government. Long ago, Matthew divined a simple but invaluable truth: Federal and state governments do a splendid job of amassing useful informa-tion for the public, but a wretched job of distributing that information. As a consequence, most people are unaware that free help is available on almost any subject imaginable.

Suppose you decide that you want to manufacture widgets better and more cheaply than the current manufacturers, so that instead of charging $3.98 for them you can sell them for $1.79. Not only does the federal government have a report on how to manufacture and market widgets, it has an expert on the product. You can call this expert up and say, "Dave, I need everything you've got on widgets: how many widgets are used in the U.S., who manufactures them, what the average price is, how many are being imported, and any trends that are developing." And Dave will send you everything he's got, either free or for a nominal charge.

But how do you find Dave? Enter Matthew Lesko.

Working out of resources in the public library, poring through government source documents, Matthew determines who the experts are. Then he finds them, talks to them, and evaluates them. And then he puts them in a book called Information USA, which is as thick as the Manhattan telephone directory and provides readers with a master index of what help is available.

You may have seen or heard Matthew on one or more talk shows, because he's been on all of them, including mine. When he goes on radio or television, phones ring off the hook. To order his book, you can call free of charge. The number is 1-800-32-LESKO.

Information USA is a sourcebook, not a how-to book. You can't learn how to manufacture widgets by reading it. What you can learn is where the sources of information are.

Rule Two: Work for Someone Else First

If you want to start a restaurant, work for a restaurant owner before you set out on your own. If you're going to start a car repair business, get a job in a mechanic shop first, even if it's only part-time. Your apprenticeship needn't always be a long commitment; in some cases, two or three months might do the trick.

Working for someone else at the outset will give you on-the-job training and prevent you from making a whole range of errors once you start up your own firm.

It might seem logical that your first step would be to learn what you can about the industry through reading rather than going to work for someone in the field of your interest. The two approaches are complementary, but neither can replace the other. Reading about a field will tell you about the competition and the market, but it won't tell you about the amount of capital you'll need or the effort required. Only hands-on experience will give you a feel for that. And until you've worked for someone, you won't know the questions to ask.

Rule Three: Be Selective

In selecting what you want to do, it's advisable to decide on one thing rather than several things, and to learn how to do that one thing very well.

I learned that lesson at a very early age from my Uncle Bob. Seated at the dinner table one evening, he picked up a fork and said, "Steve, if you devoted your entire life to selling this fork, figuring out who needed it, and then buying it and selling it, you'd be a big success."

Dabbling in a wide variety of deals, you're not going to make money. You must have a focus.

Rule Four: Choose a Business That Will Hold Your Interest for a Considerable Amount of Time

Most entrepreneurs have a passion for doing something well, whether they are making a product or offering a service. For many years, a former client of mine named Marty Lifland manufactured the kind of webbing that's used to make seat belts, parachutes, and other such products. Webbing would never excite me, but Marty had a passion for the textile industry, and was never happier than when he was getting his hands dirty in his factory, working alongside his employees, to whom he communicated his passion.

I know a woman in Miami who coaxed her husband into signing a promissory note so that she could start a limousine service, working out of her laundry room. She made a mistake by not working for a limousine company before starting her own, but she more than made up for her omission by the zeal she brought to the enterprise. The week she opened for business, she called every limousine service in Miami and asked them to think of her if they had more business than they could handle. Within two months she was booked solid, with the crew of "Miami Vice" as her principal client. The last time I spoke to her, she was operating five limousines, and her husband was planning to quit his job and work for her.

Today 80 percent of start-ups are by entrepreneurs offering a service rather than manufacturing a product. Very often the entrepreneurs are a husband and wife who determine to start a business together, working from their home. The energy that such couples can muster is often equal to that of four or five employees brought in to start up a firm. And when these "love–work partnerships" work well, they are a marvelous antidote for the estrangement and lack of communication often found in a dual-career marriage.

Rule Five: Start with the Lowest Possible Overhead

Writers are ideal entrepreneurs from the standpoint of overhead because all they need is a computer and a telephone. Self-employed salespersons are nearly as ideal; to the computer and telephone they just add an automobile. Neither the writer nor the salesman needs to lease an office for five years and hire twenty people. They can work in their homes, and by themselves. They pay no employee benefits or Workmen's Compensation.

As a CPA, I specialized in helping people launch small businesses. I was intimately involved in efforts to raise money, start the enterprise, stimulate sales, and control expenses. Few of my clients appreciated how great expenses can be during the first few months. I've had dozens of clients who wanted to open restaurants. Some were qualified. Most were not. They all believed that running a restaurant was a snap. They had no idea of the potential for disaster. I remember one group of young restaurateurs who bought $5,000 worth of live lobsters and seafood for their grand opening. But they'd neglected to install an alarm system on their restaurant, and overnight, someone broke in and stole all the food.

Rule Six: Never Get Discouraged

Entrepreneurs share one characteristic that sets them apart from other people. They don't see failure as an option or a possibility. I know that I don't. If my company went bankrupt today, I would start a new one tomorrow. I know that the power of doing it is within myself. So did Mark Payden.

In 1976 Mark and a friend, Steve DeToy, both then in their early twenties, called me out of the blue, told me they'd been referred to me by a local banker, and asked for an appointment. At our meeting, they explained that they'd arrived a few days earlier from Minneapolis. They'd come to Providence, they said, because they wanted to open an outlet for Earth shoes. Earth shoes, at that time, were a big fad. They featured a negative heel—the heel low and the front high, so that you walked with your heel down and your foot sticking up. Earth Shoes, the company, had a central manufacturing plant that supplied franchise stores all over the country; Mark and Steve had run the store in Minneapolis, where it had been so successful that customers lined up to get inside. They had driven to Providence knowing nothing about the area, only that there was a franchise available in the city. Being so innocent, they thought that the way you started a company was to find a city with an opening and walk into the local bank and ask for money. They had no money, they told me, but their parents and relatives were willing to stake them. I told them I would help them make an application to the Small Business Administration, which, if approved, would guarantee their loan up to 90 percent. We projected all the revenues and expenses based on other Earth Shoe stores, whose figures were enumerated in a packet of information on the franchise. In due course their loan was approved, and they opened for business to a considerable fanfare from the local business press.

At first, everything seemed wonderful. They did a flurry of business. What they hadn't counted on, and couldn't have known, was that the Earth shoe concept had just begun to wane. Earth shoes might or might not be beneficial. There was no question that they were not attractive shoes. To some, they looked like clown shoes. That, coupled with delivery problems, doomed the young men's franchise operation.

At that point Mark Payden might have told himself that he wasn't cut out to be an entrepreneur, that no one would take him seriously any more because he'd started a company that had gone under. But Mark didn't take it personally. What he told himself was that the failure hadn't been his fault; he couldn't blame himself either for the fading of a fad or the problems of the supplier. And he immediately created another opportunity. Over the months, he'd become aware of a new fad: customized T-shirts, with messages written front and back. He liked Providence; he wanted to stay. He decided to make himself "the king of T-shirts."

Today, Mark Payden is a phenomenal success, having built himself an empire out of virtually no money. His secret is his positive attitude. I've never seen him without a smile. It's not phony; he's just a happy, positive, forward-moving person.

I can't think of a more important quality for an entrepreneur than the ability to come up off the floor and continue fighting. In truth the main ingredient to success in any small business venture lies in your heart and mind. It's a combination of ability and perseverance often called stick-to-itiveness. Once again, I'm speaking from experience. Since that day in 1981 when I left my partnership to start on my own, I've been slapped in the face countless times. I was so broke at one point that I couldn't even pay my household bills; not only my electricity but the water to my house was shut off, and I had to flush my toilets with water from the swimming pool. On the way to work one day, I ran out of gas. I had no money and no credit card that a nearby gas station would accept. Luckily, I had enough change to call my cameraman, who picked me up and took me to the office. But I looked upon these episodes as severe cash shortages, not signs of failure, and I kept on plugging because I knew the customers loved the product. As long as I could prove that to investors, I could raise more money.

If You Want to Start a Business . . .

In chapter 2, I noted that nine out of ten people dream of quitting their jobs and striking out on their own. Owning a small business is part of the American dream—in the minds of most people, the key to independence and freedom. Today, about one in fourteen members of the work force, some 10 million Americans, call themselves "Boss." Fear is what most often stops others from becoming entrepreneurs, and why shouldn't it when we read that four out of five small businesses fail in their first two years?

Actually, these reports are greatly overstated because they're based on filings of new corporations and new businesses, most of which never even get to the launching stage. Royal Little, the founder of Textron, the first true conglomerate, firmly believed that failure was a component of success and that all he had to do to become a multimillionaire was succeed 55 percent of the time. In his lifetime, he lost more than $100 million, but he made far more than that with the ventures that succeeded.

What follows is based on the assumption that you too have thought at one point in your life, however idly, of having a business of your own. Perhaps you dreamed of going into business with your spouse; some of the most successful small businesses launched in recent times have been started by couples. Perhaps you thought of sweetening your life with extra income from an endeavor to which you'd devote only part of your time; one Boston couple I know who wanted to own a small business decided not to quit their jobs, first because they enjoyed what they did, second because they knew the only way they could raise the capital for their small business would be if they continued to work. After two years of searching, they decided on a dry cleaning franchise, a high-profile business in a growth area; they bought the business and turned a profit their first year. (In spite of their bad press, franchises have a much higher success rate than any other kind of business;

if you're contemplating an entrepreneurial career, you might consider testing the waters with a franchise business first, before starting a business of your own from scratch.)

Most small businesses that fail do so because there's not enough capital initially, and no fallback position. For this reason, all financial planning for a small business start-up should use a worst-case scenario. There's a rule of thumb to the effect that you should double even your most pessimistic projections about the amount of capital you'll need. If you've projected a worst-case need for $250,000, figure on $500,000.

In 1981 I made the mistake of launching my company with insufficient capital. I thought I could enter the broadcasting business with $250,000, when the need was ten times that much. For a CPA, that was an inexcusable error; I can only be grateful that I made it in my own behalf and not in behalf of a client.

Nothing really went wrong. I committed no major errors, nor did members of my staff. It just took two years longer than I thought it would to get our financial news service mounted. My sense of how long it took to get things done had been completely unrealistic. I had assumed that everyone would be as highly motivated as I was, which not only was not the case, but was completely unrealistic on my part. I'd also assumed that customers would respond to our product the moment it went on the market, and that wasn't the case at all.

Most businesses require two years at an absolute minimum to become profitable. It takes that long for others to realize you're out there, to warm to your product and buy it. The world doesn't operate on an entrepreneur's timetable; it operates on the world's timetable. You may be the exception, of course, but if your experience is typical, customers or clients won't be beating a path to your door in the second month of operations.

But first things first: You won't be worrying about profitability timetables if you can't find the capital to finance your start-up.

I urge you to think twice before using all of your life savings or borrowing from a bank against the equity on your house. I've seen too many people who hit upon a great idea for a small business invest everything they had and wind up with nothing. It takes a long time to recover from that kind of an experience.

The only time you might consider borrowing against the equity in your house is if the equity is tremendous and you have a modest venture in mind, such as a window-washing service you intend to operate with your spouse out of your basement. But if you aspire to build a business of any conse-quence, involving employees and stockholders, don't tie up all your per-sonal assets.

If you're not using your savings or borrowing against your house, where will the money come from?

Finding a Financial Angel

Angels are people who help you raise money or who put up money themselves in exchange for financial participation in your company. If you have a sound idea for a profitable venture and know how to present it, there are thousands of angels out there who could conceivably want to be involved.

Angels make their living primarily by raising money and funding small companies in exchange for a fee, a piece of the action, or both. They are motivated by pride and greed. They get tremendous satisfaction from seeing a company grow and knowing that the company couldn't have grown without them. If the company succeeds, they stand to make enormous profits. The reason they're called angels is that very often they seem to drop from the sky when you're most in need, and offer you deliverance.

One morning in 1984 I calculated that I was seven days away from bankruptcy. That day, while doing a story on financial planning, I happened to interview a stockbroker named Ellen Margaretten, a partner in a small investment banking firm in North Miami Beach, Florida. After the interview, Ellen, an extremely observant and sensitive woman, said, "Steve, you have a funny look on your face. What's wrong?"

"I'm not too happy right now," I confessed. "I'm working eighty hours a week, I have a wonderful product, everybody loves it, but I just didn't have enough money to get my corporation off the ground."

"Well, tell me your story," Ellen said. She listened to me for five minutes. When I'd finished she said, "How much money will it take to bail you out right now and put a smile on your face?"

"Seventy-five grand."

"Well, you stop by here on Friday. There'll be a check made out to Steve Crowley for seventy-five thousand dollars."

Angels come in all sizes. On the smaller scale, an angel can be one individual and a secretary, working out of a home or small office. On a larger scale, angels are investment bankers with big staffs and fancy offices and seats on the financial exchanges. Many investment bankers are also brokers. They function as the bridge between the small entrepreneur and the stock market, or the small entrepreneur and individual investors who are eager to fund a company. Sometimes the brokers invest their own money, but most often they raise the money from clients.

It often starts with a "private placement." Suppose you need $500,000 to start your company. The angel finds ten people to put up $50,000 each, or puts up $50,000 himself and raises $450,000. Why will investors put up that kind of money in your company? Because they assume that if the company prospers, you'll want to take it public. In that event, their money will be converted to stock at a predetermined price that will yield them a profit, usually no less than 100 percent and often a great deal more.

The investment scenario just described is played thousands upon thousands of times each year throughout the United States. It's how our economy operates. It's how companies like yours get started. The money you raise through a private placement goes directly into your company's checkbook. If your company doesn't prosper, the investors lose their money; that's the risk they take in exchange for the opportunity of getting in on the ground floor and positioning themselves for those huge potential profits. Angels and the investors they find are sophisticated and seasoned people. They enter every private placement with the expectation of making money, but they know that many new ventures fail.

Angels use two terms more than any other. The first is "leap of faith." The second is "burn rate."

Investors won't touch a private placement meant to fund a poor idea that's poorly thought out and presented. But even a well-conceived, well-presented idea won't inspire them to make a "leap of faith" and risk their money unless they believe in the individual behind the project. It's the same dynamic at work when you go to your Uncle Joe and Aunt Sally and ask them for $25,000 to help you open a restaurant. What your aunt and uncle will be asking themselves is whether you have the knowledge, understanding, drive, and staying power to make your restaurant succeed. In the end 75 percent of all private placements are based on character.

The "burn rate" is the amount of money a month it will take to keep an enterprise going during its start-up phase. A small enterprise might have a burn rate of $10,000 to $25,000 a month; a large new corporation could burn millions. As an entrepreneur, you have to think in terms of "burn rate," as well. If you're projecting a loss of $15,000 a month for a year, you may wish to allow for a "burn rate" of $20,000 or even $25,000 a month in the budget you present to your angel.

In pitching angels of any kind, be they banks, investment bankers, relatives, or friends, it's important to remember that it's much easier to raise $400,000 at the outset than it is to raise $200,000 at the outset and another $200,000 down the line when you've discovered that your initial projections were too low.

Small service business excepted, there are few businesses today that don't require seed capital of at least $250,000. Most investment bankers aren't interested in anything smaller than $250,000. Many won't consider an investment below $500,000. Two hundred fifty thousand dollars used to be a lot of money. It isn't any longer—at least not to the investment community.

❖   ❖   ❖

Angels aren't at all difficult to locate. In most major cities, you'll find them listed in the yellow pages of the telephone directory, usually under "Investment Securities" or "Stockbrokers."

But before you make a cold call, try the following approach. First, make a significant deposit in a bank of your choice. Then buy your banker a good lunch. During that lunch, tell him exactly what you plan to do, and how much you think you'll need.

It may be that your bank will have an investment banking department, in which case your banker will send you there. But that may not be the best place for you because investment bankers employed by banks tend to think like bankers first and investors second, which means that they may not demonstrate the willingness to risk required in your situation. Should that prove to be the case, your bank executive will almost certainly know the better angels in your community, some of whom may be depositors, and he can refer you to them.

Whether it's your banker who makes the contact or not, you are usually just a few telephone calls away from a proper introduction to an angel. Someone you know knows an angel, or several angels; by networking with friends or colleagues with business or investing experience, you can develop a recommended list of angels. Perhaps no one you know has direct knowledge of an angel; in that event ask to be introduced to any of their friends or acquaintances who are presidents or vice presidents of firms in their area.

It will pay you to interview a number of angels until you find one with whom you're comfortable, not simply from a business, but from a moral, standpoint as well. In looking for my angels, I went to New York several times over the course of a year to interview a dozen smaller investment bankers. I've already mentioned Gordon Gecko, the character in *Wall Street* played so indelibly by Michael Douglas that he won an Oscar. I met a few such men, and didn't like them. You don't need any special knowledge to determine whether you want to do business with an angel; you'll know the first time you talk to him or her face to face. It probably cost me $50,000 to find a quality investment banker who would stay with our company and be our *consigliere*, but it was money well spent; today, he's an integral part of the company, not only an angel but a mentor. But my cost was far more than you'll probably need to spend, and it could wind up costing you nothing.

Once you've found a qualified angel, it's up to you to persuade him or her that your project is a sound and exciting investment. There's only one way to do that.

Creating Your "Package"

The first step in starting a company of any size is to put together what everyone involved in new ventures—CPAs, lawyers, investment bankers, angels—calls "the package."

Packages come in several varieties. Some look like college term papers, others like the outline for a book or the treatment for a screenplay. Some are

typed and presented in loose-leaf binders, others printed and bound. Whatever form the package comes in, it offers an organized plan describing the
purpose of the enterprise, its plan of operation, where it's going to be
located, the number of employees it will have, projected costs and revenues
over a five-year period, and the anticipated need for capital. In addition, the
package makes an argument for the success of the proposed enterprise,
suggesting, among other things, why this service or product or project is
better than the competition. Finally, the package describes the background
of the people involved in the prospective enterprise.

It's the package that represents you to investors and lenders and tells them
whether they want to size you up in person.

Putting a package together will take time, but it will save you far more
time in the end because potential lenders will all be asking for the same
information, and you'll be able to send them the package without making a
presentation until you're certain of their interest. Additionally, in putting
your package together, you'll have put myriad bright ideas and potential
problems through your mental meat grinder. In short, you'll have a powerful
and formidable business plan, which should be followed closely and updated periodically.

It's said that a prospective buyer of your house will make a decision
within fifteen seconds after entering your front door. Frequently, the decision process is virtually complete *before* the buyer comes inside.

It's the same with business proposals. I once pitched a show to ABC that
had the president of the network jumping up and down within a minute.
"This is great," he said, "this is the kind of program I want on ABC." He
called several of his executives out of their meetings and into his office and
said, "I want you to make this show right away." That's when I discovered
that presidents of corporations don't always have the last word, because his
executives didn't share his enthusiasm, and the show didn't get made. But
that doesn't obscure my point: I wouldn't have had so much as a chance if I
hadn't gotten the president of the network excited about my concept within
the first minute of my pitch. In a business proposal, the equivalent of that
first minute is the summary sheet of the package.

Every proposal should have one sheet of paper that summarizes in five or
six short paragraphs what your concept and intentions are: the corporation
you're starting, the product or service you're marketing, the amount of
money you'll need, the potential for profit, and the quality of the people
involved. Anyone interested in your proposal will eventually read it all, but
almost no one will read beyond the first page if they're not hooked on that
page.

The proposal must be well and clearly written, with a narrative style that
tells a story. Nothing convoluted, no big words, just plain, specific talk.

Any local or regional office of the Small Business Administration will
provide you with a folder that includes everything you need to know to

create a business package. And you certainly can create such a package yourself. But to try to do it yourself would be foolhardy, in my judgment. This is the time when you need the help of experts, first a CPA with experience in launching small companies, and second, a lawyer with the same kind of experience who's a whiz at writing proposals.

In Praise of Expert Help

The period when you're attempting to organize a venture that's going to preoccupy you and make your dreams come true if successful is no time to cut corners. You would certainly never consider going into business today without buying a computer—or at least you shouldn't. Trying to save a few thousand dollars by doing without an accountant and a lawyer is as sure a prescription for failure as are undercapitalizing, underestimating initial expenses, neglecting customers, and buying champagne and caviar on a beer and pretzels budget.

Here's just one example of how a qualified CPA can help you. Suppose you're starting a very modest enterprise, one you really can finance by yourself without compromising your personal assets. And now suppose that from this $50,000 or $100,000 you've put up, you begin to draw $200 to $300 a week in living expenses. Should you pay income tax on that draw? Absolutely not. It was your money to begin with. You paid tax on it when you earned it. But you *will* pay tax on it again unless someone sets your new venture up as an "S Corporation," the term for a small business corporation.

Paying taxes they shouldn't pay is the biggest mistake novice entrepreneurs make. A competent CPA will divide your initial investment into both shares of stock and loans payable back to you with interest. This assures that during your start-up phase, when the company is still losing money, you're paying no income tax on your draw and no payroll or social security taxes either.

As to lawyers, I've probably heard the same jokes you have, but the truth is that a good lawyer specialized in small business ventures can not only help you with your proposal, he or she can keep you from breaking the law. You may be the world's most law-abiding person, but if you don't know the laws governing business activity, you may unwittingly violate them, and to such a degree that you'll be out of business. Two women I know started a catering business, working out of their homes. In due course, they became remarkably successful, so successful, in fact, that they hired employees, mass-produced food, and had delivery trucks pulling up to their doors. Guess what? They were in violation of every zoning and health law on the books. Not that they were unclean. To the contrary. But by working out of their homes without the proper permits, they had avoided inspections by local health authorities. They were forced to move to a storefront, and fined so heavily that they almost lost their business. One hour with a qualified lawyer would have avoided the problem.

So, in starting up an enterprise, spend what it takes to do it right.

The most important job of the CPA at this time is to tell you how much money you're going to need to successfully launch your venture. If you're not a CPA yourself, you'll need one to show you how to estimate what your revenues and expenses will be. If you prepare yourself thoroughly in advance, amassing all the data you can, you'll be able to get invaluable advice at a reasonable cost. Whatever you do, don't go to a CPA without a preliminary set of numbers, because you'll just be wasting money.

Very often when you take an investment project to a CPA, he'll tell you all the reasons why you shouldn't do it. That's because CPAs are not entrepreneurs. Their job is to point out all the risks in the venture you're contemplating. Your job is to listen attentively, assess their qualifications to give advice, change your plan when and if the advice makes sense, and not be deterred overall if your basic program is a sound one. (CPAs, of course, won't be the only naysayers in your world. They'll be joined by your attorney, members of your family, and friends.)

Once your CPA has satisfied his conscience by telling you all the reasons why you shouldn't proceed, he's going to want to help you put your business proposal together, since that's the way he makes his money, and we all operate to some degree on greed.

A CPA qualified in launching small companies can put all the numbers together and help you formulate a business plan. But he can't, as a rule, write the package. For that you need a lawyer well versed in the narrative form traditionally used in the writing of business proposals, which investors are accustomed to and expect. I have not met many CPAs who are good writers. I have met lawyers who are great writers.

A qualified CPA will know of a qualified attorney and, in all likelihood, will have worked with him before. Just make certain that the man he takes you to is, in addition to being a great writer, a great attorney, because when you deal with other people's money, everything must be done according to the letter of the law.

How Much Control Must You Give Up?

Whenever you ask other people to invest their money, you are going to have to give up a measure of ownership and control. The question is, how much?

It's the job of your attorney and CPA to tell you how much you'll have to give up in order to raise the money you need to start your enterprise. It's your job to tell them how much you're *willing* to give up. Even though they are working for you, it's important to impress upon them that you're a together, savvy, smart person and a hard negotiator. They won't respect you if you say, "Gee I don't know what I should give up. What's normal?" You have to say,

"Look, I'm willing to give up x percent of this company to raise this money." In all likelihood, they'll say, "No, you're going to have to give up y percent." And then you negotiate and wind up with a compromise.

Obviously you want to retain as much ownership and control as you can. It's always desirable to attempt to retain at least 51 percent, and when you're starting small with a group of friends, each of whom is putting in $10,000 to $25,000, that can usually be accomplished. When I started my company, it was with three close friends. But because we were friends didn't mean that I didn't have to negotiate. I wound up with 58 percent of the company, and they shared the remaining 42 percent, a fair deal given that I would be doing all the work.

It's very important that the entrepreneur have control and some degree of ownership. You want to be very careful about how much of yourself you give away at the outset of your effort. I doubt that you'd be comfortable giving away 80 percent just to get the seed money you need for a venture that's going to preempt your working life. On the other hand, if you're starting a business that requires a great deal of capital to get it off the ground, and that's the business you've dreamed of, you may have no other option. It turned out that I didn't. If I wanted to be the president of my company, but was unwilling to risk my personal assets, I had to raise money through outside sources.

While retaining as much control as you possibly can is your objective, you don't necessarily have to have 51 percent of your venture, or anything close to it, to make your dreams come true. As the entrepreneur, you will own a considerable number of shares in your own venture. Should the venture succeed and should you take your company public, you stand to earn a tremendous profit. Most companies that go public are start-up operations; wealth is created when the original owners of a successful company sell their stock to the public at many times the price they paid for it. I put less than $100,000 into my corporation at the outset; four years later, my shares were worth a million dollars.

Incidentally, it's good psychologically in any business you're starting to have some of your own money on the line. It needn't be a lot. But investors are comforted by the knowledge that you're risking alongside them.

STEP THREE: GAINING SUPPORT FOR YOUR PLAN

The moment you announce to family and friends that you want to make a change, you're going to get a lot of resistance—particularly if that change involves a move to a new locale. You'll be told that you shouldn't do it, that it won't work, that life won't be as good there, that it's not right to leave your family. And it won't be easy, because the tradition of remaining close to parents and grandparents is a deeply rooted one. But if you're to be happy, you have to live the life that you want to live and not the life that other people want you to live. Living life as they want you to live it makes them happy, not you.

When I made up my mind to move to Florida, I told myself that at the very least I would discover who my friends were. I assumed that any number of people would maintain that I'd gone off the deep end. I couldn't have been more right. By that point, I was something of a celebrity in Rhode Island because of my television work. I also had a lot of money. Between the two, it seemed that everybody wanted to be my friend. After I announced my intentions, people actually crossed the street to avoid talking to me. It was as though, in determining to leave Warwick, I had somehow disparaged the life they were living.

Only one man didn't desert me. His name is Ernie Baptista, and he was and is a partner in a consulting firm that specializes in managing employee benefit and pension plans. He invited me to lunch one day—the first invitation I'd had in weeks—and he said, "You're doing exactly the right thing. I really admire you. I've thought of leaving Rhode Island myself, but my wife would never leave, and I love my wife." He believed that I'd shown promise in television, and that I had the talent to go national, an ambition I'd hoped to fulfill by setting up a small company that would syndicate features about money. "How much will it take to start that TV production company down there?" he asked.

"Probably $250,000 to get it off the ground," I said.

Ernie's reply astounded and thrilled me. I remember it word for word. "Well, when you get down there," he said, "there'll be a cashier's check for you for $100,000 from myself and a friend, and we'll send the rest later."

The worst thing you can do is to make an abrupt announcement of your plans without preparing those your decision will affect. It takes a fair amount of planning.

During the transitional phase I made as many contacts as I could in my new profession. In addition, I identified my mentors and angels. To friends and acquaintances who didn't know how seriously I'd been plotting my new life, it appeared, when I announced my plans, that I had little, if any, support. That was because I couldn't afford, before the fact, to publicly commit myself, because if I had, I would have immediately lost all my clients. If you start telling people that you're planning to become a television broadcaster, they are not going to ask you to do their tax returns.

If you are happily married, it's imperative that you not only inform your spouse of your thinking from the outset, but attempt to convey your enthusiasm and the reasons for it. If your spouse doesn't support your plan, you've got to weigh the marriage against what you want to do with your life.

Fifty-five percent of all married women have careers of their own, so you may have a case of one profession pulling the other. In most cases, money is the overriding factor, because when one spouse is making $120,000 and the other $30,000, weight would have to be given to the larger earner. Usually, it's the man who earns the larger salary, but I've seen a number of situations in which it's the woman. Where you don't gain support from your spouse and children, you put the entire family in serious jeopardy. The Big Six accounting firms are notorious for moving people around a great deal, very often against their wishes. A friend of mine had no sooner become a partner in Providence than they moved him to Boston, and then to Miami, and a short time later to New York. The promotions made him a great deal of extra money, which they're thoroughly enjoying, but the several moves put a lot of stress on the family.

Expect to get the most resistance from your spouse and children. Your spouse will have ties in the community, either professional or social or both, that she or he will be loath to relinquish. As for your children, nothing is more important to them than their friends, and nothing more threatening than the prospect of entering a strange community where social circles, formed since the early years of their peers, are extremely difficult to penetrate.

As to parents, they frequently follow once they realize that you're settled in to a good environment, doing well, and have no intention of returning to your hometown.

Chasing your dream can be a lonely business because you're dealing with your personal desires and goals, almost to the exclusion of loved ones. Yet psychologists tell us that only when we've developed ourselves to our fullest potential on all levels can we present ourselves to family and friends as someone worthy of their love.

II

THE MAKEOVER

5

Learning How to Spend

SPENDING is the forbidden apple of the financial Garden of Eden, where all our troubles begin.

Spend too much and you fall into debt.
Fall into debt and you can't save.
Fail to save and you have nothing to invest.
With nothing invested, you're up the inflation tree.

The following chapters will challenge the way you handle every aspect of personal finance: debt, saving and investing, how you buy your homes and cars, how you provide for your children's college education, how you protect your family, shelter your income, and provide for your retirement. But it all begins with spending, because only when you've learned how to spend for maximum enjoyment with minimum damage does everything else begin to fall into place. Your objective will be to cut your spending by anywhere from 5 to 20 percent, so that you can direct excess money that you would have paid to other people toward the things that make you happy: a nest egg that will give you freedom, college for your children, a down payment on a house.

Impossible, you say? Easy, I say, once you know how to do it. It's like panning for gold, sifting through your expenses until you find five dollars here and fifty dollars there, buying only what you need at the best available price.

THE SYMPTOMS OF MINDLESS SPENDING

Most people have no idea where their money is going. They know only how much comes in. Two out of five Americans today have neither a checking nor a savings account. They live from paycheck to paycheck, cashing each check the moment they get it, usually at those check-cashing stores that have proliferated in recent years, then buying money orders to pay their bills. When you pay 2 percent each week to cash your paycheck, that's more than one week's pay thrown away every year. Why would anyone pay such a penalty? Because it takes money to open a bank account, and these people spend theirs so fast they almost never have any left. What few dollars that might be left are spent on lottery tickets, the greatest rip-off ever perpetrated on the working class.

One of the symptoms of the mindless spending that has become rampant in our society is the emergence of pawnshops as one of the hottest financial service businesses in the country. A few miles from my home is a pawnshop that's open 24 hours a day; every Friday the cars—some of them Mercedes and Cadillacs and BMWs—roll up to the pawnshop door and their drivers go inside to hock their Rolexes so that they'll have enough money to take their wives out for dinner that weekend.

There's a myth in our society that well-educated, sophisticated, upper-income people like doctors and lawyers are somehow immune to this kind of hand-to-mouth living; in fact many such people are the most chronic overspenders in our society.

As a private pilot, I fly in and out of many airports. At every one of them, I see rows of empty planes tied down. Most of those planes are owned by individuals; most were purchased for $50,000 or more, cost $3,000 a year to maintain, and are flown about forty hours a year. A comparable sight confronts me when I visit a marina: hundreds of boats tied to their slips, many of them purchased for $100,000 or more, and costing their owners $10,000 a year to dock and maintain. Those boats don't get a great deal more use than the airplanes. If the owners of those planes and boats can afford the expense of buying and maintaining such heavy-duty items, well and good. But four times out of five, that isn't the case.

It's said that Elvis Presley once had twelve cars in his driveway. That's twelve cars to garage and maintain and pay insurance on, and repair when they break down, as well as one or two full-time employees to make sure it all gets done. Instead of providing pleasure, the cars become an emotional drag. Maybe Elvis didn't feel that way, but I certainly did when I owned my Mercedes, BMW, and Cadillac in those flush years in Rhode Island.

That's what makes this spending binge we've been on for the last two decades so ironic: So much of the money goes for items that bring the spenders little or no satisfaction, and may not even be good for their health. I've lost count of the people who have complained to me that they can't find two thousand dollars a year to set up an Individual Retirement Account—one of the greatest tax-saving bargains ever offered—yet continue to smoke, drink to excess, and take lavish vacations.

Parents who smoke and drink to excess set a terrible role model for their children. Why should it surprise them—as it so often does—that in spending to excess they are setting an equally terrible role model in a vital aspect of life? Perhaps I'm a little more aware of this than I might otherwise be because I'm the father of two extremely young boys, but what I know for a fact is that when young children, from their very first memory, see Mommy and Daddy buying goods and services at an almost uncontrollable pace, they will grow up with very little regard for the value of a dollar.

One of the reasons that we adults have so little regard for the value of the dollar today—I say "we" deliberately because I don't wish to put myself on a pedestal; I must constantly remind myself of my own advice to others—is that we rarely transact our expenditures with actual dollars. In the overwhelming number of instances we write checks or pay with a credit card. Bankers love it when we pay with such noncurrency means as credit cards and debit cards—those cards that immediately debit your bank balance by the amount you've spent. Why do they love it? Because they know that as difficult as it is for us to visualize the real dollars we're spending when we write a check, it's even more difficult when we pay with plastic.

When I urge the parents of small children to pay for goods and services with real dollars in their children's presence it's with two thoughts in mind. The first thought is that it will provide the children with a vivid example of what real dollars are and how difficult they are to earn. The second thought is that it will make the parents think twice or even three times before making their next purchase.

If that doesn't do it, perhaps what follows will.

THE CRUX OF THE MATTER: FUTURE SPENDING POWER

The government tells us that the annual rate of inflation has averaged 4.5 percent. Very often when I lecture, I'll ask my audience how many of them believe that their cost of living is rising only 4.5 percent a year. Not a hand is raised. Then I'll ask how many believe their cost of living is rising at a higher rate. Every hand in the room goes up.

One of the problems with the government's inflation rate is that it's based so heavily on the prices of agricultural and petroleum products, which tend to be stable over long periods of time and rise dramatically only in times of emergency (witness the price of oil following Iraq's invasion of Kuwait in August 1990). What the inflation index doesn't reflect as well is what you and I spend our money on each day: clothing, movie tickets, a Domino's Pizza, batteries for a camera, computer paper, getting a suit or dress cleaned. When the cleaner raises the price of cleaning a man's suit, it rarely goes from $4.50 to $4.75; from $4.50 to $5.50 is far more likely.

For certain individuals, the cost of living can increase between 7 and 10 percent annually, and even more if the goods and services that matter most to them rise steeply in price. Not long ago, I attended a financial seminar on inflation, which speaker after speaker pegged at 4 percent. I pointed out to the organizers of the seminar that in one year they'd raised their fee from $200 to $300—an increase of 50 percent.

No matter what your age today, if you live a healthy life, don't contract cancer, and don't get killed in an accident, one day you'll retire and live on your pension. The question you've got to ask yourself isn't merely what kind of a life your pension will buy you on the day you retire, but what kind of a life it will buy you twenty years later. The answer, deplorably, is 25 percent of what it bought at the outset.

As noted earlier, the value of our money gets cut in half every ten to twelve years. Suppose you're about to retire with a pension of $100,000 a year. Sounds good, doesn't it? Ten years from now, the pension will be worth only $50,000 in terms of today's dollars. Ten years later, you'll be living as you would today if you had only a $25,000 pension.

I know a woman whose husband died many years ago at the age of fifty-eight, leaving her with $300,000 to last her the rest of her life. Today, her $300,000 has grown to $400,000, but she's miserable because she knows how much less the income from her capital buys her than it did years ago, and she is terrified of the future.

A friend of mine in San Francisco owns a beautiful home in Pacific Heights with a spectacular view of the bay and the Golden Gate Bridge. At the height of the big run-up in California real estate prices, his realtor told him that she could get him $1.5 million for his home. My friend, a freelance technical writer, had always dreamed of writing fiction, but had been reluctant to dedicate his life to it because he realized he might never sell what he wrote. Now, at fifty-five, he thought he saw a way to finance his dream. He calculated that if he sold his home and bought another one for cash for a fifth of the price in a small community in the Pacific Northwest, a place he'd always wanted to live, he'd have no debt whatever and $600,000 in the bank after all his taxes and selling costs were paid. Without debts, he could easily live on the $50,000 to $60,000 his money would earn, he told me. What did I think? I told him that I was a great believer in chasing one's dreams, but I urged him to think about the downstream consequences. Ten years later, his $50,000 to $60,000 would be worth $25,000 to $30,000 in terms of today's values, and twenty years later it would be worth $12,500 to $15,000. Along the way, he'd pick up Social Security, but I asked him to consider whether even that would be enough to buy him a comfortable life. If not, he would have to make provision for some additional income.

I know of a man who was once extremely wealthy and was used to living very well. For some time now he has had to dip into his capital to maintain his living standard, in the process of which his many millions have dwindled to less than two million. Should his capital diminish to less than a million, he's said, he intends to commit suicide. However sad a commentary that is on the state of our values, it does illustrate how not even the very wealthy escape the ravages of inflation.

The important thing to remember about inflation, however, is that you can control its impact to a considerable degree by the way you spend your money. Your future spending power is influenced by many things: how much you earn, how much you save, how well you invest, the strategies you employ to cut your taxes. But as I said at the beginning of the chapter, it all begins with spending, because your spending habits today influence to a great degree your spending needs tomorrow.

CALCULATING YOUR PERSONAL INFLATION INDEX

Your Personal Inflation Index (PII) depends on what goods and services you buy most often, and where and how you choose to live. What it tells you is how much more money you're going to need next year to live as well as you're living this year. If to live comfortably you need $30,000 this year and your PII is 8 percent, you'll need $2,400 more next year—8 percent of $30,000. If your income doesn't change, and your PII is 8 percent, in real dollars your salary drops by $2,400. Just to stay even, you'll need a raise of 8 percent.

There's a trick in finance you may have heard of called "the Rule of 72." Divide the rate of return you're getting on an investment into 72 and you can determine how long it will take your money to double. If you're earning 8 percent, after taxes, your money will double in nine years. Using the same rule, you can divide your PII into 72 and determine how long it will take for the value of your money to be cut in half. If your PII is 8 percent, and your income remains constant, your purchasing power will be cut in half every nine years. If you're earning $30,000 today, and your PII is 8 percent, you'll need to be earning $60,000 nine years from now, and $120,000 eighteen years from now, just to maintain your current life-style.

Suppose I told you that twenty-five years from now you'll pay four times more for a Chevrolet that costs $12,000 today—i.e., $48,000. Would you believe me? Probably not. But a little more than twenty-five years ago, I paid $2,850 for a Chevrolet—a fourth of what the comparable car costs today.

In the old days, of course, those of us fortunate to own homes and other assets were able to diminish inflation's impact, and overall might come out ahead. Our 8 percent PII might have meant an annual increase in living costs of $5,000, but if we owned a $200,000 house and the value of that house increased even 3 percent a year, we were up by $6,000 on the assets side of the ledger, and $1,000 to the good. If you owned an $80,000 house and real estate prices were rising by 6 percent a year, then you had $4,800 to offset other rising costs. With that kind of increase, you were undoubtedly getting a free ride on the inflation gravy train.

The problem today, and for the foreseeable future, is that the inflation ride may be over. As we've seen, rather than increasing in value, real estate in many areas is decreasing in value. We not only have nothing against which to offset our rising expenses, we're losing ground on a second front.

The one good thing about owning a house, even in a down market, is that to the extent your money is going to service a fixed mortgage payment—and that's where most money goes—inflation isn't hurting you. To the contrary, each year the mortgage payment in real dollars gets smaller and smaller by whatever rate the overall value of the currency diminishes.

Depending on what you spend your money for, you're insulated in other ways as well. If the price of milk goes up by 20 percent this year, but you don't drink milk because it disagrees with your digestive tract, you have more need for a gastroenterologist than you do a financial consultant. If you're retired and living in Florida and driving fifteen miles a week like most of your neighbors, you're probably filling your gas tank up about four to six times a year. It really wouldn't affect you a great deal if the price of gas were to double.

But what if you own a boat or an RV, and are paying 14 percent on your loan? And what if, in addition, you're accustomed to charging many goods and services on credit cards, and then allowing those balances to slide instead of paying them off each month, thereby incurring a finance charge of 18 or 19 percent? Then your Personal Inflation Index is going to be far above the government's inflation index, because your PII is tied directly to the amount of interest you are paying.

Calculating your PII exactly would require you to determine what proportion each of your expenses was to your overall expenses, a difficult, tedious, and unnecessary operation. All you need is a ballpark figure to alert yourself to how much your annual costs are increasing, what a serious problem that is, and why it behooves you to do something about it. First and foremost, that means learning how to spend.

THE CASE FOR SMART SPENDING

In college, my "Economics I" professor always talked about money in terms of human pleasure. Whether one was buying necessities or luxuries, each purchase supposedly produced "happies."

"Happies" are units of personal gratification gained from the pleasure that spending brings. A major part of the pleasure is knowing that what we've bought is something we both need and can afford. One without the other does not produce a "happy." We've all read stories about the great shoppers of Fifth Avenue and Rodeo Drive. The truth is that most of these shop-til-they-drop people get a high from shopping, perhaps as reassurance that they can have anything they want, but go into a deep depression the moment they get home and look at what they've bought.

I seriously question whether people buying Louis Vuitton luggage today even though they can't afford it are getting their "happies" worth. Not only does it strain their budget, it will deepen their depression the moment it gets banged up. There's an added problem: fancy luggage points a well-to-do traveler out to thieves. Really wealthy people, the kind who don't need to make a statement to reassure themselves about who they are, use old, often battered, luggage.

When we talk about smart spending, we're not promulgating a monklike life involving abstinence, or even sacrifice. What we're talking about is squeezing the most satisfaction out of the fewest dollars—and in the process freeing up money for the very "happies" you want more than any others. How do you get these satisfactions? To use a phrase made familiar by the late and great John Houseman, you get it "the old-fashioned way," by shopping for bargains.

One day a few years ago, a friend of mine picked me up in a gorgeous Mercedes that looked like it had just been driven out of the showroom. "Gee, Bill," I joked, "I didn't know you could afford this kind of a car on your salary."

"Actually, Steve," he replied, "this car cost me $11,000."

"I don't believe you," I said.

"Believe me," he said. "It took me six months to find it."

What he'd done, Bill said, was to pore through the classified sections of newspapers and haunt Mercedes dealerships in an effort to find a Mercedes he could afford. He found it at last at an estate sale, the property of an elderly woman who had recently passed away. Not only had the car been well cared for, it had been driven fewer than 10,000 miles. Bill will drive that car for five years, possibly ten, and, when he sells it, get his $11,000 back.

In my business I come across people all the time who are able to live immensely fulfilling lives by taking great pains not to overspend. They find a hundred different ways to cut their spending—even recharging old batteries instead of buying new ones—and what they get in exchange is an affordable life and peace of mind.

The most important question on any cruise, no matter where its destination or what the weather is like, is how much the person in the next cabin paid for his or her ticket. Small wonder. The passenger in 256 paid $2,000 for his accommodation. The passenger in 258 paid $800 for hers. She shopped hard and he didn't. Any travel agent can sell you a ticket at full fare. The art is to find an agent who belongs to a consortium that has deals with the cruise lines for vast reductions in fares. How do you do this? Call the cruise line and get a quote or a pamphlet on the list prices. Then make as many calls as you have to until you find a travel agency that specializes in cruises. The agencies that get deals with the cruise lines are invariably those that send a lot of business their way. It's as simple as that. All it takes on your part is half a dozen telephone calls and a little bit of patience.

It's the same with air travel. Since the time of deregulation, the price you pay for an airline ticket has had little to do with the distance you were traveling, and much to do with competition between the airlines. It's a complex game, but one that the best travel agents know how to play. An agent for an airline wants to sell you a ticket on that airline, and may or may not give you the best deal. A travel agent who wants your business will do a computer search for the best available fare to your destination at the time you want to travel, irrespective of the airline, and *then* compare your fare to the best fare available. If there's a big difference between what you booked and what's possible the agent will attempt to get you the better rate.

The master of cut-rate travel is a man named Tom Parsons. Some time ago, I went to a hotel to interview Tom, who is the author of *Best Fares*, a fat newsletter on discount travel. I found him in the biggest suite in the hotel. "Wow," I said, "what did you have to pay for this place?"

"Eighty-nine dollars," he said. On his arrival, Tom had asked to see an assistant manager. Identifying himself as a member of the Marriott's upgrade program, he'd told the assistant manager that he had his family with him and needed a suite but didn't want to pay for one. If by any chance there was an empty suite that night, would the assistant manager be willing to let him have it for the price of a regular room? Seeing an opportunity to create good will at no cost to the hotel—he knew the suite wouldn't be sold that night— the assistant manager obliged.

The travel industry calls the hotel room that remains empty overnight, or the airline seat that flies without a passenger, or the unoccupied cabin on a cruise, the "most perishable commodity" in the world. The most perishable commodity in our lives is the dollar we didn't have to spend, either because we overpaid or we didn't need what we'd bought.

A while ago, Bill Blass, the famous designer of men's clothing, went on a television interview wearing his trademark blue blazer and slacks. When the interviewer complimented him on how well he was dressed, Blass, who makes a living selling clothes, confessed that his blazer was eight years old. "Buy quality," he advised.

The fact is that we can only wear one suit of clothing at a time, and if we take good care of our suits, they will last for years. An expert in men's clothing once told me that the biggest mistake men make is having their suits and slacks and sports coats constantly cleaned. Over time cleaning will destroy the garments. This expert recommended that men should rotate their suits and have them pressed three times as often as they have them cleaned.

Women are constantly criticized for buying an inordinate number of suits and dresses, and much of that criticism is justified. But men are often just as guilty. Ties today cost as much as shirts. Imagine: fifty and even one hundred dollars for a tie. Most men own far too many ties. Rather than pay such outrageous prices, they could send their old ties to companies that not only clean but remodel them—making them fatter or leaner depending on the style—for a fraction of what a new tie would cost.

When I owned my speedboat, I could easily afford it, and it did give me a measure of "happies." But I would never consider buying a large powerboat again because all sorts of rental companies have sprung up in recent years that will rent me a boat by the hour or day for a fraction of what it would cost me to maintain and insure the boat and pay the bank installments. If you want to take your family on a two-week sailing trip, you don't have to own a sailboat; you can rent it, and use the thousands of dollars you've saved in other, more rewarding ways.

BREAKING THE SPENDING HABIT

How do you break the spending habit? The way you break any undesirable habit: You retrain yourself in manageable increments.

Suppose you look in the mirror one morning and conclude that you've got to take off some weight. You resolve to skip breakfast for a week, have a fruit plate for lunch and forego those predinner cocktails. By midafternoon you'll be fighting to stay awake, and by the time the cocktail hour rolls around, you'll say to yourself, "Tomorrow." That martini will do more than add 150 calories to your waistline; it will convince you that you haven't got it in you to change.

So with spending. Try to reform yourself in a day, denying yourself all those pleasures all at once, and you'll fall by the wayside within days. It's the same with spending. Try to lick bad spending habits cold turkey, and you won't last a week.

Suppose you're a tennis player or a golfer, and you want to transform your game. The way to do that, as previously noted, is to stop playing for an interval of several months, take lessons, and practice without the stress of competition. Only in this manner will your bad habits be replaced by good ones. Too much pressure before the good habits have been ingrained, and you'll revert right back to the old ones you were trying to kick.

So we're going to start with a warm-up, just like we do in athletics. Rather than denying yourself anything, you're going to learn how to maintain the same life-style on a sizably diminished budget.

Here are the rules:

1. Always shop in supermarkets, never in convenience stores, no matter how convenient they are. You'll save a minimum of 10 percent and as much as 20 percent. No exceptions.

2. Don't go into a supermarket without a batch of discount coupons. They can save you up to 30 percent on groceries and personal care products. When you get a flyer in the mail or your newspaper, read it. If your newspaper carries a special food section—very often, it comes with the Thursday paper—go through it. Many supermarkets maintain a coupon bin at the entrance to their store for the convenience of customers. Go through it before shopping—and, incidentally, take a look at the supermarket's most recent newspaper ad, which will be visibly posted at the entrance.

3. Avoid high-markup stores in fashionable areas.

4. Shop the sales, and shop them early. Virtually every department store in the country has a white sale at least once a year, usually in January. That's the only time you should buy your towels and sheets. If you maintain a charge account with a local department store, you'll get a notice of a presale for clients. Don't delay; go then.

5. Shop the specialty discounters. Most urban areas have at least one men's store where suits, sport coats, slacks, and overcoats can be bought at a deep discount over what you'd pay in the more fashionable shops. In New York, BFO is a popular outlet. In Los Angeles, it's Dorman-Winthrop. Sym's stores are all over Florida and elsewhere as well.

Filene's basement store in Boston is world famous, and deservedly so, not only for its quality but for its bargains. Articles of clothing that haven't sold fast enough or are out of season are moved to the basement and retagged at superlow prices. For the Boston branch and many others, it's an opportunity to salvage something out of the merchandise and reduce their inventory so that they'll have room for new, seasonal items. For the customers, it's an opportunity for unbelievable bargains. An $800 designer sports jacket can be bought for $125, a $600 women's suit for $175. The only problem with Filene's bargain basement is that it sometimes becomes a battleground for shoppers.

6. Eat at home, not in restaurants. Even food chains have to build rent, salaries, utilities, and profit into the simple hamburger. In a fancier restaurant, the tip you pay your waiter would more than cover the cost of the ingredients for your home-cooked dinner. For the same reasons, brown bag it to lunch.

7. Do it yourself. Start replacing outside service jobs with your own muscle and sweat. Wash and wax the car, mow the lawn, change your oil, launder your shirts, shine your shoes, and wash and set your own hair. Try to learn a little about home upkeep and maintenance—painting, paperhanging, and making minor appliance repairs. If you don't know anything about it, there's a whole shelf of home-repair books in your local library. For inspiration, recall that when electricians and plumbers increase their hourly rates, they don't do so in terms of the inflation index. Their increases are on the order of 10, 12, or 15 percent.

8. Shop for a better bank. Banks are in trouble. They need your money. They'll offer inducements to get it. Maintain a certain minimum balance, and they'll pay you interest, even on a checking account. If you can't keep the balance up, and know you'll pay charges, make certain that the bank you choose has the lowest checking and service charges around.

9. Shop for the best credit card. If your credit is excellent you may qualify for a lower interest charge card. Not everyone charges 18 percent.

10. If you move, do it yourself. Forty three million people, about one in five of us, will move sometime in the coming year. We move, on average, eleven times in a lifetime. Moving without the help of professional movers used to be something only the ambitious would try. Today, it's something most of us try. Four out of five of us now move ourselves, and for good reason: We can save three-quarters of the expense. A study by Ryder Truck Rentals says the average cost of a household move between 100 and 200 miles is $1,332 using a national van line. But using a rental truck, the same move would cost $349, a savings of $983, or 74 percent. New tax rules make do-it-yourself moving even more attractive from a financial point of view, because it's tougher now to get a break for our job-related moving expenses.

11. Buy used—and sell what you no longer use. Before you put out a thousand dollars or more for a new dining room table and set of chairs, or pay $500 for a coffee table, check the used furniture stores in your city. In many cities, you'll find shops with stunning collections of used men's and women's clothing in terrific condition, selling at a fraction of what they cost new in the leading stores. In chapter 9 we'll be talking about how to buy a luxury car in mint condition and with low mileage for 30 percent less than a new one would have cost, saving yourself $10,000 to $20,000 in the process. Flea markets are a great place for bargains; my wife paid $80 for a pair of sunglasses, then found an identical pair at a flea market for $27. There's no shame attached to tracking down bargains; it's always in vogue.

The other side of buying used is to eliminate unnecessary items from your life, and profit in the process. That used furniture and clothing came from well-to-do households; one reason they're wealthy is that they convert possessions they no longer need to cash.

A yard or a garage sale is a great place to find bargains. It's also a way to empty your closets and attics of clutter and wind up with some cash. Is there a guitar no one's touched for a dozen years? Sell it. As you'll learn in chapter 11, that $200 or $300 you get for the instrument can double in six years. Did you buy a personal computer and find out you didn't need it, or couldn't master it? Sell it. The same for that VCR on which you were going to tape all those television programs. If you've never learned how to program it, don't feel guilty; most VCR purchasers don't.

12. Buy in bulk—another savings habit that's gaining popularity. Warehouse shopping clubs, born in the west, have swept eastward and can now be found in many parts of the country. In these supersupermarkets, you can buy a year's supply of coffee or a case of toothpaste, knocking the unit price down by as much as 20 percent. Bulk shopping can be a great time-saver, as

well. Instead of shopping for staple items every week, you're shopping once a month or even once every few months. When you're working for yourself, time really is money.

THAT NASTY "B" WORD: BUDGETING

Budgeting is a word that makes many people cringe. They think of it as something negative, and virtually impossible to do. The fact is that it's an easily acquired habit that accomplishes two vital objectives.

The first objective is to make certain that we have enough money each month to buy our necessities and pay our obligations on time. My mother was—and still is—a marvelous budgeter. Every payday, she took the money my father brought home and divided it into a dozen white envelopes: rent, electricity, taxes, groceries, etc. When the monthly bills came due, the money was there to pay them. Simple, but it works.

The second vital objective of a budget is to help us track our spending— absolutely essential knowledge when we want to cut down. In the fall of 1990 we did a money makeover for a young couple who wanted to gain control over their spending and couldn't account for $800 a month. Both worked, and both often arrived home late—too late to fix dinner. So they'd call for a pizza, or go out for dinner, even if just for a hamburger. What they discovered was that $600 of that $800 was paying for fast food and convenience dining. They also discovered that by allotting themselves a fixed sum each week and making simple pasta and vegetable dishes at home on those nights when they ran late, they could cut the $600 by $300 and put the other $300 in the bank.

Because this husband and wife had no idea where their money was going, I urged them to begin paying as much as they could by check. I'd give the opposite advice to someone used to paying by check or credit card and anxious to cut down on spending. That person should immediately begin to pay with cash. It's so easy to write a check or charge a purchase when that's what you're used to doing. See new shoes you like? No problem, even if you don't need them. But vow to pay cash for everything you buy and when the moment to hand over those greenbacks arrives, you'll have very different thoughts.

6

Debt: How to Control It
Before It Controls You

DEBT is a wonderful tool when you know how to use it. It can destroy you if
you don't.

The more educated and stable you are, and the higher your station in life,
the more susceptible you are to trouble. Doctors are notorious for their
financial problems because they live big, their taxes are high, and their
credit rating is usually good—perfect circumstances for getting buried in
debt. Some of the finest physicians in New England were clients of mine; too
many of them were mired in debt. Who's going to turn down a loan for a
doctor with a thriving practice? To bankers, such a person is golden. Man or
woman, the doctors would come to me and say, "I don't know how it
happened, but I owe an extra $70,000 for income taxes this year, and I don't
have the funds to pay it. Could you get me a discount loan at a bank?" The
implication was that if I couldn't arrange such a loan I wasn't a good CPA and
I wouldn't have their business for very much longer. And so, even though I
knew I was getting my clients into further trouble, I would arrange for an 11
percent, 90-day loan that the bank would keep renewing as long as the
interest was paid.

THE SEDUCTION OF EASY CREDIT AND THE CALAMITIES IT CREATES

Debt is like a drug. It provides instant gratification. Only later does it extract
its horrendous price.

What can be easier than "easy credit," as those who dangle the dollars
under your nose describe it? Once again, lest you think I'm speaking from
some lofty perch, let me assure you that I've been there. Remember those
young bank officers I described in chapter 2? They were being pressured to

drum up business, and I was just what they were looking for: a young professional with a great job, a rising salary, excellent prospects, and a sound credit rating. They would come upstairs to my office at Price Waterhouse and say, "Hey, let's go to lunch." At lunch, they'd say, "Do you need a new boat? Some furniture? No problem. Come on down at 4 o'clock and we'll sign the papers." And that's how I got suckered into debt very early on. Being a CPA, who presumably should have known better, didn't help me in the least.

Who among us hasn't experienced that rush of temptation when confronted with the knowledge that something we want in the worst way is ours for the charging? So we take out our American Express card or Diners Club card, either one of which, with its virtually unlimited credit, permits us to set our own credit spending habits, and off we go on that trip to Europe or Asia, and a few weeks after we get home, we receive a bill for $10,000. Do we borrow $10,000 from our bank at 12 to 16 percent to pay it off or, not wanting to embarrass ourselves with our banking officer—Lord knows when we might need him—do we let it ride at 18 percent, paying only the minimum due? Overwhelmingly, we choose the latter course; no applications to fill out, no time lost, and no embarrassment. But the cost of our vacation has just risen by the cost of the interest on the debt.

At the end of the eighties, Americans were carrying $182 billion in credit card debt alone. Since more than 100 million Americans file taxes, that approaches $2,000 per taxpayer.

It's been said that every American has experienced a major debt or credit crisis by age forty. Something happens—a lost job, a divorce, a health problem, an accident, an unforeseen problem involving children—and suddenly we're not able to make the payments, and the bills begin to pile up, and then we're tempted to use even more credit, borrowing on one credit card to pay off another, and suddenly we're pinned against the credit wall. Imagine that credit wall as one of the four walls supporting your house. When one wall collapses, a house is no longer habitable.

Those of us who work know that we get our full quota of stress in the pursuit of our professional objectives. What we seek is a private life as filled as possible with serenity. Yet what could be more stressful than discovering at month's end that we don't have the money to pay our bills? What is worse than retrieving the mail and finding nothing but overdue notices, or getting pressure calls late at night from a tough-talking bill collector?

Most people don't realize that credit is a game and like any game has to be played according to the rules. And the first rule of the credit game is that you have to pay your bills on time. There are tremendous penalties if you don't. Not only are you paying far more for an item or a service than it cost or was worth, a few months of misuse can ruin your credit for years. Recently, an executive of American Express told me that the firm was starting to cancel the cards of many clients who were now consistently past due, no matter how long they'd held their cards, or how promptly they'd paid in the past, or what their excuse. Try to get a loan after you've had a major credit card canceled.

And try to get some sympathy from your banker these days when you fail to make the monthly payment on your mortgage. Some banks have done so poorly in recent years that they're incapable of extending understanding—or, more importantly, time—to anyone who falls in arrears. Miss three payments and foreclosure proceedings begin. When I said earlier that millions of Americans who have no savings are two paychecks away from being homeless, I had the banks in mind.

Even more at risk are those homeowners who succumbed during the eighties to the enticements of these very same bankers, and took out equity loans on their houses. The bankers argued: With the value of their houses rising each year, why wait until they sold their houses to enjoy their prosperity? In some cases, of course, these increasingly popular equity loans were made necessary by an emergency, but in the overwhelming number of cases they were inspired by the opportunity to ride the inflation gravy train. Only a few states, most notably Texas, have homestead acts that prohibit home equity loans on the grounds that the home is sacred and must never be encumbered by more than a first mortgage. In all the others, homeowners are free to borrow against the equity in their homes—and to risk the consequences should anything happen to their income stream. Usually, equity loans are based on two incomes in the household. Suddenly along comes an illness or a recession and one of those incomes is cut off, and there's not enough money coming in to service both the original mortgage and the equity loan. To save the nest egg in their home, the owners have two options. The first is to borrow still more money to service their debt. If they can't borrow more money, their only solution is to exercise their second option, and sell their home.

Now comes the unkindest cut of all, when homeowners and real estate tycoons alike discover, as Donald Trump did, that the inflation gravy train has stopped, reversed direction, and changed its name to the Deflation Express. With the value of real estate falling, they've not only lost their nest egg, the sale of their house won't give them enough money to pay off their debts.

As mentioned in chapter 1, when the amount you owe on any property exceeds the value of the property, we say that you are "upside down" on that property. If you sold the property to pay off the debt, you'd have to put up additional money.

It happens on automobiles all the time. Let's say that you purchase the car with a five-year loan. Three years later, you decide to buy another car, and you ask the dealer to take your old car in trade. The dealer makes a phone call, and reports back to you that you owe more on the car than it's worth. The same problem exists even more frequently on boats and RVs, those ubiquitous boats on wheels, because the interest rate is often higher than on car loans. Virtually everything we buy on credit cards is upside down the moment we buy it, because if we were to walk straight from the store to a pawnshop we'd be offered 25 percent of what we paid for it, at best.

In the old days, we took great comfort in knowing that if things got bad, we could always sell the house and retrieve our nest egg. In the nineties, the only homeowners who can still do that are those who bought their properties many years ago in areas where real estate values subsequently escalated. Today, the sagging real estate market has put too many of us upside down on our home loans. That's no problem for those who have no need to sell, and can maintain the income required to service the mortgage. For those who must sell, it's a nightmare.

One evening in August 1990, I listened to a young man describe his nightmare to Bruce Williams of Talknet Radio. He and his wife had bought a house for $140,000. The value of the house had risen to $160,000, but had recently fallen to $120,000, below the mortgage balance. In the interim, he and his wife had separated and were planning to divorce. In order to avoid foreclosure on the house, they were both borrowing to make the payments, but falling behind by some $200 a month.

A friend of mine, an extremely successful executive, lived for years with his wife in their dream house, located in a lovely community just outside Washington, D.C. They had a beautiful life, surrounded by family and friends, with a more than adequate income stream and money in the bank. And then my friend's wife developed a terminal disease. Insurance provided for her medical costs, but not for the round-the-clock nursing she required. Over the next five years, my friend's savings vanished and he found it increasingly difficult to maintain their dream house. One day, at last, it became impossible. "Steve," he recounted some months later, "I shut the front door, put the key in my pocket, and never looked back. I don't know what happened to the house."

In southern Florida in the eighties, entire neighborhoods were created on flexible mortgages offered by S&Ls. The mortgage really should have been $900 a month, but you paid only $700 and the difference was added to your mortgage balance. As these easy terms enabled more and more people to qualify for their "dream house," the neighborhoods became overbuilt and the value of the properties went down. Then came recessionary times. Many of the homeowners lost their jobs. And one day, they began to walk away, just like my friend, and the banks wound up with their homes. Even those people who were happy with their homes and still had their jobs walked away when they discovered that their mortgages now exceeded the value of their homes.

If you buy a home at the top of the market and have to sell it two or three years later when the market has hit bottom, it could wipe you out. Exactly that happened to a couple who bought a gorgeous big home in Greensboro,

North Carolina. They'd already rented another home in Florida and were paying double overhead. Selling their Greensboro house under duress cost them their original down payment and all their home improvements.

THE OTHER "B" WORD: BANKRUPTCY

When debt becomes unmanageable, the catchall answer is bankruptcy. Americans once thought of that as bitter medicine; today it's perceived as the remedy for solving all indebtedness problems, and no longer carries as bitter a taste as it once did. For $500 to $1,000 in legal fees, you can say goodbye to sky-high loans and credit card balances, put your creditors on hold for ten years, and stop those around-the-clock calls from bill collectors. The figures tell us that bankruptcy is a solution that has come increasingly into vogue. In 1969, some 100,000 Americans declared personal bankruptcy. In 1990 more than 700,000 Americans did so, an increase of 700 percent plus in just twenty years. As the nineties began, personal bankruptcies were increasing at the rate of 10 percent a year.

Twenty-five percent of those Americans who file bankruptcy do it because they can't pay off their credit cards. The average American declaring bankruptcy today has $40,000 in credit card debt alone. Attorney Greg Messer, who runs the bankruptcy division of the national law firm, Jacoby and Myers, says he's dealt with clients who had 25 to 30 credit cards, on which they'd charged as much as $70,000 in goods and services.

When you file bankruptcy, most of your assets, investments, bank accounts, and personal property will be liquidated. Some states let you keep your home and your car. The bankruptcy stays on your credit record for years. During that period, it's cash only for the most part; no one will give you an unsecured credit card, and home, car, and personal loans can be obtained only with the greatest difficulty and at devastating rates.

The sad part is that roughly half of those people who file for bankruptcy might have been able to get rid of their debts by negotiating with creditors and adopting a leaner budget. Creditors are especially impressed when someone they're after seeks the help of a credit counselor. Bankruptcy should always be an absolute last resort.

For those seduced by easy credit, there is a price to be paid even worse than bankruptcy. More than anything else, it puts their dreams beyond reach.

GOOD DEBT VERSUS BAD DEBT

In its simplest form, good debt is any expense you charge to a credit card and pay back when the bill comes due, without paying interest. You've not needed to carry big sums of cash about, you've got a record of your expense, and you've gained a grace period in which to pay for your purchase.

In its more complex form, good debt gives you leverage to buy a property that will appreciate at a rate greater than the expense you incur. Few of us have the cash to purchase a home outright. Good debt enables us to do it.

There is nothing better than a mortgage if it's used to purchase the right property at the right price, especially if it gets you into a home that provides you with intense gratification and the special comforts that only home-ownership brings, as well as the prospect of long-term profit. Over the long haul, real estate *will* appreciate. It may diminish in value from year to year, but ten or twenty years later, you should be able to sell it at a profit. So in the best of all worlds, the leverage that *good* debt gives you enables you to control a $200,000 asset for considerably less—as little as $20,000—and to profit from its long-term appreciation.

Good debt is what you incur when you buy a small business and persuade the owners to finance the purchase on favorable terms. Go through traditional financing channels and you'll be pressed to make payments on principal and interest from the outset. Starting a business is a tenuous enough proposition; the last thing you need at such a time is undue pressure from your creditors, but that is what you'll get because their only interest is making money on their loan. If you fail, they foreclose, and sell the business to someone else. The people who sold you the business, on the other hand, have a vested interest in your success. The only way you'll make good on your purchase is if the business prospers under your management. If you fail, the sellers get the business back, but that's not what they want. If they did, they wouldn't have sold it to you in the first place. So the loan to you is good business for them, and good for you as well, provided of course that the business you're buying is a thriving one, with excellent prospects.

If the sellers don't want to finance the purchase, a bank loan in these circumstances would also qualify as good debt. You're gaining control of an asset for a fraction of its value, and this asset will earn enough to meet all financial obligations, including a paycheck to you, and still increase in value. I know a man who bought a business for $500,000 down. The day he took the company over, there was $1 million in its checkbook. In this case the seller was desperate, and needed the buyer, whom he'd known for years, to take over the business quickly before it began to fail. (Banks, incidentally, are much more likely to finance the purchase of an existing business with a good track record than they are to finance a new business. But even those loans are hard to come by; in the tight-credit mood of the nineties, many banks are turning down applications from developers offering to put 25 percent down.)

Good debt, finally, is what you incur to take that great adventure or do something wonderful for the person you love—provided you can comfortably repay the debt without risk to your collateral. More about that further on.

Bad debt is needless debt or debt you can't afford. Credit card debt is a prime example of bad debt, and the most flagrantly abused.

I'm not against credit cards so long as the charges are paid off on time. But credit card debt that rides along from month to month at 18 percent annual interest can kill you. As long as you pay the minimum amount due each month, the bank won't warn you to stop charging. To the contrary, the moment your credit balance goes over the authorized limit, a computer might churn out a letter congratulating you on having your credit limit raised from $5,000 to $6,000. Department stores play the same game. Sears, in fact, invented the revolving credit plan. Your balance is $400. Send us $25, the store told its clients. In this fashion, you could wind up owing Sears forever.

Most such credit card debt carries an 18.5 percent interest charge. In California it can run as high as 21 percent. Even at 18 percent, your cost for any item doubles in four years. Not only is the interest high, it's no longer tax deductible, except for businesses.

As insidious as credit card debt may be, stretched out boat loans are worse. Most boats depreciate rapidly in the first two years, yet are purchased with ten and twenty year financing. The more expensive the boat, the longer the financing. If your goal in life is to buy an expensive powerboat and you don't have enough money to finance it, you may find loan brokers who will help you achieve your dream for 10 percent down, but in the course of servicing that loan, you're going to pay for your dream boat twice.

The important thing to remember about any purchase bought with credit or loans is that you don't own what you're buying until you've paid the debt. It's the lender who owns it—a lesson that many millionaires have to relearn. When you miss your payments, the banks take control. All it really takes is one missed payment for your creditors to become your bosses. Who needs more bosses?

HOW MUCH DEBT MAKES SENSE?

To answer how much debt makes sense, you have to understand the difference between secured and unsecured credit.

In the seventies and eighties, unsecured credit was the norm. If you needed $5,000, you could walk into a bank—not necessarily your own— and get it without putting up collateral. All you needed was evidence of good character, a good credit rating, and permanent employment that earned you adequate income. Usually, the loan would be for twenty-four months at 15 to 17 percent. In such a permissive credit environment, many people would obtain several such loans, each from a different bank, of course, and some for as much as $8,000. But gradually, the banks discovered that unsecured loans in a mobile society characterized by high job turnover and divorce were risky business. Too often their creditors skipped town, leaving no trace of where they'd gone.

More banks today, beset by so many other problems, expect collateral for every loan they make. If the loan goes bad, the asset you pledged becomes theirs. Unsecured credit, by and large, is available only to those who don't need it, and even then its use is highly proscribed. For example, American Express offers its platinum cardholders an unsecured credit line of $10,000 or more through Centurion Bank—but the line of credit issued can be used only to pay down their American Express bills.

Secured loans come with longer paybacks, lower rates, and easier terms than unsecured loans. The most popular secured loan today by far is the aforementioned home equity loan. Close to half of all homeowners now have one. The bankers love the loan because it's secured by an asset that would bail them out should the borrower default. The borrowers love the loan because it's a hidden tax shelter. The Tax Reform Act of 1986 phased out all consumer interest deductions save those on houses; there was nothing in the law, however, to prevent a homeowner from borrowing against the equity on his house—the interest on which would usually be 100 percent deductible—and using the money to buy a car, a boat, or anything else.

Such loans may put smiles on the bankers' faces, but for homeowners they can be risky business. Any time you borrow against your home equity, you're spending against your life savings, and it's not at all wise for you to trick yourself into thinking you're doing otherwise. Cars, boats, and RVs are depreciating assets; the moment you buy them they're worth less than you paid for them. If your earnings were suddenly to be curtailed because you lost your job or became ill, and you couldn't meet your payments, your home might be foreclosed. Using stocks and bonds as collateral is one thing; lose them and all you've lost is money. Using your house as collateral is quite another matter; you could join the ranks of the homeless.

So how much debt makes sense? For unsecured debt, only as much as you can promptly service without adding greatly to the cost of your purchase. For secured debt, only as much as you can repay comfortably in no more than five years. Many home equity loans today are being written with ten-, twelve-, or fifteen-year paybacks. If the purpose of the loan is to improve your house, that's okay, because you're using the money to make your most valuable asset that much more valuable. But if you can't repay a home equity loan meant for a boat or a trip to Europe in five years at most, that means you can't afford it.

BAILING OUT OF DEBT

Here are some telltale signs that you might be drowning in debt:

1. Your unsecured debt totals more than 20 percent of your income.

2. You're paying only enough money to cover the interest on your debt, and not reducing the principal each month.

3. You're drawing cash advances from one credit card in order to pay off another.

4. You're using your credit card to pay living expenses like groceries, gas, rent, and utilities.

5. You're consistently late with payments.

6. You're being denied credit on other loans or lines of credit. Business turns down people who already have too much debt or previously had problems paying bills.

When *any* of the six signs appear, your financial ship has sprung a leak. When two or more appear, your ship's in danger of sinking. Here's a six-step, commonsense method for bailing out of debt:

Step One: Add up all unsecured debts. Suppose you have credit card debt of $8,000, store charges of $2,000, and a personal installment loan of $3,000. That's $13,000 total, which is costing you about $900 a month. By using a simple calculator, you can set yourself a realistic schedule for gradually reducing and eventually eliminating the debt.

When you simply can't afford to pay the $13,000 down any faster, a carefully constructed bill consolidation loan could be just the ticket, assuming your credit is still good. I'd find a friendly banker to rewrite the total debt over 24 months, giving you a new lower payment of about $630 a month. Bill consolidation loans will increase the interest you're paying, but in this case the cost is justified because it enables you to reduce your monthly payment to a more affordable level while you're cleaning up your bills and regaining control over your personal finances.

Step Two: Consult your creditors. Be honest with them. Tell them about your debt situation, and show them the schedule you've set up to make good. When you're honest with your creditors, they tend to be more sympathetic and willing to work with you.

Step Three: Perform. Show your creditors you mean business by making systematic and periodic payments in the exact amount and at the exact time you said you would. This should put an immediate stop to most if not all of those humiliating letters and phone calls.

Step Four: Stop using credit cards. Either cut them up or give them to someone for safekeeping—preferably someone you can't browbeat into giving them back. Using credit cards to incur new debt when you're trying to eliminate the old debt makes as much sense as skipping lunch and gorging at dinner when you're trying to lose weight.

Step Five: Eliminate all other unnecessary expenses. Keep an accurate record of every dollar you spend. Follow the recommendations for cutting down on spending detailed in chapter 5.

Step Six: If necessary, seek professional help. Most major cities have nonprofit groups that will help you devise a budget and repayment schedule. Check the yellow pages of your telephone directory under credit and debt counseling services. The Consumer Credit Counseling Service, a not-for-profit organization sponsored in part by United Way and with more than 400 offices nationwide, offers individual counseling to help people dig out of debt, set up budgets, and build their savings. You'll be asked to make a small donation, but that's strictly voluntary; the service is free. To find a branch in your area, call 1-800-388-CCCS.

CCCS works as a middleman, stepping between you and your creditors. Your counselor will work out a budget and payment schedule with you, based on your salary and present living conditions, that's also acceptable to your creditors. You, in turn, commit to sending CCCS a check, either bi-weekly or monthly, the proceeds from which CCCS then disperses to your creditors. Credit counselors can't solve your problems for you—getting out of debt, like losing weight, ultimately depends on you—but they can give you support and a systematic program.

Three corollary suggestions:

• *Be patient.* It will take longer to get out of debt than it did to get into debt. Stick to the repayment schedule and budget you or your creditor counselor have set up.

• *Stay employed.* Without income you can't pay off your debts. If your current position isn't paying you enough, you should consider looking for a better-paying job or taking a second job until you're out of the hole.

• *Pay yourself.* Just as important as getting out of debt is getting into the savings habit. It's so important that even if all you had to work off your debt was $100 a month, I'd rather see you apply $50 toward the debt and deposit $50 in a savings account. Why? Because if all you've done is pay off your debt, you wind up with no debt and no assets—and no sense that you're any different from the person who got into debt in the first place. A savings account will change that poor self-image. More about this in chapter 7.

THE BANKER'S SECRET REVEALED: HOW AN EXTRA PAYMENT OF $100 A MONTH CAN SAVE YOU THOUSANDS IN INTEREST

Marc Eisenson, a bright and engaging young man, is the author of a book called *The Banker's Secret.* The day I was to interview him on television, he arrived with three plastic houses, the kind you put on a train set, and set them on a table.

"What are those for?" I asked.

"To illustrate 'the banker's secret,' " he said. "When you buy the house in the middle, using a bank mortgage, the amount of money you'll eventually pay back will be equivalent to the purchase price of all three houses."

How can this be possible? Let's assume you're making a payment of $1,000 a month to the bank on a $100,000 mortgage. At the outset of your loan, only $23 of that goes to repay your principal. All the rest is interest. Over the life of the loan, you're going to pay back $288,000, which is $12,000 less than it would have cost you to buy three $100,000 homes for cash.

"When you take a loan," Eisenson writes, "you agree to pay back the amount borrowed plus interest. That's fair. But you've probably never realized how much that interest can be. For example, on a $75,000, thirty-year mortgage written at 10 percent interest, the total payback will be almost $237,000. That's nearly $162,000 in interest charges on a $75,000 loan. More than twice what was borrowed. One house for the price of three."

What the bankers don't tell you, Eisenson states, is that anyone can save tens of thousands of dollars in interest payments by sending in a small additional payment on a systematic basis, to be applied to the principal. As the principal decreases, so does the amount of interest you pay on the loan. The amount of your regular monthly payment doesn't change; what does change is the amount of your payment that goes toward interest, and the amount that goes toward principal. The balance tilts in your favor by tiny increments that eventually add up to a giant leap out of the debit pit.

When you put an extra $25 a month into your mortgage, what you're doing is investing that money at whatever rate your mortgage has been charging. Assuming you have a 10 percent mortgage, all of a sudden you've turned a 10 percent debt into a 10 percent investment. Instead of costing you 10 percent, your $25 is earning 10 percent risk-free. In addition, that extra $25 automatically reduces the amount of interest the bank can collect from you the following month and every month thereafter. More of each regular monthly payment therefore goes toward reducing the loan rather than in payment of interest. When this reduction is compounded through the life of the loan, the effect is stunning. By making a single extra payment of $50 at the outset of an $800 a month loan, you'll save $750 over the life of the loan, and shorten that life by a month.

To get started on a prepayment schedule, you must first okay it through your lender. In some states, you automatically have the right to prepay, but even in those states where the right isn't on the law books, your lender will almost certainly oblige, and waive any prepayment penalties. When you prepay in such small amounts, the paperwork and time spent to collect the penalties makes the exercise unprofitable.

Before signing your prepayment agreement, get hold of an amortization schedule. You can obtain it from your bank, or an attorney, or from Eisenson for $12.95 by calling 1-914-758-8249. The schedule will help you decide what amount is best for you. It will also show you how many years away you are from paying off your loan. Be sure to check the schedule carefully. Even a discrepancy of a few dollars can pyramid into a significant amount over the term of your loan.

Keep an accurate record of your prepayments. And keep your schedule as regular as possible, not only to avoid confusion but to get the loan paid off more quickly. Many loans have prepayment penalties, but the truth is that it costs the lender too much to collect the penalty on such a small amount to make the effort worth it.

KEEPING YOUR CREDIT RECORD CLEAN

Your credit rating is your most valuable money tool. Without a good rating, your ability to function in society will be seriously impaired.

Everyone has four or five money crunches in a lifetime, when there's a sudden, urgent need for cash. It may be something positive, such as a great investment opportunity. You decide that your company's going to do extremely well in the coming year and you want to buy some shares. Or a successful friend you admire and trust invites you to invest in a promising business venture. Or a piece of land becomes available on which you'd like to build your dream house ten years down the line. If you don't act, the land will be gone. On the negative side, the loss of a job or a sudden emergency can provoke an even more urgent need for cash. Whatever the need, you have the option of using your savings or borrowing.

It's almost never a good idea to take money from a savings program of any kind if you can possibly avoid it, because it's extremely difficult to replace savings once the dollars have been withdrawn. If your savings are in a retirement plan, retrieving the money can be a tedious process. Borrowing money in the expectation that you'll repay it promptly is a much better idea.

Because credit, used appropriately, can dramatically enhance your life, and even be a lifesaver, it behooves you to keep your credit rating clean.

There are only two basic steps to acquiring and maintaining a good credit rating. The first is to buy on credit, or borrow money from a bank. The second is to pay off your debts in a timely manner.

To give you an idea of how important timely repayment can be, let me tell you a story about a young attorney in New York City, a recent law school graduate with no net worth to speak of, who determined to establish an excellent credit rating so that he could borrow money to make investments. His first move was to borrow $10,000 from a bank on a thirty-day demand note. Twenty days later, he repaid the loan, with interest, explaining to the banker that things had turned out a little better than he'd expected them to. Bankers love borrowers who make early paybacks; this banker was so impressed that he told the young man he would increase his credit line to $25,000. A few weeks later, the attorney reappeared and asked for a $25,000 loan. Not only was the loan granted without question, it was on better terms than the first loan. Once again, he repaid the loan early. So it went for a year, the lawyer borrowing ever greater sums of money at better and better interest rates, and repaying each loan early. The first half-dozen loans were negotiated through the same bank, but eventually the lawyer went to other banks, where he used the first bank as a reference. By this point, the first bank was singing his praises. After one year the young lawyer had built a $1 million line of credit at half a dozen banks, and could get a significant loan with a phone call. Not once had he actually used the money he borrowed; his only purpose was to establish a reputation, and his only cost was the interest on the loans, a pittance compared to the credit power he had gained. For the rest of his life, he used his credit line to invest in Manhattan real estate and wound up a multimillionaire.

Theoretically, it would be possible for anyone to do what that attorney did, but it would be more difficult today, given the wariness of bankers and the tightness of the money market. Assuming your credit needs aren't excessive, such extreme measures would also be unnecessary, because as long as you maintain a good credit record you'll most likely be able to borrow money when you need it.

What you want to avoid are the small mistakes that put you on the books as a credit deadbeat. One common mistake is to let a small balance carry over on a credit card or department store bill, on the assumption that it won't matter if you pay it, along with other charges, the following month. It will matter. To the credit raters, the amount of the balance is immaterial; what goes on their books is that you failed to make timely payment.

Sometimes you can get a black mark on their books through no fault of your own. Suppose you're shopping for a car, and visit half a dozen showrooms. At each showroom, you tell the salesman that you intend to purchase on credit. The salesman, without your knowledge, checks your credit rating. On the books, it shows that a number of "inquiries" have been made about you in a short period, a blemish on your record. When and if you do decide to buy a car, your credit application could be turned down.

The consumer credit business is gargantuan. As the nineties began, credit services were keeping tabs on $720 billion of total consumer debt. The job falls to three major credit reporting agencies: TRW, Inc. in Orange, California, Trans-Union in Chicago, and Equifax in Atlanta. By and large, they do a good job, but in this field any mistake at all can adversely affect lives and cause needless humiliation. Imagine the feeling if you'd just made a purchase in a department store, only to be stripped of your credit card. Credit industry leaders maintain that fewer than 0.5 percent of errors are found in individual credit records, but a study conducted by Consolidated Information Services in New Jersey suggested that as many as 60 million Americans may have one or more errors in their credit history files.

Whether or not you have immediate need for a loan, therefore, it's a wise idea to check your credit rating. To do this, look up "credit reporting agencies" in the yellow pages of your telephone directory, call and ask for a credit report form. There is a charge of five to twenty-five dollars, unless you've been denied credit in the last 30 days, in which case the service is free. Don't be surprised if you find one or more inaccurate items on your record. Most people who check their ratings do find errors, which is why it's such a good idea to check.

Here are some of the most common glitches:

- Cross-merged files, in which people with similar names or addresses have their credit histories mixed in with yours.
- Out of date information.
- Erroneous or inaccurate information supplied by creditors or consumers.
- Incorrect reports of missed payments. Lenders are notorious for filing such reports.
- Credit histories of ex-spouses linked together long after the divorce.

If you're unable to interpret the information, the credit bureau is obliged by law to help you.

If you find an error, notify your local credit bureau immediately. Under the law, the credit bureau must investigate and correct any mistakes. Generally, the industry recognizes thirty days as a reasonable amount of time to investigate the potential error. If the error is found in your favor, the credit bureau must send an updated report to any business that has requested your file during the previous six months.

If you do find a negative report, you have the right to enter a 100-word statement on the bottom of the report, giving your side of the story. Credit managers usually don't put much credence in such statements, but if there was a reason why you didn't pay on time, it's important for you to make it part of the record. At a minimum it demonstrates your appreciation of a good credit rating and your determination to maintain yours. If you make a statement, write it in clear, businesslike language.

Contrary to popular belief, there isn't a single "credit rating" in your file. Decisions about your credit soundness are up to the individual lender, and are based upon interpretation of your file. While one late credit card payment may not make a difference, a pattern of delinquencies will. A warning: Delinquencies remain on file for as long as seven years. If you know you won't be getting an "A" on your credit report card, let your potential lender know. Lenders are generally more sympathetic to those who bring such matters to their attention than to those who don't.

The best way to guarantee a healthy credit rating, of course, is to maintain excellent credit habits. In this regard, you should keep six goals in mind:

Goal One: Pay on time.

Goal Two: Pay within three months. When you charge that $600 stereo to your credit card or department store card, have it in mind to pay the extended charge off within three months, if possible. Six months is the outer limit.

Goal Three: Always pay more than the minimum balance due. The last thing you want is to go on the credit records as a person who always pays the minimum.

Goal Four: When making a major purchase, always put at least 20 percent down; 30 percent would be better, and 40 or 50 percent better yet.

Goal Five: Make an all-out effort to find the best possible loan. The man who sells you your car may not have the best deal. Try banks and loan brokers on your own. And resolve, in the process, to get no more than a five-year loan for cars, and a ten-year loan on boats. The shorter the term, the less it costs you.

Goal Six: Whenever possible, stay a month ahead on your payments.

CHOOSING THE RIGHT CREDIT CARD

Once more, there is nothing wrong with credit cards if you pay the charges on time and avoid interest payments. As stated earlier, credit cards preclude the need for big sums of cash, they give you a record of your expenses, and they provide you with some stated interest-free grace period before you have to settle up. As every credit card holder knows, there are tangible fringe benefits as well. Rent a car with a major credit card, and you don't have to pay that pesky additional insurance charge called "CDW"; your credit card company picks it up. Charge your air fare to certain credit cards and your life is insured for the flight, up to half a million dollars. Sometimes the right "affinity" credit card can entitle you to free gifts through the accumulation of bonus points. The benefits keep getting sweeter as the competition for your business increases.

If you travel at all, it's critical to have one major travel card. Assuming you pay your bills on time, that card can give you tremendous clout when you're far from home. Travel agencies and hotels pay attention. You can cash checks or draw money from ATMs.

But all credit cards aren't created equal. American Express is extremely popular abroad, but many establishments in the United States won't accept it because it charges them more than other cards. Variable charges for the consumer are another major difference. Some card companies charge an annual membership fee, others don't. Some offer grace periods, others don't. Interest rates on credit balances vary as well.

In shopping for a credit card, you should compare grace periods, annual percentage rates (APR), and membership fees.

If you're used to paying your balance off on time, the interest rate is immaterial to you. Choose a credit card with a low annual fee, or none at all, and a lengthy grace period, which can give you up to fifty-five days of what, in effect, is an interest-free loan. Forget about finance charges. They won't affect you.

If you leave an unpaid balance each month, choose the card with the lowest interest rate available. Don't concern yourself with grace periods or annual dues.

If you pay in full some months and leave an unpaid balance in others, you'd do best by having two credit cards. Use the no-annual-fee, long-grace card when you plan on paying in full at the end of the grace period. Use the low-interest card when you know you'll be paying over a period of time.

IS IT WISE TO LIVE DEBT-FREE?

When my grandparents built their house in New England in 1912, mortgages were considered a luxury. You were expected to have the money to buy a house before you bought it. People who didn't have the money didn't buy houses. At a minimum, you put down 50 percent. The mortgage was short-term, and the interest was 2 percent, 3 at most. How times have changed.

There is no question that mortgages have made homeownership possible for millions upon millions of people in the time since my grandparents paid for their house. But in the interval, a curious belief has arisen: You ought to have a mortgage even if you don't need one. Given the reality of inflation, this argument holds, you'd be paying for your house with ever cheaper dollars. Tax deductions add further incentives to borrowing money to buy a house rather than paying cash, especially to those in the higher brackets. But since the new tax-reduced tax rates went into effect, the most you can save on every dollar that goes to interest payments on your home mortgage is about 30 percent. And with home mortgage rates at 9 to 11 percent, the cumulative interest is so high that you've paid for three houses instead of one, as we've seen.

Despite these changes, the notion persists that getting into debt is a good idea. I see this most often in the communications and entertainment industry, where performers and newscasters can go from earning respectable salaries to enormous salaries in a brief amount of time. Suddenly, they're making more money than they can possibly spend, at which point they'll come up to me and ask whether it would be a good idea to pay off their mortgages and credit cards. My answer never changes: "Absolutely."

Living debt-free should be your ultimate goal. At that point, you're paying for the goods and services themselves, and not for the use of the money. The only thing debt does is make us pay more for what we're buying. Living debt-free, you're no longer paying an extra 5 or 10 percent or more—sometimes a great deal more—for everything you buy. You're free of what a friend of mine calls "monkey books," those loan coupons you have to send in each time you make a payment. You're free of the harassment of your creditors.

I'm not suggesting for a moment that you need to live a completely debt-free life, although that would be the ideal. What I want you to do is use debt as a tool that can improve your life rather than dominate it. George Burns, who celebrated his ninety-fifth birthday in 1991, drinks two or three martinis every evening. But he doesn't drink six or twelve.

Using credit cards is a good idea, provided you pay the charges in full every month, because they can help you establish a good credit rating. And very few of us could buy a house without a mortgage. But the ideal life is the one in which everything else—car, furniture, appliances, recreational vehicles—is paid for.

The first advice financial planners give to newly wealthy clients is to pay off all their debts, mortgages included, because the interest paid on debt of any kind increases their personal inflation rate more than any other factor. Debt is useless expense, avoidable inflation. There's not a loan that doesn't contain both an inflation factor and a profit for the bank.

If you were making a million dollars a year why would you want a mortgage? If you can afford to buy a car for cash, why would you want to lease it? If you were wealthy why would you want any debt at all? What could be more desirable than owing nothing to no one?

7

Systematic Savings: The Key to Every Dream

AMERICANS are terrible savers, compared to the rest of the developed world. We spend a far higher percentage of our incomes. The average American has $10,800 in his or her bank account, the average Austrian, $16,800, the average Swiss, $23,400. Who leads the world? One guess. In Japan, bank savings accounts average $40,100—nearly four times what they average in the United States.

Ninety-nine percent of all working Japanese have their paycheck deposited directly into their bank, a practice virtually guaranteed to enhance savings. In Germany, it's 95 percent, in Scandinavia 92 percent, in Great Britain 70 percent. Who's that in the rear echelon? One guess. In the United States, only 17 percent of the working populace has paychecks sent directly to the bank, one of the worst records among 82 countries surveyed.

Financial planners are unanimous in their conviction that every working person should save at least 10 percent of his or her disposable income. In the sixties and seventies, Americans saved, on average, between 6 and 8 percent a year. Today, we're saving 1 to 4 percent, on average, which means that millions of us are saving virtually nothing at all. The average family head between twenty-five and thirty-four saves 1 percent of his or her disposable income, according to 1988 figures, the latest available. The head of a family in the thirty-five to forty-four age range saves 0 percent. From forty-five to fifty-four, savings rise to 8 percent, because by that point panic sets in. From fifty-five to sixty-four it falls again, to 6 percent. And from sixty-five on, it's minus 3 percent.

What these figures prove without question is that the overwhelming majority of Americans working today will be unprepared for a secure retirement at sixty-five. What the figures also demonstrate indisputably is that these same Americans are living on the financial edge.

Three out of four people who tell me their stories could not live more than two weeks without a paycheck. They're spending money like it's going out of style, gambling the rest, and absolutely ignoring the future. They don't want to acknowledge the new, hard truths of American society in the nineties and beyond: that corporations are downsizing and replacing older workers with young ones; that pension and health and welfare benefits are dwindling and in some cases disappearing altogether; that Social Security won't remotely cover their retirement years. Among those Americans who are paying attention are many frightened people in their fifties and sixties who own nothing but their homes—and even those are mortgaged. Not one of these people has a meaningful pension plan. One alarmed woman came to me and said, "Assuming I don't get fired or replaced by some thirty-year-old, I have eight years left. Then my income stops. Please show me what I can do." So we sat down and she told me how much she'd need to live on, and I calculated that in order to have that much income she would need to save $1,500 a month from this moment forward. She was crestfallen. "I can't do that," she said. Some months later, she married a fairly well-to-do man. She married him, I believe, out of fear.

I'll say it again: The number one mistake nine out of ten Americans make is not having a sum of money equal to six months income set aside as a buffer. And this, too, bears repeating: Hundreds of thousands of outwardly affluent Americans are precariously close to homelessness, because banks throughout the country with millions of dollars of bad loans on their books are foreclosing on homeowners who fall three to six months behind on their mortgage or equity loan payments, or both. Some banks have been known to seize homes on which two payments have been missed.

The *absolute* minimum you should set aside as a buffer for loss of your job, or an illness, or a divorce is the equivalent of three months' income. You should have money squirreled away that not even your spouse knows about. I'll say this once more as well: You're a far different person getting out of bed each morning knowing you have $25,000 in the bank than you are knowing you have nothing. Your outlook on life, your career, your marriage, your children, your environment, the place you live, would be totally different. Even a boring passbook account, in which you've made just $150 a month in interest on a $25,000 deposit, heightens your sense of self-esteem.

That's swell, Steve, you're probably saying at this point, but exactly how do I do it when I'm barely scraping by as it is?

The answer is in three parts: first, attitude; second, habit; third, a proper savings program.

Attitude

Whenever I ask psychologists and psychiatrists why they have so many patients, the first word out of their mouths is "Money." They cite the absence of money as the cause of emotional stress, separations, and divorce. I'll never forget the comparison made by one psychiatrist between Latin cultures and ours. For the Latins, he said, masculinity is gauged by the shape of your body and how handsome you are, whereas in the United States, masculinity is measured by money and what money buys—by women as well as by men. On more than one occasion in my own office, I've heard young women state that they want to marry a man with a Mercedes and a Rolex.

What's more important to you, feeling potent, or feeling that you're in command of your life? You don't need a Porsche to get where you're going. You can get there in a Beretta. If you buy cars for cash, the more expensive car will deprive you of $15,000 to $20,000 in income your money would be earning during the life of the car. If you buy cars on credit or lease them, you're out even more.

The irony is that when you owe money you feel helpless, as though you're possessed by your possessions—not a very potent feeling. A certain amount of leverage can be beneficial, but too much can destroy you. Water is essential to life, but if you drink too much you drown.

The first step in developing a savings program is to decide to live by your own values. That one decision can make all the difference in the world.

Habit

There's only one way to save successfully, and that's to do it every day. The habit is more important than the amount. A dollar a day put away for a child from birth will send that child to college. I knew a young man who came from India to the United States to go to college with barely enough money to live on. When he graduated four years later, he had investments in five mutual funds worth $75,000. "How did you do it?" I asked him. "Oh, five dollars here, and ten dollars there," he replied. Remember my friend Ernie Baptista, whose first goal was to save $100,000? He didn't put it away a thousand dollars at a time. He put away $20 and $50 at a time. His favorite words are "systematic" and "periodic."

But words like those would be foreign to countless Americans today. Many have trouble understanding the concept of saving, or the meaning of the word. Their parents never taught them, and they've never picked it up. They not only know nothing about banking, they don't even put money under the mattress. They can't distinguish between "savings," the noun, and "saving," the verb. "Do you save money?" I've asked shoppers while doing interviews in malls. "On what?" they'll reply. One woman said, "I save money by buying the store brands and not the name brands." Another said, "Yes. I shop at discount stores." When I asked these women if they saved for the future, they seemed genuinely puzzled. Others I've interviewed who understood the concept of saving didn't appreciate its essential purpose. "We're saving for a boat," they'll say, or "We're saving for a stereo." They don't realize that saving to *spend* money is not a true savings program, because the objects they buy won't hold their value.

True savings are funds invested in such a way that they will grow in value, rather than get used up. An investment in a house would qualify, if the house is held for many years. An investment in education would qualify because the spending of this money increases your child's earning power.

When you save money, it *is* important to know what you're saving for. Mindless saving makes no sense. If you have no idea how the money is going to translate into future well-being, you have no motivation. But it's also imperative to understand that saving for a boat or some other object comes fourth, after three more imperative objectives have been met.

The first objective is to accumulate that emergency reserve I keep harping on: three to six months income, $5,000 to $25,000, no less but no more, stashed away in a bank account or a money mutual fund, preferably both.

The second objective is to accumulate a nest egg for retirement, a program that should start as early as possible but *never* later than age forty-five.

The third objective is to accumulate money for such essentials as a down payment on a house or your children's education.

Does this mean that you can't save for a boat until the first three objectives have been fully funded? Yes and no. You've *got* to put that emergency reserve away before anything. But there is no reason you can't save for a boat—or a trip to Kenya—at the same time you're building your retirement nest egg and the kids' college fund, *provided* you understand that contributions to the pleasure fund come only after you've contributed to your retirement, house, and college funds.

A Proper Savings Program

Saving is the mirror image of borrowing, and savings the mirror image of debt. Instead of spending tomorrow's dollars today, we're saving dollars for tomorrow.

Just as my mother used to put dollars into budget envelopes to pay the family bills, so a proper savings program utilizes a number of different pockets. Each objective should be matched with a specific investment to which funds are added weekly or monthly. Before we get to those specifics, let's raise a few cheers for compound interest, the basis of all investing.

COMPOUND INTEREST: THE EIGHTH WONDER OF THE WORLD

Someone supposedly asked Albert Einstein what he considered mankind's greatest invention. And the great scientist replied without hesitation, "Compound interest." To many other savvy investors it's known as the eighth wonder of the world.

What *is* compound interest? It's interest that itself earns interest. Suppose you invest $100 at 10 percent. After one year, you've earned $10 and you have $110. In the second year, your $100 continues to earn 10 percent—as does the $10 you earned in interest. So instead of $120 at the end of two years, you have $121. Doesn't sound like much, does it? But after 7.2 years, instead of having $172, you have $200. And in 14.4 years, instead of having $244, you have $400. And in 21.8 years, instead of having $318, you have $800.

By its very nature, compound interest needs time to really kick in. That's why it's so important to start a savings program as early in life as you can. The time to start saving for your child's or grandchild's future is when the child is born, not when he or she is about to enter college. Consider this: If you put away a dollar a day from the moment the child was born, and the money were to compound annually at 8 percent, you'd have $17,361 to give that child on his or her twentieth birthday. Your contribution would have totaled $7,300.

Just for the sake of illustration, let's suppose that for some reason the child didn't need the money and you offered to continue contributing a dollar a day until he or she reached thirty-five. That would be another $5,475 from you, for a total of $12,775. On your child's or grandchild's thirty-fifth birthday, he or she would have $65,373, almost six times more than you contributed.

At that point—again for the sake of illustration—let's suppose your grateful child or grandchild cried, "Enough! You've taught me how to do it. Now I'll take it from here." By putting a dollar a day into the fund for the next thirty-four years, an additional $12,410, he or she would have exactly $1 million at age sixty-nine.

In sixty-nine years $25,185, saved at the rate of a dollar a day, and compounded at 8 percent, becomes a million dollars. Can there be any more dramatic example of the miracle of compound interest? As a matter of fact, there can. In chapter 12, we'll be showing you how to compound your money at 12 percent—the rate at which your money should grow if you want to stay ahead of inflation. At that rate, the magic of compounding kicks in a good deal faster. Applying the Rule of 72 once again, in which we divide the interest rate into 72, we find that instead of doubling every nine years as is the case with an 8 percent return, our money doubles every six years—not just the money we've invested but also the money we've made.

But whether it's 8 percent or 12 percent or some lower or higher figure, the earlier in life you begin to save, the better off you are. And you absolutely must begin by the time you're forty-five. Forty-five is the last outpost; if you haven't begun to provide for your retirement by then, you're going to really have to cut back on your life-style in order to put enough away—unless you plan to work until you drop and have the stamina and opportunity to do so.

But why put yourself in this predicament? Why not start to save today? It seems so difficult when you think about the tremendous sums you'll need as well as your current obligations, but it's so easy once you know the secret.

THE SECRET OF A SUCCESSFUL SAVINGS PROGRAM: PAY YOURSELF FIRST

Every month of our lives, we pay our mortgage loan, car loan and perhaps a personal loan, and our electric, gas, and other bills, but we don't include ourselves in the list of monthly expenses. We've never said to ourselves, "I'm writing all these damn checks each month, why can't I write a check for $50 a week for myself?"

"Pay yourself first" is the primary rule of saving. Just as there are two sides to a balance sheet, so are there two sides to the process of making yourself whole. As noted earlier, it's far better to engage in a simultaneous savings and debt-reduction program than it is to work exclusively on paying off your debts. To all the good feelings you get when you've got money in the bank must be added the reinforcement it gives you to continue to save.

So when you pay your bills each week or month, think of yourself as your most important creditor. Every time you receive a paycheck, consider that you owe yourself no less than 5 percent of that check, write out a check for that amount and deposit it in the bank or any of the other savings programs we'll be discussing momentarily. Actually, 10 percent would be ideal, but 5 percent is a good starting figure, so that you don't feel strapped at the outset.

I know people who are rich today because they paid themselves first; instead of paying their debt off at the rate of $100 a week, they paid off $50 a week and put $50 in the bank.

If you were to begin to put $50 away each week, and the money earned 8 percent compounded, after twenty years you'd have contributed $52,000 and you'd have $217,000. (This assumes you've been able to defer the taxes, a subject we'll deal with in chapter 11.) In twenty years $217,000 may not be an impressive amount of money, but you'll be far better off having it than having nothing at all.

If you're one of those fortunate people who has no debt other than your mortgage, you should be writing a $100 check to yourself every week. There are few people who couldn't cut $100 a week from their spending with a few adjustments in life-style. Given the cost of dining out these days, you could cut a good part of the $100—or even all of it—by eliminating one restaurant meal a week. One hundred dollars saved a week, as in the example above, would give you $434,000 after twenty years, on a contribution of $104,000.

If you're positive you can't save $50 or $100 a week, then pick a sum you can manage, even if it's only $15. Raise the sum six months later, and raise it again after a year. You'll have plenty of reinforcement when you begin to see those bank statements. For added reinforcement, treat yourself to a simple financial calculator on which you can figure how fast your money compounds at various interest rates and deposit amounts.

Once again, the key words are "systematic" and "periodic." Make a payment to yourself every Friday, or every Monday, or every payday. Or put one-seventh of your weekly payment into an envelope each day, and take the envelope to the bank at the end of the week. Or play a game with yourself: Every evening, as you're preparing for bed, deposit all your change and one-dollar bills into a small box. If you have no one-dollar bills, you have to deposit the five-dollar bills, or if you don't have any, deposit the ten-dollar bills. You'll never miss the money, and you'll be amazed at how quickly a significant sum accumulates.

What about those bad moments when a large, unexpected expense or a check that fails to materialize plays havoc with your budget? Here's the rule for times like that: Let the other payments slide, but never fail to pay yourself. No excuses.

TEN SUREFIRE WAYS TO SAVE

There are styles to saving, just as there are styles to living. Some we go for, others we reject. There are so many ways to save that it's virtually impossible not to find one that appeals to your temperament.

Here are ten savings programs, some quite basic, others with flair but all of them capable of getting the job done.

1. *Set up a bank passbook account.* The bank is admittedly the least exciting place to save. It offers the lowest return. But it's a great collecting point, because it's so accessible and it will accept any sum of money for deposit. Into your passbook or statement savings account you can put $25 or $50 or $100 a week, until you've got $5,000. At that point, you can buy a certificate of deposit, which will give you a better return than the passbook, the only proviso being that you don't cash the certificate in before the due date. If you do, you'll pay a penalty. Some money market accounts will accept deposits of no less than $100, so if you're paying yourself less than that, put the money into a passbook account, and transfer it when you've got enough.

Be sure that the bank you choose compounds savings daily. The money you deposit on Monday will have earned four days' interest by Friday.

2. *Join a payroll deduction plan at work.* A painless way to save. You don't write a check, you don't even see the money. It's deducted from your paycheck and goes straight into your account. Have as much deducted as you can afford. If you never see the money, you'll find it easier to live on what you end up taking home.

In addition to contributing as much as possible to any pension plan your employer offers, open an Individual Retirement Account as well. Even if IRAs are no longer tax deductible in your situation, the funds accrue tax-deferred. You can contribute up to $2,000 a year, $4,000 for married working couples.

3. *Have your employer put your money into a 401K or SEP plan.* These

are popular plans and with good reason. They enable you to defer taxes; you pay no income tax on the amount you put away until you take the money out. And they're portable; you can take them from job to job. Both plans are fairly simple, and most employers today offer one or the other, if not their own specialized pension or profit-sharing plan.

The term "401K" comes straight out of the tax code; it's the section number authorizing the plan. "SEP" stands for Simplified Employee Pension and simple it is—think of it as an employer-sponsored IRA. Basically, under both plans you should be able to sock away up to 15 percent of your total income with an annual cap of around $8,000. Plans vary, depending on the amount your employer will contribute. Some employers will put in 50 percent of your contribution—an incredible deal. Where else could you earn 50 percent interest on the day you make your deposit?

It's important to realize that under both plans your adjusted gross income *and* your taxable income will be reduced by the amount of money paid into the plan. So, in effect, they're like tax deductions—the money comes right off your total wages. Let's say your salary is $40,000 a year, and you'd like to pay 10 percent, or $4,000, into a 401k. Your total W2 wages at the end of the year will show not $40,000 but $36,000—and you have sheltered a healthy chunk of income from Uncle Sam by jumping through a legal loophole.

If your employer doesn't have a 401K, SEP, or some other beneficial retirement plan, demand one. If the employer doesn't comply, consider moving on.

4. *Buy United States EE Savings Bonds.* You can buy them at work or through your bank. They're purchased at half their face value—a $50 bond costs $25—and ten years later, you get double your money back. You pay no tax on the interest until you cash the bonds in. Since savings bonds aren't convenient to cash in on a short-term basis, they should definitely be purchased for the long term. Once you've bought them, forget about them until they reach maturity.

A new law, which took effect in 1990, allows tax-free interest on EE savings bonds when they are cashed in to pay college tuition bills. To qualify, the bonds must be bought in the parents' names. For most parents, this benefit will end up boosting the equivalent interest yield from a lowly 6.5 or 7 percent to 9 or 10 percent.

5. *Buy life insurance with investments attached.* When you buy a universal or variable life insurance policy, part of your premium goes into an investment account. You get insurance protection for your family, and an opportunity to let your money grow tax-free until you cash in your policy. Most insurance companies will bill you every month or quarter for the premium, so that you don't forget to save. Although the bulk of your life insurance should be term insurance, the least expensive available, a small permanent policy can be a valuable addition to your savings program. (We'll get into life insurance more thoroughly in chapter 14.)

6. *Buy investments.* This is an ideal savings program for those of you who would rather spend than save. In this case, you're spending money, but what you're buying has the power to multiply your money. There's risk attached to this form of saving; wise investments, however, traditionally make money.

Buy ten or a hundred shares of stock at a time in companies of which you have personal knowledge, or whose performance impresses you. Some years ago, a friend of mine who has a home in the High Sierra of California noticed an increasing number of Subarus on the highway. He called his broker and asked him to investigate. At the time, the stock was little known, and selling for $6 a share. The broker never got back to him, and my friend forgot about it. Had my friend bought ten shares of Subaru on his own and held them, he'd have a tidy sum today.

Buying ten shares at a time will cost you extra commission, but by year's end, you'll have acquired an impressive portfolio, in effect your own personalized mutual fund. Another, perhaps easier, way to do it is to buy shares in an existing mutual fund. As we'll see in chapter 12, investing in several high-quality stock mutual funds is a must; they've been outpacing other investments by a wide margin.

Another investment worth considering is a tax-free municipal bond fund, especially if you're in the top tax brackets and like tax-free interest equivalents of about 10 percent.

Are you the kind of person who wouldn't put money in a bank account but would buy gold coins on a regular basis? Fine. Once a month you can buy a one ounce American Eagle gold bullion coin. In 1991 the coin would have cost you about $375. What it will be worth in 2001 will depend on the price of gold at that time. While I don't counsel speculation on a grand scale in gold or other precious metals, I love the kind of investment that you won't touch.

Whatever investment vehicle you choose, when you combine investment spending with other forms of savings, you'll achieve diversification, an objective of every good savings program.

7. *Pay off your first house faster.* If you're planning to refinance your house, take out a fifteen-year mortgage instead of a thirty-year mortgage. The difference in the monthly payment will surprise you; it's not that much higher. But what a difference in savings! Not only will you save a bundle in interest over the years, the equity in your home will build at a much greater rate.

Another way of accomplishing the same objective without refinancing is to make an extra payment toward the principal each month, as we discussed in chapter 6. As long as you don't have a prepayment penalty built into your mortgage, a small extra principal payment once a month is an outstanding form of savings.

8. Buy a second house and rent it out. Investing in real estate is one of the best ways I know to save when you're not the "saving type." Start small. Make sure you can get enough rent to pay your monthly mortgage and cover cash flow. Then let your tenants help you pay the bills while you're building equity. More on this in the next chapter.

9. Start a personal car fund. Need any more be said about the killing costs of interest payments? Any time you can avoid them, you're saving money. Start digging yourself out of the debt trap now by starting a personal car fund. Each time you make your car payment, put $100 to $200 into a bank account. When the time comes to buy your next car, you'll be able to pay cash or, at a minimum, make a substantial downpayment.

10. Start a collectibles hobby. Pick a hobby, any hobby, so long as it's based on items that normally appreciate in value: rare coins, stamps, manuscripts, autographs, antiques, classic automobiles, art. A friend of mine who didn't like to save money loved to buy art. He specialized in rare prints. One day an art dealer told him that Norman Rockwell, the famous illustrator of those great *Saturday Evening Post* covers, would not live more than another year. My friend bought ten signed prints for $500 each. He sold them after Rockwell's death for nearly $2,000 apiece—quite a rate of return for one year.

Not long ago, I met one of the richest men in America. He gave me a tour through his mansion, reputedly the largest home in the United States. There I saw evidence of his great preoccupation, collecting. Over the years, he's collected everything from antique gasoline pumps to model trains. He is so involved and so knowledgeable that every collection he assembles gains in value.

If collecting is what it will take to get you to save, then by all means do so. Pick an item that interests you, talk to dealers to find out what you need to learn and how much money you'll need to get started. The most important question to answer is whether your investment will have a chance to grow. A wisely chosen collecting hobby is the most enjoyable savings method I know.

III

THE NUTS AND BOLTS OF A SECURE, DEBT-FREE LIFE

8

Homes: Playing by the New Rules

WE'LL call them the Fosters. He's an attorney. She's a buyer for a major department store. They both work in Los Angeles. They both make good money—but not enough to buy the kind of home they'd like in one of the city's good neighborhoods, which, even in a soft California real estate market, would cost them $600,000, require a down payment of $120,000 and mortgage payments of $50,000 a year. "Steve," Marjorie Foster said, "we don't *have* $120,000, and we wouldn't feel comfortable paying $50,000 a year." Looking in an ever-expanding circle, the Fosters had finally found a house they liked and could afford in neighboring Pomona, 25 miles east of downtown Los Angeles. They liked Pomona, as well. What they didn't like was the prospect of a long daily commute. "We've made a life-style decision," Marjorie told me. "We don't want to drive an hour and a half each way in heavy traffic on the Pomona Freeway just to be able to say that we own a home. So we're going to continue to rent in Los Angeles. But we've always been told that it's better to own your home than to pay rent. Are we making a terrible mistake?"

"Before I answer," I said, "let me ask you a question. Do you and your husband have a favorite vacation spot, a place you absolutely love?"

"We do," Marjorie said. She told me about a small community in the High Sierra of northern California where they had vacationed in both winter and summer.

"Could you see yourself retiring there someday?"

"Absolutely."

"One more question: What are real estate prices like?"

"Tempting. We looked at a three-bedroom condominium last summer for $81,000."

109

"Then that's where you want to invest your real estate dollars. You can't afford Los Angeles real estate, but that's where you need to live, so the only solution is to rent. On the other hand, this is a great time to buy real estate, because prices are so depressed. Buy the condo while it's cheap, and fifteen years from now you'll have a free-and-clear retirement home worth three to four times what you paid for it."

The solution I proposed to the Fosters—which they followed with good result—illustrates at least three new rules of the real estate game as played in the nineties, rules that apply to anyone who wants to get in the game. Let's consider those rules in order.

RULE ONE: BUYER, BEWARE

Caveat emptor—let the buyer beware—is one of the oldest rules of commerce, but it will qualify as a new rule to anyone who participated in the hot real estate market of the seventies and eighties. During those two decades it wasn't all that serious if you overpaid for a house; a year after moving in, you'd almost surely be able to sell it for a profit. Today—as I've been suggesting since chapter 1—buying a home has become a dangerous, potentially ruinous game. In each of the foregoing chapters, we've looked at homeownership from a special perspective. Here, we're going to put all the pieces together, so that you can know exactly what process to go through in deciding whether homeownership is right for you. I can't think of any subject more deserving of all the attention we've given it because, next to determining whether you're going to work for someone else or go into business for yourself, buying a home is the most important personal financial decision you'll probably ever make.

Estimates place home equity as the number one asset held by most American families. In fact, it represents nearly 50 percent of personal wealth in this country. The growth in home equity has served as a form of enforced savings for millions of Americans who otherwise might not have saved a nickel. In addition, homeownership has provided incalculable psychic income.

Homeownership has been the heart of the American dream since before the inception of the republic. Ancient prohibitions on landownership had fueled revolutionary movements in many European countries and inspired thousands of Europeans to migrate to the New World. The right to own land became one of the provisions guaranteed by our founding fathers—every one of them an immigrant or a descendant of immigrants. That right was further institutionalized by the United States Congress in 1862 when it passed the Homestead Act, which made public lands in the west available to settlers without payment, provided they moved onto the land and developed it. To this day, Congress maintains its affection for the homeowner, an affection tangibly demonstrated as recently as 1986 when mortgage interest and property taxes were preserved as tax deductions during a tax reform that eliminated many other deductions.

What that act of Congress said to consumers was that for the foreseeable future at least, buying a home would increase their net pay. While the standard tax deduction for a married couple is less than $6,000, with home ownership itemized deductions automatically climb over $10,000, saving the couple approximately $1,500.

But tax savings are only one of many elements that must be considered today in determining whether becoming a homeowner is a wise idea, and not nearly as important a consideration as they were when one could deduct 50 percent and more on interest and property taxes rather than today's 28 percent. Of far greater importance are the matters that have made buying a house today an uncertain proposition. To understand why this is so, let's review the basic considerations involved.

Virtually everyone who buys a house does so with the aid of a mortgage, usually 80 percent but often 90 percent and occasionally 100 percent of the purchase price of the dwelling. The most compelling argument in favor of a mortgage—even if you don't need one—is that each year, as a consequence of inflation, you will pay off your indebtedness with less valuable dollars.

If you were the only one who understood this economic fact of life, you'd be way ahead of the game. Unfortunately, the banks understand it even better than you do. Because they know they'll be receiving fewer and fewer real dollars each year as you make your fixed payment, they're going to charge you a lot more for the total loan.

When banks calculate how much interest they'll charge you for a loan, they add the rate of inflation nationally to the amount of profit they want to make. In the case of an 11 percent mortgage, a 4 percent inflation rate is added to a 7 percent premium—the amount of gross profit, less the inflation rate, the bank wants to realize on your loan.

Over the life of a thirty-year loan, as we've seen, you wind up paying almost three times for one house. On the other hand, because you've paid with ever cheaper dollars it's not nearly as bad as it seems. The big difference—the difference that determines whether you've made money or lost money—is what happens to the value of your house between the time you buy it and the time you sell it.

In the seventies and eighties, dozens of self-proclaimed real estate experts assured us that real estate would always appreciate, and that we could make ourselves rich by riding the prices up. One West Los Angeles broker took this philosophy a step further, urging homeowners in his area to "trade up." With prices appreciating so swiftly, he pointed out, they would make even bigger profits on a more valuable home.

It worked, and for such a long time, and with such regularity, that we all did begin to believe that prices could only rise. So swift was the ride on the inflation gravy train that we were loath to disembark, lest we miss out on next year's profits. Who cared if mortgage rates were 11 and 12 percent if values would rise 10 or 20 or even 30 percent in a single year?

But finally there came a year when the values didn't rise and then a year when they receded. That house for which we paid half a million dollars would fetch only $400,000—exactly the amount of our mortgage. If we had to sell today, we'd lose our $100,000 down payment.

Leverage, the ability to control a large asset with a relatively small amount of money, works only if the asset is going to appreciate. There is absolutely no economic virtue in controlling a big asset that's dropping in value.

The degree of impact on you depends on what percentage of your income is allotted to shelter. In the old days, 28 to 32 percent of your net income could go to housing, depending on how lenient your bank was willing to be. Each bank defined that cost differently. Some included insurance and property taxes, others simply the cost of servicing the mortgage. Over the years, as the cost of housing rose, banks become more lenient, to the point that housing costs could comprise 40 and even 45 percent of net pay. We'll soon know whether that figure will go back down toward 30 percent in the wake of the savings and loan crisis.

As long as you're able to make your payments and hang onto your home, it doesn't matter what percentage of your income is going to shelter—assuming, that is, that you've got enough left over for your other needs. Nor does it matter what happens to the short-term value of your home. But if you were temporarily incapacitated so that you fell a few months behind on your payments, you could lose your home. If you were forced to sell in a down market, you would have to keep dropping the price until you found a buyer, and, if the market sagged badly, you would become "upside down" on your house, unable to sell it for enough to retire your indebtedness. Your house may be a splendid one, worth every penny you're asking for it, but if the builders in your area have overbuilt, your housing market has been destroyed. If the biggest employer in your community suddenly decided to relocate, hundreds and thousands of homes would go on the market, driving the price of real estate down. If you guessed wrong and something happened to the neighborhood, you could end up being stuck with a home you no longer wanted. Yet again, I'm speaking from experience. When I first moved to Fort Lauderdale in 1981, I bought a beautiful home with a circular driveway and an in-ground pool within walking distance of the beach for $125,000. It seemed like a great buy at the time, but soon after I moved in a change in the zoning regulations permitted the construction of apartment buildings, which made the area less desirable to homeowners. A number of us bought elsewhere, then found that we couldn't sell our original homes. Not only were buyers resistant to the new environment, they now had other options. In the interim, builders had turned their attention to undeveloped land ten miles to the west, where, profiting from less expensive land, they began to build homes twice as large as those near the beach but still in the same price range. And of course, the buyers bought those homes in preference to homes like mine—which I'd be hard-pressed to sell for $125,000 today, and have put on the rental market as I await a buyer.

The dream of owning a house still has such a powerful hold on the American psyche that owners of condominiums and town houses rarely display the same pride of ownership as owners of detached, single-family homes. But given all of the foregoing, it should be obvious that while the gratifications of homeownership are inarguable, the realities of the nineties have made it a dicey proposition. The first question to ask yourself is, "How long, realistically, am I going to live in this house?" The shorter the period you intend to live in the house, the greater the risk you create for yourself in buying. If you buy a house one month and have to sell it the next, you've already lost 6 percent of the house in real estate commissions.

If you're involved in an enduring relationship, and both you and your partner are living where you want to be and doing what you want to do and you have no thought whatever of moving on, then by all means, buy a home—and buy it now because it's important to buy real estate today that you may not be able to afford tomorrow, and anyone who has followed the real estate market in recent years knows that it's the best buyers' market to come along in years.

If you're in this category, I have three words of advice for you: Location. Location. Location. Always buy the lesser house in the better location in preference to the better house in a lesser location. In the lesser location, values will depreciate with the market. In the better location, values will either hold or actually rise even in a down market. You have to investigate with care, because conditions vary city by city and neighborhood by neighborhood. In Austin, Texas, during the great real estate bust of 1990, prices were still climbing. The rules that apply in Pompano Beach, Florida, which was suffering a real estate recession in the first part of 1991, have little to do with the rules that apply in Boca Raton, ten miles to the north. Boca Raton has the impressive name and the track record to match, and people will readily pay a million and a half dollars, because they're buying prestige, and recessions don't faze them any more than they faze the residents of Bel Air, California.

If you're buying a principal residence for the long pull, and you really want to be thorough, look up the rates of population growth in your state and community, as well as whether incomes are rising or falling. Expanding populations and rising incomes generally forecast higher real estate prices over the long run. For proof, examine the records of California, Florida, and Texas over the last 20 years.

But if you're not buying a home for the long haul, if your career is such that it requires you to move every few years, or you're not where you want to be, doing what you want to be doing, or if you're uncertain about your relationship, then buying a home may not be a good idea at all and could even be disastrous.

In 1987 a physician and his wife bought a home in Los Angeles. In 1990 he was offered a tremendous job in Atlanta—a department of his own, money for research, and an exceptional salary—that he couldn't turn down. His wife found an excellent job as well. And because real estate prices in Atlanta are about half what they are in Los Angeles, the physician and his wife were able to make a great buy on a new home. Everything seemed perfect until they tried to sell their Los Angeles house. They'd bought it for $395,000. They offered it at $495,000. Not only did they get no offers, they got no prospective buyers. When the time came to move to Atlanta, the house still hadn't sold. But by this point, they'd closed escrow on the Atlanta house. For the next six months, they had to carry both houses. Nine months after listing their Los Angeles house, they finally sold it for $375,000—$20,000 less than they'd paid for it in 1987. To this loss they added the 6 percent commission on the sale, another $22,500, and the six months of double mortgage payments, another $10,000 at least. Their $50,000 plus loss represented their entire savings. When I talked to them, they were in a daze. "Gee, Steve," the husband said, "I was taught that people who rented were stupid, that when you bought you saved on taxes and when you sold you made a profit. So what happened? How did I just lose money?"

What happened was that these people got caught in a down market, caused in part by overbuilding and in part by loss of consumer confidence. That loss of confidence wasn't caused simply by the economic certainties that began to gather at the end of the eighties. The reality is that owning a home today is no longer perceived by the public as the financial panacea that it was.

For millions of Americans today, owning a home in the city where they work is more a fantasy than a realizable dream. In New York, Boston, San Francisco, Los Angeles, and a number of other major metropolitan areas, real estate prices rose so dramatically during the eighties that people like the Fosters, with good jobs and solid futures, were nonetheless priced out of the market. Others who did manage to scrape up the down payments found themselves impossibly in debt. Not only were they making payments they could barely afford, they were going even further into debt to furnish all those rooms with furniture, draperies and carpeting, and to buy television and stereo equipment. For these people, as for the Fosters, there are more creative solutions.

RULE TWO: CONSIDER RENTING YOUR PRINCIPAL RESIDENCE

For many years, a social stigma attached to people who rented apartments. They were thought to be second-class citizens, and often they thought that about themselves. They had the impression that if they marked the rent box on credit card applications they would be perceived as poor credit risks, or at least inferior to those who owned their own homes. Out of that sensibility came the popularity of duplex apartments following World War II. People who might not otherwise have been able to carry mortgages bought two-family homes, lived in one and rented the other. Renting was such a stigma that people would often go to any length to find the smallest condominium or town house, only to discover when they wanted to sell their property that it had diminished in value. The worst blow of all was discovering in attempting to rent their condos or town houses that the rent they could get didn't even cover their monthly carrying charges.

Today, not only have all those lessons been absorbed, sharp changes in social perceptions have made renting seem compelling.

If you could afford it, a suite in a good hotel would be the most carefree existence imaginable. All of your problems would be taken care of for you. All your utilities would be paid for. You wouldn't even have to change a light bulb. Renting today can be a close second to that ideal existence. The inability of so many people to come up with the down payment on homes in urban areas has not been lost on developers. They have moved into the market with gorgeous apartment complexes, beautifully landscaped, featuring spacious units, many with fireplaces, as well as amenities few homes could offer: tennis courts, swimming pools, Jacuzzis, health clubs. Some of these apartment complexes adjoin golf courses, boat ponds, and jogging trails. In many, the rent includes all utilities. It doesn't matter how much gas or electricity or water you use because at the end of the month you have only one bill to pay, and the amount is the same for the duration of your lease. Best of all, your maintenance cost is zero. Anyone who has ever owned a home knows how much it costs to maintain that home each and every year. Yes, you get better income tax deductions when you own a home, but the cost of a new roof or a paint job or a new furnace can greatly exceed your tax savings. And even if nothing goes wrong, there is always the cost of maintaining your grounds, which can be substantial even if you do it yourself.

When you rent, moreover, you don't pay property taxes, at least not directly. There is a theory that property taxes are built into your rent payment, but the truth is that you're always "behind the curve" in this situation, and getting at least a partial free ride in the community.

But the most delicious freedom of all is the knowledge that whatever goes wrong can be taken care of with a phone call. Your time can be put to more profitable use—earning money or just enjoying life. Living in a smaller arena, life becomes exquisitely simple; you're no longer straining to keep up with the Joneses, which, let's face it, has a lot to do with the popularity of large homes.

It gets better. So many developers have recognized the changing perceptions about renting that they have overbuilt. The result is a tenants' market, in which developers will not only rent reasonably but on a three-, six-, or twelve-month lease. In many instances, renting is so economically efficient that you find yourself spending far less money than you did as a homeowner, and in possession of many more dollars to invest. For sure, you've got the money that would have paid the down payment on your home. Best of all, when you decide to move on, there's no 6 percent real estate commission to pay.

Many former owners of single-family residences, having experienced the psychological benefits of ownership and perhaps some economic benefits as well, find it difficult to move to a rental unit when they sell their homes. For them, buying a condominium represents a more realistic next step. It certainly makes good economic sense to buy another property, even one with a lesser value, when you sell your home at a profit, because you diminish the amount of profit on which you'll be taxed.

But anyone contemplating such a step should consider carefully the non-economic benefits to be derived from living a hassle-free life. Those who buy into condominium units have their first experience with people I call "condo commandos," who set up rules and regulations to control condominium life. Moreover, using profits from the sale of a home to buy a condominium often locks up a couple's life savings, whereas not buying anything but paying the tax instead frees them to do anything they want. Rather than see their lives wrapped up economically with the life of the condominium, I would rather see them bite the bullet, pay the capital gains tax, and invest the remainder so that it throws off enough income to enable them to enjoy their new-found freedom. What could be worse than to enter a new life with a whole new set of mortgages and taxes to pay?

Is renting a better way to go? In addition to all the above considerations, the answer is yes if:

- You're likely to move in five years or less, because it'll take that long to recoup on closing costs and sales commissions
- Homes in your area are renting for half of one percent of their market value per month or less, and will continue to do so even after anticipated rent increases
- You expect home prices to lag behind inflation

RULE THREE: BUY A VACATION HOME

Having warned you just a few pages ago about the dangers of buying a principal residence, I'm going to turn around and urge you to consider the purchase of a vacation house within the next two years. Buying a vacation house in a place you love and might one day retire to is a great idea for everyone who can possibly swing it, and particularly for those who find they've been priced out of the urban house market. There are at least seven reasons why.

It's a Bargain

Not in a long while has there been such a buying opportunity as exists in real estate today—particularly in areas associated with retirement living. In Tucson and Phoenix at the beginning of 1991, developers were almost giving homes away. No down payment, just take over the mortgage. A home in Phoenix once valued at $250,000 was available for $110,000. Anyone who liked the desert climate and wanted to buy a retirement home could take advantage of a market that might never be repeated.

In Hilton Head, South Carolina, an exclusive area, two-bedroom, two-bath condominiums were selling for $60,000 to $65,000, and you could buy them for 10 percent down. South Carolina is in the same latitude as Los Angeles, which means that it has temperate winters. There are furnished condominiums in Palm Aire, a resortlike area of Pompano Beach, Florida, less than a mile from my home, that sell for $60,000.

One of the best areas I can think of for a future retirement home is southwest Florida, more specifically Fort Myers. There are several reasons why. First, home prices are incredibly affordable there; they start in the high fifties. Second, it's a planned community, which means amenities, maintenance, and controlled growth. Third, the weather is generally warm. Fourth, Florida has neither an income tax nor an inheritance tax—yet.

Obviously, no vacation home is right for you, no matter how great a bargain it is, if it's not in the right location. If you're accustomed to taking your vacations in the summer and wish to continue to do so, Tucson isn't the best place to buy because the summers there are ferocious. Choose the right location first, and you're almost certain to find bargains corresponding to the above examples.

It's Potentially a Great Investment

In the strictest economic terms, you can't look at vacation or future retirement property as an investment. It has to be looked at as a consumable item because each and every month it's going to cost you a certain amount for the mortgage payment, taxes, insurance, utilities, and maintenance. Nonetheless, there is suggestive evidence that any real estate bought at current bargain prices in areas catering to retired people will double and triple in value over the next 10 to 15 years.

In 1987 my wife and I were in Honolulu on a brief vacation and decided to look at some town houses. We saw several that appealed to us, selling for $125,000. I was on the verge of buying one, but changed my mind because I was concerned about maintaining a property that was so far from my home. My concern was appropriate, but my decision was regrettable because I was convinced that those town houses would quickly appreciate in value. Shortly thereafter, cash-rich Japanese began buying Hawaiian real estate in a major way, and today those same town houses are selling for $350,000 to $400,000. Had I bought a condominium for $125,000, I would have a paper profit today of $225,000 to $275,000—and a return of 1,800 to 2,200 percent on my down payment of $12,500.

As this is being written, I'm shopping for a home on Marco Island, along the Gulf of Florida. It's one of the most gorgeous places I know, situated next to placid waters and with an excellent climate. As in many other desirable locations around the United States, developers got carried away and overbuilt. As a result, I can buy a lovely home there on a deep-water canal, with a dock, for $250,000. Ten years from now, in my opinion, Marco Island will be to western Florida what Balboa Island is to southern California, a precious residential area. Already, the word is out in places like Chicago and Buffalo; talk to CEOs and board chairmen in such cities and they'll tell you either that they have a place on Marco Island already or are looking to find one.

If you buy right in the right area, you could be sitting on a tremendous capital gain fifteen years from now. For $15,000, you can control a smaller piece of property (not on a canal) worth $150,000 today—and $500,000 by the time you've paid it off.

It's a Tax Deduction

Suppose you were able to buy a vacation home in an area you loved for $75,000. And suppose you put 20 percent down, and arranged financing at 9 percent for 15 years. Each month for the next 180 months, you'd pay $609, most of it interest at the outset. Over the fifteen years, your interest payments would total $49,500, every dollar of it deductible. Assuming you were paying federal taxes at the rate of 28 percent, the tax savings to you would be $13,900. Property taxes would be deductible as well. If you were to buy your vacation home in an area where prices are currently depressed, the appreciation on your property would almost certainly exceed the amount of interest you'd pay over the life of the loan, and might even cover your property taxes as well. If you were to buy in an area with a highly promising future, interest and tax payments would be insignificant compared to the gain you'd realize.

It's Paid with Depreciating Dollars

The "cheaper dollars" argument may not be compelling enough when you're considering the purchase of an expensive principal residence costing several hundred thousand dollars or more, given all the other imponderables, but it's still a valid consideration in any real estate purchase. Since inflation diminishes the value of the dollar by half every ten to twelve years, the value of the dollars you use to pay off the mortgage in the fifteenth year will be worth between 40 and 45 percent of the dollars you used to make the down payment.

It's an Enforced Savings Plan

We've seen that homeownership can no longer be considered the fail-safe savings device that it was twenty and thirty years ago. Given the prospect of longer life, you can't assume that the $200,000 nest egg you've amassed in your house will get you through retirement; you can spend that much in a nursing home in two years. But as part of a savings program, a house is still important—provided you buy at a good price and in the right location. With these qualifications, a small vacation or retirement retreat, financed with a fifteen-year, fixed-interest mortgage, is a fantastic savings tool. In the last years of the mortgage, especially, most of the monthly payment is applied to the balance of the loan. And by the time the loan is fully paid, your investment, like any good investment, will in all probability have appreciated.

It's a Free Vacation, Any Time You Want It

Have you ever added up how much you spend each year on vacations? Transportation aside, a week for two at a nice resort can run $2,000 to $4,000. Multiply these numbers by two, three, or four, add in the cost for children, if you have them, and you have a truly staggering number. And how about long weekends—that four-day ski trip in February, or that long weekend to the shore over the 4th of July? That's all goodbye money, with nothing to show for it but memories and increased debt.

But suppose you were to buy an all-seasons vacation home in New England or the Rocky Mountains or the Far West. You'd save thousands each year on hotel rooms and expensive restaurant meals and laundry and all the other items that add to the price of the average vacation. That money you'd save would easily pay for the cost of maintaining a vacation home—mortgage, taxes, insurance, maintenance, and utilities.

It's a Paid-up Retirement Home in the Place You Love Best

If you can't live and work in the place you love best, the next best thing is to spend all your free time there. By the time you're ready to quit work for good, you've not only had all those great vacations, you've got a paid-up retirement home. Acting now makes it all come true.

A caution: I know that many people who buy vacation properties do so with the objective of leasing them out when they're not using them, putting them into a rental program. And I know that it can sometimes work spectacularly. A Los Angeles lawyer bought a condominium in Vail in 1970 for $65,000. Every year since then he has earned more money in renting it out than it costs him to maintain, and the condo today is worth a million dollars. But for every story like that I've heard a dozen where it didn't work out. The profits were small and the aggravation great. In some cases, the profits had to be used to restore the property to a livable state.

GETTING IN THE GAME

Whether you're buying a principal residence or a vacation home, the best way to get into the housing market is to start talking with real estate agents, sellers, and developers. Find out what kind of financing deals exist and where the most motivated sellers are located. Even when interest rates are relatively low, it's tough coming up with enough cash for the down payment, those expensive points, closing costs, and out-of-pocket expenses, not to mention all the money you'll need to furnish your new house. So you need to negotiate the best deal you can.

If cash is tight, try getting a mortgage through the Federal Housing Authority (FHA), or even a Veterans Administration loan, if you qualify. Closing costs are minimal, as is the down payment. Or check the classified ads for low assumable mortgages with very little down and no qualifying requirements. Even if you're working with a real estate agent, some sellers are motivated enough to work out a private financing deal with you. The agent can help you on this score, telling the seller how much cash you have to work with and putting together a creative mortgage package with or without a bank.

If at all possible, avoid the banks when financing your house. In the past ten years, I've bought two houses; neither purchase involved a bank. I let real estate agents do my work for me. I told them how much I wanted to pay for the house, how much I wanted to put down, and how much interest I'd pay to the seller who would carry the mortgage. I said I wanted a mortgage that I could pay interest only on each month, if I so chose, or retire in part or in whole any time I wanted to. Within a week, the agent had lined up three houses, and before we were finished we'd looked at a dozen—every one of them owned by people who were happy to finance my purchase based on my conditions. When we closed the deal, there were no points or closing costs and there had been no credit check.

Here are three other ways to get in the game when you don't have sufficient savings.

Equity-Sharing

Equity-sharing involves co-ownership of a home by two or more parties. One party occupies the home as his or her principal residence. The terms are worked out between the co-owners. One owner can make the down payment while the other makes the monthly payments. Or the down payment and monthly payments can be shared in equal or unequal amounts. Tax benefits are shared as well. When the property is sold, profits or losses are shared according to the percentage of ownership.

Equity-sharing enables you to get into a home you might otherwise not be able to purchase. Your partner in the venture, on the other hand, makes a clean investment without maintenance or management hassles, and with guaranteed occupancy.

Parents, siblings, friends, and employers are all potential partners in an equity-sharing arrangement. Many doctors and dentists are looking for a surefire investment, and what could be more surefire than a house that someone's living in? Some communities have firms that specialize in matching investors with prospective buyers. Real estate agents or real estate attorneys may also be good sources.

Lease-Option Agreements

If you're a prospective buyer with limited cash, a lease-option agreement may be a good deal for you. Under such an agreement, you the renter have an option to buy the property you're living in at a later date. Both you and the seller sign a purchase agreement outlining the price, terms, and closing date, and specifying for how long the lease option is to run. With a lease option a portion of your monthly rent may be applied to the down payment of the home. In addition, you are required to put up "option funds," usually 3 to 5 percent of the purchase price—the figure is negotiable. If you decide to buy the home, the option funds are applied to the down payment. If you decide not to buy the home, the option funds are retained by the seller. So a lease option can't be a frivolous venture on your part; you should really want the house. While you may be hesitant about risking thousands of dollars on a house you may eventually decide you don't want, you have to give the seller an incentive to take his property off the market and lease it out to you.

To get a lease-option agreement, you may be asked to prequalify for financing, so that you can prove to the seller that you'll have enough money to complete the purchase on the closing date. If you decide not to buy the house, you must notify the seller, in most cases between thirty and ninety days before the lease runs out.

If you're the buyer, the lease-option agreement offers you several remarkable advantages:

1. It permits you to take immediate possession of the home, while accumulating your down payment and closing costs.

2. You immediately begin building equity, particularly if the value of the house appreciates during your lease-option period.

3. If the real estate market should rise, you're still locked into the lower price you negotiated.

4. If the real estate market should go down, you have the option to refuse purchase.

5. You can investigate the quality of life-style in your new home and neighborhood to see if it matches your needs.

6. If you're an out-of-town buyer, you can move into your new house without delay while you're trying to sell your old house.

If you're the seller, the lease-option agreement offers advantages as well:

1. It may enable you to negotiate a higher price for your house because you're offering more favorable terms to the buyer.

2. It gives you monthly income during a period when it may take a long time to sell your house because of the great quantity of houses for sale in your area.

3. The monthly income enables you to cover mortgage payments, taxes, and insurance.

4. You have someone inside your house providing much-needed security and upkeep.

Contract for Deed

This arrangement takes the lease option to the next level. You contract with the seller to buy his property, you take physical possession of the property, but you don't take title to the property until some later date, specified in your agreement, when the property will be refinanced in your name. Under this arrangement, you assume responsibility for the mortgage payments to the bank, and you make a partial payment on the difference between the selling price and the amount owed to the bank. Suppose you agree to buy the house for $180,000. The mortgage is $140,000, which you agree to service. That leaves $40,000 representing the seller's equity in the house. You haven't got $40,000, but you do have $10,000, and he's willing to take that amount and give you a second mortgage for the other $30,000, on which you'll pay interest only for two to five years and then liquidate with a balloon payment at the end of the term. Why would the seller agree to such a deal? Because he needs the money to make his own payments current, or because you're the only buyer, or both.

Whatever kind of financing arrangement you make, and for whatever kind of dwelling, keep in mind that when you reach forty or forty-five years of age, it's time to stop thinking about thirty-year mortgages. At that stage of life, a fifteen-year mortgage is the longest you should consider. The monthly payment will be about 20 to 25 percent higher, but the savings will be astronomical. Banks love fifteen-year mortgages so much that they'll make it worth your while to agree to one, charging you a quarter point less than they will for a thirty-year mortgage. If your bank won't do that, find one that will.

If you're in the forty to forty-five age range now and working off a thirty-year mortgage, you don't have to refinance. Just run a new mortgage schedule that shows you how much additional you have to pay each month on the principal to pay the entire loan off by the date you wish. Then make those extra payments and, voilà, by the time you're sixty you'll have no more monthly payments. Making extra payments, incidentally, is a great way to knock down the cost of those 11 to 14 percent adjustable rate mortgages, if you're stuck with one of those, without incurring the significant cost of converting to a fixed-rate loan. If refinancing will lower the interest rate by 2 percent or more (1.5 percent on loans of $150,000 or more) *and* you intend to stay in your home for at least three to five years longer, then it may be worth the time and expense to formally refinance. But five minutes with a calculator will tell you if you can't accomplish the same thing without cost or fuss by paying your principal down each month.

It should be obvious by this point that I'm a great believer in shorter paybacks on any loan you negotiate. If you can't afford the short payback, perhaps you can't afford to borrow the money in the first place.

GETTING THE MOST OUT OF REALTORS

Finding the right buy, whether it's a principal residence or a vacation home, is a demanding task. Most of us can't give it the time it rightfully requires. That's where a good real estate agent can be a blessing, particularly one who specializes in the area in which you want to live.

To get the most out of a real estate agent, you have got to be as specific as you can possibly be about exactly the kind of house you're looking for, what condition it must be in, which neighborhoods are acceptable, how much you can put down, how much financing you require, and whether you prefer to make a financial arrangement with the seller or wish to deal directly with a bank. Without this information not even the best agent can do a good job for you. But if you can be specific, a realtor will do all the groundwork and not charge you a dime—one of the greatest bargains around.

Following this game plan, a New York City woman who never believed she could afford to buy a house anywhere in the five boroughs turned her problem over to a real estate agent. It took six months, but the realtor found her a home for $90,000 in the Throg's Neck area of the Bronx, a short commute from her job in Manhattan.

Always remember, however, that the agent—even your agent—is working for the seller, not the buyer. It's the seller who pays the commission. So if you're the buyer, you need a professional on your side. That professional is a lawyer. Never buy a house without one.

If you're selling a house, real estate agents will probably attempt to convince you that the standard 6 percent commission is not negotiable. That's not true. In the competitive real estate market of the nineties, commissions of 4 and even 3 percent are possible; the greater the value of your property, the lower a commission you can demand from your broker. Your broker will want an exclusive contract. That's fair, because he or she will be putting both time and money into the effort to sell your home. But don't give an exclusive listing for more than 120 days. If your house hasn't sold by then, it's time to evaluate the job your realtor is doing.

Brokers often earn their money, but they take a big chunk of your equity in doing so. Six percent of the purchase price may not seem like much, but a $12,000 commission on the sale of a $200,000 home could represent 25 percent or more of your equity, and even a 4 or 3 percent commission subtracts a substantial amount from the equity.

So before listing your home with a broker, you might try being a "Fizzbo," the industry's nickname for owner-sellers. (It comes from the acronym FSBO, for sale by owner.) Prepare well. Make certain, above all, that you have a good idea of prices in your neighborhood for houses comparable to yours. The best way to gain that knowledge is to go to as many open houses as you can. You then have to decide how much you think your house is worth, and what price you won't go below. Once you've made those decisions, put a sign out, advertise in the local newspaper, and give yourself at least 90 days. If you're successful in finding a buyer, make certain that you retain an attorney who specializes in real estate to draw up your agreement with the purchaser.

If you're eager to avoid giving such a big chunk of your equity to a real estate broker, you might want to look for an agency that specializes in putting buyers and sellers together. For a one-time fee of several hundred dollars, these agencies will match you up by computer with prospective buyers, almost like a dating service. A young man I know named Scott Eckert pioneered this "buy owner" service in Florida and Chicago, and received such a good response that he plans to expand to other parts of the country. A similar service was recently offered in Dallas.

However you choose to sell your house, make up your mind to spend what it takes to spruce it up before putting it on the market. Buyers are said to make up their minds about a house in thirty seconds or less. What do they see in those thirty seconds? First of all, the landscaping and plantings in front of your house. Dollar for dollar, that's the best investment of your money. The next best investment is a fresh coat of paint and new wallpaper where needed. What sells a house is showcasing, like a nice front door.

TWO CHEERS FOR TIME-SHARES

The burden of this chapter is to show you how to gain a beneficial equity in a real estate market whose rules have been virtually transformed almost overnight. But I can't end the chapter without raising at least two cheers for a country cousin of homeownership.

Time-sharing was developed by some very bright people who figured out that instead of selling a building for $250,000 to a single buyer, they could divide it up into 40 units and sell each unit for $25,000, thereby quadrupling their money. Today, some time-shares are returning three and four times what they're worth. Although the prices are somewhat inflated, many people who bought time-shares are very happy with them. I once went to interview the inhabitants of a time-share in Fort Lauderdale, Florida, expecting to find a great deal of dissatisfaction. Of the thirty people I interviewed, not one of them spoke against it. Many extolled the level at which the facility was being maintained.

Overall, however, it's estimated that three out of four time-shares that have ever been built or sold are now up for resale, proof enough that the majority of buyers regret that they bought. Perhaps the area in which they bought didn't live up to expectations. Or the rigidity of the time-share requirement—needing to spend the same week or two in the unit each and every year—didn't work with the buyer's schedule. Whatever the reason, this disaffection has created an extraordinary opportunity for people who don't want to buy a vacation home but are absolutely certain where they want to spend their vacation each year.

When the time-share market collapsed a few years ago, a "secondary" time-share market developed. In this market, a buyer who paid $15,000 a week for his time-share will offer to sell all rights for as little as a quarter to a third of what he paid for it. *That* is a bargain.

If I could buy a time-share at a deep discount in an area that I was absolutely certain I wanted to return to year after year, and the purchase entitled me to a week or several weeks without further charge in a facility I really liked, I would have no hesitation about buying the time-share. On the other hand, I wouldn't delude myself into thinking that I'd done myself anywhere near the same amount of good as I would have if I'd bought a vacation home.

Whatever the recent history of real estate prices, it's clear that most real estate properties will continue to appreciate in value over long periods of time. They have been doing so since the founding of the country 215 years ago. It's also clear that pockets of recession and even depression will appear periodically because of slow demand or overbuilding. In those occasions, dramatic drops in prices will provide bargain basement buying opportunities for shrewd investors and house buyers alike. Just don't get caught by shorter-term market swings that can and will wipe you out. Real estate investing during the nineties will be exciting and demanding—definitely not for the faint of heart.

9

Cars: Buying Them for Keeps—or at Least for Five Years

NOTHING wipes out savings faster and destroys our credit ratings more thoroughly than buying and trading expensive new cars every few years. No consumer wins that game because he or she always buys a car at retail and sells it at wholesale after the value has dropped—a double hit. Never has the risk of loss been greater than it is today, with automobiles costing as much as houses cost in the fifties.

After houses, automobiles are our second biggest expense. For those millions of Americans who have been priced out of the urban housing market, automobiles are *the* single biggest purchase they will make in their lifetime. More properly, that should be purchases, because these are the people who habitually buy a new car every two or three years—cars whose sticker price will frequently exceed the purchasers' annual take-home pay.

Of all the money makeovers, transforming the manner in which we buy and use our cars may be the easiest, as well as the most profitable, resulting in savings of several thousand dollars a year, and as much as $100,000 in a lifetime.

WHY CARS COST SO MUCH—AND WHAT YOU CAN DO ABOUT IT

Believe it or not, there was a long period in American history when cars were reasonably priced. In the years following the invention of the automobile by Henry Ford, the increasing efficiency of mass production plus heavy competition drove prices down to a point where cars were extremely affordable. With the exception of the Great Depression, most working Americans could manage to put 20 percent down on a car costing $1,500, and make payments on loans of 7 percent until the car was paid for. You could still buy a new car for $1,200 in the years following World War II, and as recently as 1965 a Chevrolet sold for $2,700 and a Cadillac for $3,500.

Over the last quarter-century, however, the overall cost of driving has risen considerably in absolute terms, meaning that it takes a great deal more of our income to put us in the driver's seat. Some of that increase is due to inflation, but most of the increase is due to the manufacture of increasingly more elaborate products, reflecting the conviction of American and foreign automobile manufacturers that consumers want ever more powerful and sophisticated cars. I've read reports to the effect that on an inflation-adjusted basis, new cars actually sell for less than they did twenty-five years ago. I don't consider this relevant or significant even if it's true, which I seriously doubt. The unvarnished truth is that, conditioned by television, motion pictures, and the media, and given the opportunity by stretch financing, we have increasingly been buying fancier cars than we need or can afford. It makes no economic sense. The loss in value of the car in years one and two is gigantic, and the cost of liability and collision insurance has gotten totally out of hand. Along with the increased price of automobiles has come an increase in the cost of maintaining them. Remember when our lube and oil change at the local service station cost less than $10? Today that same service can run $50, and even more if we follow the maintenance schedule prescribed by the manufacturer and have the work done by the dealer. Any problems not covered by the warranty can set us back a week's pay.

The great exception to automobile expenses is gasoline, which sells for less today in absolute terms than it did fifty years ago. In 1940, premium gasoline sold for 18 cents a gallon, equivalent to $1.78 in today's dollars. But in mid-1991, premium gas was selling for less than $1.50 in most metropolitan areas. When it comes to filling the tank, these are the good old days.

The biggest cost of maintaining an automobile, however, has nothing to do with service, repairs, or gasoline. It has to do with the cost of the money we borrow to buy the car. Not only is the amount we must borrow greater by far today than it was twenty-five years ago, the rate at which we borrow is much higher, and we can no longer deduct the interest on the loan or the sales tax.

As the price of automobiles increased, and they became increasingly more difficult to purchase, the only response dealers and finance companies could make to encourage sales was to diminish the cost of monthly payments. It got to the point where the average buyer no longer asked the price of a car or how much the interest would be when he or she walked into a showroom. The only question asked was, "How much are the payments?" Salesmen being salesmen, their reply would be, "How much can you afford per month?" The purchaser might say, "Well, I'm paying $280 now, but I guess I could go to $350 for the car of my dreams." And the salesman would ask, "Could you stretch to $375? For $375, I could put you into your dream car."

The corollary to the concern over monthly payments was that car loans had to be stretched over four, five, six, and even seven years to keep them low enough for the consumer's wallet. A few years ago when I was shopping for a car, I was pressured by the finance manager at the car dealership to go with a seven-year loan. He said, "Look, this is the wave of the future. Keep those payments low. Why do you want to have all your money tied up in cars?" I didn't take his advice.

You don't want *all* your money tied up in cars, certainly, but the more cash you pay the better off you are. The longer a loan becomes, the more expensive it is. By stretching the financing out over five, six, or seven years in order to get the monthly payment down to a number the consumer can afford, a $17,000 car winds up costing upward of $23,500. The shorter the term of your loan, the lower the price of the car, the less interest you pay, and the less the car costs you. When the payments are stretched out over anything more than three years, the finance charge goes through the roof. Even medium-priced cars today have finance charges of more than $5,000 attached to them. And because the first years of the payback are almost pure interest, when trade-in time rolls around, most Americans find they are upside down on their car loans: The amount of the loan is greater than the value of the car.

Today, automobile manufacturers are paying for pushing an amount of debt on society that society couldn't handle. They are paying with rebate checks and zero financing.

I said earlier that sluggish automobile sales in recent years weren't so much a reflection of consumer fears as they were of increasing awareness, provoked by the new tax laws, of how much more expensive a car has become. Now, I believe, that awareness has reached the next step. I think that Americans are ready to change their entire approach to the purchase and care of cars. Instead of viewing them as commodities to be traded in every two, three, or four years, they're going to think of them as valuable, expensive pieces of equipment to be held for five, six, or seven years or even longer, as long as they can be well maintained.

In 1975 my uncle married a Rumanian woman. He came back from Bucharest with a lot of photographs, some of which, taken in the early morning, showed all the cars parked on the street covered with canvas. When I asked him why all the cars were covered, he said, "Because in Rumania, a car is a very valued possession. You just don't run out and buy one. It takes ten years of salary to buy a car, and there's a waiting list. So when you buy a car you know it's going to be your car for a long time and you'd better take care of it."

In the summer of 1990, in front of my office in Fort Lauderdale, I watched one of my TV producers, Genevieve Schmitt, pull a custom canvas cover over her newly purchased Toyota. It's happening, I told myself. We've begun to think of cars not as disposable items but as valuable pieces of equipment we're going to have to hold on to and care for for many years.

How can we think otherwise, when cars cost so much and the payments are so expensive and continue for so long? How can we not change our car-buying strategies, knowing that the $22,000 car we're eyeing right now could cost $35,000 in six years? The money spent on interest for a $35,000 car plus the depreciation, particularly in the first two years when the value drops the most, will be thousands more than it will cost to keep a good older car in mint condition.

If we're going to hold on to our cars, it behooves us to buy the right ones at the outset, and to pay no more for them than we have to.

HOW TO BUY THE RIGHT CAR AT A ROCK-BOTTOM PRICE

For most of us, an automobile is a whole lot more than transportation. It usually reflects our personality and makes a personal statement about how we want to be perceived by the world. The multiple choices available as to color, power, style, size, performance, safety, cost, and operating economy—and combinations thereof—make choosing the right car a formidable job. Unfortunately, emotions and lack of knowledge hinder our pursuit of the "perfect" car at the "right" price with the best possible financing, and most of us make enough mistakes at the dealership and wind up paying so much money to the dealer, and eventually the bank, that we become disillusioned with the car soon after we've bought it.

A successful car salesman once told me that even today, many people come into the showroom and don't ask for a discount. They'll just pay the sticker price. They're either afraid to negotiate or don't realize that they can and should negotiate. Older people can be especially reluctant to do so; one salesman told me of a senior citizen who came into the showroom and said, "How much is that Pontiac, over there?" The salesman said, "Nineteen thousand four hundred." "I'll take it," the man said, unaware that with the slightest effort on his part, he could have bought the car for $17,400 or less.

Buying a car is a game—a very expensive game if you lose. The key is to stay in control both mentally and emotionally.

Several years ago, my wife and I, vacationing in Los Angeles, saw Robert Mitchum drive up to the Beverly Wilshire Hotel in Beverly Hills in a BMW 735i. Then and there, we both fell in love with the car. She was pregnant at the time, and I wanted her to have a big, safe car to drive that would protect her and the baby in an accident. For me, big and safe go together. As a television reporter, I covered one of the worst accidents in the history of Miami. A truck had blown a tire, crossed a grassy median, and crashed into three oncoming cars. All three cars were American compacts, and all three drivers were killed. On another occasion, driving a rented Cadillac, I was hit by a car going forty miles an hour. The driver, who had run a red light, crashed into the passenger door of the Cadillac, and went through the windshield of his Pinto. I opened the left door, got out, and brushed the glass off my suit. On another occasion a Dodge Dart with four young kids in it went through a stop sign and broadsided me. This time I was driving a big Pontiac Bonneville, and once again I emerged unscathed.

When my wife and I returned to Fort Lauderdale from Los Angeles, I bought a number of automobile magazines and satisfied myself that the BMW was one of the safest cars in the world. I also read as much as I could about the features of the car, and I got an excellent idea of what it cost the dealer and how much profit he would try to make.

At 3 P.M. on the last Saturday afternoon in January, I went into a BMW showroom in Pompano Beach. My timing was deliberate. January is traditionally a slow month for new car sales. By the last Saturday of the month the salesmen would be itching to make a sale; a customer who appears in the final hours of the month puts a lot of pressure on them—particularly at this dealership, which was not open on Sundays. I was absolutely certain about the car I wanted to buy, but the salesman—we'll call him Ralph—was the last person who would ever know that. For nearly an hour I focused my attention on another model, asking questions, sitting in the car, even taking a test drive, until I had Ralph believing that that was the car I wanted. Just as Ralph, certain he had a live one, began to try to make a deal, I walked over to the 735i and said, "Well, this is pretty nice, how much is this?" He said, "Well, the sticker is $41,000." I said, "Well, I know I can't afford that. It's too rich for my taste." Later, I would learn that they'd sold the very same model car earlier that day to a wealthy woman who'd walked in, asked the price, and bought it on the spot—for $41,000. I said, "Give me your best offer on this car, the absolute lowest you'll go." Ralph went off to see the manager, and came back a few minutes later. "Steve," he said, "we can put you in this car right now for $37,500." I said, "Well, we're way apart." Ralph said, "Well, how much can you afford to pay for this car?" I, of course, said nothing. I just kept shaking my head. Finally, I said, "I'm thinking much lower than that. I really couldn't pay anything close to that." But instead of giving a figure, I shook hands with Ralph and started for the door. By this point, Ralph was extremely nervous. He said, "Let me go back to the manager. I'll put the pressure back on him." Ten minutes later, he came back and said, "We can sell you this car for $36,000, and you don't even have to buy it today. You can take it home and drive it around tomorrow. We'll just fill out a rental slip, and you can either bring it back in on Monday or come in and close the deal." I said, "No, I don't want to do that." And again, I headed for the door. "Wait," Ralph said, and ran off to see the manager. Within minutes the price was down to $35,000, and minutes later to $33,000. And I just kept saying no. "Would you be willing to buy this car by the time we close today?" he asked. I said that yes, I was prepared to do that, but $33,000 wouldn't do it and there was no sense in talking any more. And once again, I started for the door. At this point, Ralph panicked. He said, "Steve, please come back here. I'm sure we can do something. Please tell me what it will take for you to buy this car today." I said, "It will take $31,000 for me to buy this car today, and I'll buy it right now." Two minutes later, Ralph was back with an offer from the General Manager of $32,000, and this time when I walked out I actually made it to my car. Just as I was getting in, Ralph came running up to me, and he said, "Will you buy the car right now for $31,000?" And I said, "Yes, I'll sign the papers and give you a check right now." He said, "Come on back in. You've got a deal."

Inside, I wrote out a check for $100. Ralph wrote out the contract and gave me a receipt for the $100. I grabbed the agreement, with the deposit slip attached, and handed him my check.

On Monday morning, the sales manager informed me that he couldn't sell me the car because it had already been sold to someone else. I advised the manager that I had a good lawyer, that I would call the Consumer Advocates Division of the Attorney General's Office to explain how the dealership had reneged on a bill of sale I had in my possession, and that I'd also tell my story to the local newspapers. Two hours later, the manager called back to tell me that the car hadn't been sold after all. That day, I completed the purchase of the $41,000 BMW 735i for $31,000.

If nothing else, what this story should suggest is what tremendous room for bargaining you have when you purchase an automobile. Realistically, I knew when I walked into the showroom that I could get the car for somewhere between $35,000 and $37,000, because I'd established that BMWs were usually discounted at least $4,000 to $5,000, and that discount was, in fact, offered, after I'd been in the showroom for an hour. By sticking to the rules I've laid out for my viewers, I was able to pick up another $5,000 to $6,000—not a bad payoff for an extra hour's work.

Let's break the car-buying process down into its several components.

BUYING THE CAR: STEP BY STEP

Preparation

Begin your search in the fall, when the new models are announced. Plan to have all your facts assembled by January of the following year. That's when consumers are hurting the most, still recovering from Christmas, and with the prospect of property and income taxes ahead. A prospective buyer in an automobile showroom late in January gets reverential treatment. Never wait until the spring, when the entire country gets into a car-buying mood.

Start by reading all the magazines: *Automobile, Road and Track, Car and Driver, Motor Trends,* and *Consumer Reports.* See what the professionals have to say about each car that has caught your eye. Your priorities should be safety first, durability and resale value second, and style and power trains third.

Reconnaissance

When you go car shopping, leave your checkbook at home. You'll get a better deal by not committing yourself on the first visit.

Never shop alone, if you can possibly avoid it. If your spouse can't accompany you, take along a friend.

Visit at least three dealerships. Take test drives until you get a good feel for the make and model you really want and can afford.

Once you have a good idea of which car you want to buy, procure an up-to-the-minute buying guide from your newsstand or bookstore and check out the retail (sticker) and wholesale (dealer) price of the car, as well as the cost of all available options.

Second Visit

Act totally uninterested and emotionally detached. Put the pressure on the dealer and take it off yourself. If you're interested in car X, pretend to be interested in car Y.

Act confused. Let the dealers think they have you. It puts them off guard—just where you want them.

Fend off their questions. It's none of their business what you do for a living. Nor are you obliged to tell them whether you intend to trade in your old car, or intend to pay cash for the new car, or finance the purchase. You don't even have to tell them whether you intend to buy today, tomorrow, or next year. If they pressure you for answers, tell them you don't want to be pressured and walk out of the showroom.

Say, "No, I don't want to drive the car home tonight. Yes, I'm shopping price and dealers."

Always tell them you can't afford the car you intend to buy, as much as you'd love to own it. NEVER tell them how much you can afford to pay for the car.

Don't make an offer. Force them to make the offer. Even then, don't counter. Just say, "That's ridiculous." If they don't lower their price, leave the showroom. If at any time during the negotiation you feel yourself losing control, leave the showroom.

Don't agree to any deal at this time, no matter how insistent the salesman is that the price he's offering is a "today only special." It's a ploy. You'll be amazed at how much lower an absolutely rock-bottom price can get if you just practice a bit of patience.

Third Visit

By now, you're ready to let the salesperson know that you're a serious buyer and not merely a "buster," as window-shoppers are known in the industry.

Tell the salesperson exactly what model and optional equipment you'd like and ask for his or her best price. If asked about an extended warranty plan, financing, or trade-in, tell the salesperson that you'll discuss these items after you agree on the price for the vehicle. Say you really haven't decided to trade or not at this point and that a relative or friend might buy your old car. Ask the salesperson what would be a fair price to charge for the car. The salesperson will almost certainly give you the retail and wholesale price from his NASD Blue Book—information you'll be able to use to great advantage in bargaining later on. Don't haggle on the price of the new car at this point. Just get the price and leave. Then visit at least two other dealers to compare notes.

In the comfort and safety of your home, compare your quotes with the dealers' wholesale cost. Any dealer is entitled to a fair profit, but their definition of fair may differ from the dictionary's. Figure a few hundred dollars markup as fair.

Have an ideal figure in mind, a price you'd be willing to pay.

Fourth Visit

Head out again, checkbook in hand, but this time instead of going directly to the showroom make a detour to your bank or credit union.

Check out financing rates and terms with your bank before going back to buy. Remember, you're not obligated to take the bank loan, but it will give you the bargaining power of the cash buyer. American automakers offer superfinancing incentives from time to time in order to stimulate sales, so if the dealer's interest rate offer is substantially lower than the bank's or credit union's, by all means take it. But don't commit until after you've agreed to a price.

At the showroom once again, make the salesman an offer for the car. Start with the dealer's cost. After the salesman recovers from the shock, you'll probably be able to agree on a fair price.

Once the price has been negotiated, make certain that it includes every extra. Get a written offer, and then walk out, carrying the offer with you. The deal will still be there tomorrow. There are millions of cars out there. Make sure that you still want this one after a good night's sleep.

Keep this one thought in mind and you'll get a great deal: The salesman has to sell you the car in order to make a living; you don't have to buy it.

TO TRADE OR NOT TO TRADE?

You're always better off selling the car yourself.

My preference, by far, is to sell my old cars privately to relatives or friends—provided, that is, I know the car is in good shape. If that doesn't work, and you have time, place an ad in the newspaper. Always be honest about the car no matter to whom you sell it because even private sales carry an implied warranty.

If you can't find a buyer and you must trade in your old car, negotiate the lowest net price for the new car *before* discussing the trade. Only when you've made a deal on your new car should you ask how much they'll pay you for your old car. Make sure the car is spotless and in good working order when they see it and drive it. If they say they don't want to take your old car, say goodbye and walk out. They'll then make you an offer on your old car. It will be ridiculously low, so laugh and say, "No thanks," and again prepare to walk out. When they finally make you a reasonable offer, compare that price to the NASD Blue Book value. Don't take their word for it. Demand to see the Blue Book. Hold it in your hands. Take your time, making certain that all extras on your car have been added to the trade-in value.

A few years ago, knowing that the trade-in value of most domestic cars drops greatly after 50,000 miles, I would have recommended that you trade your car in when the odometer hits 40,000 to 45,000 miles. Today, my recommendation would be that you maintain your car in top condition, following the manufacturer's service schedule religiously, so that you can run it until it hits at least 80,000 miles, and more if you can. Some conscientious owners, with 200,000 miles on their cars, wouldn't dream of buying a new car until the old one can no longer be repaired in a cost-efficient fashion.

DRIVING IN LUXURY AT TWO-THIRDS THE PRICE

If you want to drive a great car but can't afford to pay the price, you should consider buying a high-quality, high-value used vehicle two years after someone else has taken the big depreciation hit. The value of a car drops by 10 to 15 percent when you drive it out of the showroom; even a one-year old car will be significantly lower in price than a new model. Given the realities of the nineties, luxury on a budget makes eminently good sense.

I once spent an illuminating day with David E. Davis, the editor of *Automobile*, a consumer magazine, doing a story about the extraordinary values available in used luxury cars. We went looking for late model domestic and foreign automobiles that were one to five years old. Most of the cars were low-mileage, one-owner vehicles, and showed that they'd been given loving care. In some cases, the cars were in such good condition that you could scarcely tell they were used; this was particularly true of those foreign cars that don't change styles from year to year. Dream cars tend to be looked after much better than other cars. Many even have a pedigree: a clean, printed maintenance record, exactly what you look for when you're buying a used airplane. Our findings: You could buy BMWs, Cadillacs, Mercedeses,

Jaguars, Lincolns, and Porsches, three to five years old, at up to half their original cost. At a minimum, you could save $10,000 off the vehicle's list price when new, and if you negotiated you could save $20,000. Most of the cars were in mint condition; many—particularly those models that don't change every year—could scarcely be distinguished from new showroom vehicles.

The majority of the cars came with reasonable warranties; Mercedes now offers a two-year factory warranty on selected used car models and also has an excellent in-house financing plan.

In most cases, you can make a better deal for a used car because dealers buy them cheaply and have lots of room to negotiate. In January 1991 I culled several examples from my local newspaper:

• A 1987 420SEL Mercedes "cream puff" listed at $24,995. With a very small investment of time and effort, you could have bought the car for $23,000. To buy the equivalent car new today would cost you $70,000 with the new luxury tax added on. Which car represents the better value, the low-mileage, mint condition Mercedes, one of the finest and safest cars made, or a 1991 Cadillac or Lincoln costing $5,000 to $10,000 more?

• A gorgeous 1984 Jaguar XJS, the sporty version, listed for $8,995. Take 10 percent off the price, and you're driving a car that's indistinguishable to all but the most discerning from a 1991 model.

• A clean 1988 Cadillac Coupe de Ville with low mileage, listed for $12,688. With 1991 versions going for $30,000 plus on the sticker, how can you go wrong?

Here, in sum, are ten reasons to buy used cars, trucks, and vans:

1. You can buy more luxury for the money.

2. You can buy a finer, safer automobile, one that will last longer and, in the event of an accident, keep you lasting longer too.

3. You can reduce your per-mile driving cost.

4. You can avoid the federal luxury tax on new cars costing over $30,000.

5. You can reduce your sales tax on the purchase.

6. You can avoid that major new-car depreciation hit.

7. You can lower your insurance premiums.

8. You may be able to eliminate your collision premiums by self-insuring—assuming the risk of fixing or replacing the car in case it's stolen, destroyed, or damaged. If you can handle the risk personally, it's not a bad idea.

9. You can lower your registration fees as well as your property tax bills in those states where cars are assessed. Rhode Island, for example, taxes the value of cars as personal property every single year, and it does get expensive.

10. You can keep your financing costs down.

If you do decide to buy a used car, make certain you get a look at the vehicle's service history. Avoid any car that appears to have been in an accident. And never pick out a used car at night, in the rain, or both. Used cars look their very best on rainy nights and the wear and tear is nearly impossible to spot.

LOANS FOR LESS

Here's the answer to one of the questions I'm most frequently asked at seminars and on the street: The cheapest way to buy any vehicle is to pay cash for it—unless you can invest the cash you'll be spending on the car to give you a higher rate of return than the cost of the loan. There are very few guaranteed rates of return that will match the interest charge on a car.

The next cheapest way to finance a car is to pay as much down as you can and finance the remainder over the shortest possible period. One year would be best, two years would be excellent, and three years would be adequate. You should do everything you possibly can—not to exceed three years on a loan. Forty-eight- and sixty-month loans carry an awful lot of interest—an expense devoutly to be avoided now that tax reform has phased out deductions for nonbusiness auto interest. Try not to trade your car or sell it until the loan has been paid off. If you try to do it sooner, you might discover that you're upside down on the loan.

Whatever kind of financing you arrange, you should attempt to secure a simple-interest loan. Those horror stories we've all heard about the people who attempt to trade in their one-year-old cars, only to discover that their huge loan has diminished by less than $100, are traceable to loans written under compound-interest rules that pack even more interest on the front end of a loan than a mortgage and scarcely diminish the principal at all. With simple-interest loans, the amount of your payment that goes to interest and the amount that goes to principal are in much more reasonable balance.

Once you've paid off your loan, you should plan on keeping the car for another year or two. During this period without payments, you should set up a separate savings account, and deposit an amount identical to the loan payments each month for the next twelve to twenty-four months. By the time you need a new car, you'll have a substantial portion of the money with which to buy it.

Negotiate the financing yourself. First, try a credit union. Second, try your bank. Ask for their lowest "preferred customer" rate. Sometimes a direct debit against your checking account for the payment will shave a half-point off the rate.

Shop several banks and S&Ls in town. Don't be shy. Ask lots of questions. This is a good time to be building bank contacts, regardless of where you get your loan.

SCALING DOWN INSURANCE COSTS

Insurance rates have gone up about 9 percent a year since 1980, much faster on average than inflation. In major cities like Boston, Detroit, Los Angeles, and Philadelphia, annual tabs can run more than $3,000, and if you happen to be a twenty-five-year-old male driving a high-powered car, the tab can rise to $5,000. These annual increases have sent many of us running to our insurance agent to find sensible ways to trim our bill.

The best way to lower our car insurance premium is to raise our deductible—the amount of money we agree to pay for any loss or damage before the insurance kicks in. Deductibles range anywhere from $50 to $1,000 for both collision and comprehensive coverage. Choose the highest deductible amount you can afford if you were to get into an accident. Raising a zero deductible to $1,000 or higher could reduce your insurance premium by 35 percent.

If your car is more than five years old, you may want to drop collision and comprehensive coverage altogether. By then, most American car values drop to no more than a third of their purchase price. Insurance companies will pay only the value of the car or the cost to repair it, whichever is lower. For example, if the car is worth $1,800 and we have a $500 deductible, the most we can collect is $1,300 even if the repair bill is more than that. A good rule of thumb: If the current collision premium cost exceeds 10 percent of the car's current market value, consider dropping the coverage. You can get the current value of your car from the Blue Book used by every car dealer. Your insurance agent may have such a book as well.

Here's one more argument for getting your car loan paid off as soon as you can. No bank or finance company will permit you to drop collision coverage on a vehicle that's used as collateral on your loan. The vehicle has to be free and clear before you can consider this premium-cutting option.

When you shop for a new car, make sure to find out how much it will cost to insure it. What you discover may change your mind about the kind of car you want to buy.

Insurance companies tailor their rates to makes and models of cars that are most likely to be stolen or cost the most to repair. Sports cars like Chevrolet Camaros, Pontiac Firebirds, and Nissan ZXs are favorites among thieves, so they carry heftier insurance premiums. But inexpensive cars may have high rates as well, because they cost so much to repair if damaged.

Many insurance companies offer discounts for flawless driving records—10 percent or more shaved from the bill. Some companies offer a 10 percent reduction for young drivers who have completed an approved driver's education course. There are discounts for driving cars with automatic seat belts and air bags. Some companies offer cheaper rates to nonsmokers, as well as to doctors, lawyers, and other professionals who as a group tend to have good driving records. And, of course, if you own more than one car, you should be able to obtain a multicar discount by insuring your vehicles with the same company.

One type of insurance never to skimp on: liability coverage—both for property damage and bodily injury. It's mandatory in thirty-nine states and covers the costs of damage we do to others. It also pays for court costs and judgments against us. Carry too little liability and you risk losing your home and wages to settle a claim.

TO LEASE OR NOT TO LEASE?

New-car leasing was born in California more than a decade ago, as a means of getting secretaries and store clerks who couldn't afford them behind the wheels of fancy cars. In these times of banking and credit scrutiny, you'll need a good credit record to qualify for a "cash-saving" lease. Even so, one in fifty leases goes bad.

There are only two good things to be said for leasing. The first is that it enables you to obtain the use of a car when you haven't got much cash. The second is that it gives you the pleasure of driving the automobile of your choice. But it's an expensive pleasure. When you borrow money to buy a car, at least you own the car when the payments are finished. When you lease a car, you normally make payments for several years and wind up with nothing. To be sure, the payments on a lease will cost less each month than payments on a loan, but not so much less that you come out ahead. You don't.

Leasing is a game of numbers and mirrors about which nobody likes to tell the truth. In the old days they used to say, "Lease your car and get a tax write-off." The truth is that there's no special relationship between leasing and tax write-offs. Anybody who uses a car for business can write off the car, within the limits set by the IRS, whether it's leased, financed, or owned outright.

When you pay cash for a car there is no middle man. When you finance the purchase of a car, there is one middle man. When you lease a car, there is typically a second middle man. All middle men must be paid.

Every leasing agreement, moreover, has lease fees and restrictions, designed to protect the leasing company, that raise the amount of your monthly payment. In some cases, you're bound by mileage restrictions, and often you're required to pay higher insurance premiums to cover the leasing company's exposure and to meet its rule.

People who lease cars for five years never stop to think that in the fifth year of the lease they're paying new-car rates to rent a car that's 4.5 years old.

Before you lease, make sure you compare the cost of leasing to the cost of buying the same car with sensible financing. Understand what leases are, how they operate, and don't lease for less than five years.

And don't let yourself be victimized by a popular scam in which the dealer uses the prospect of a no money down lease as bait. It works like this: You fall in love with the car, only to learn 48 hours later that you can't qualify for a lease. At this point the salesman, catching you at your most vulnerable moment, offers to sell you the car on decidedly unfavorable terms. To salve your wounds, you agree to the deal. Don't fall for it!

❖   ❖   ❖

Summing up:

Find the car you'll want to drive for five to seven years, or longer.

Drive a hard bargain, using the suggested steps. If you buy right and keep the vehicle a long time, even your dream car becomes more reasonable.

If at all possible, pay cash.

If you can't pay cash, borrow—but shop for your loan as well.

Don't lease unless you absolutely have to—and absolutely want to.

10

Feeding the College Monster

ALL of us with children and grandchildren know what kind of a world they're entering: one in which they can't prosper without a college education. Twelve million young Americans are currently studying in institutions of higher learning; we enroll twice as many of our students in postsecondary studies as the Soviet Union, ten times as many as France, fifteen times as many as the United Kingdom. A single number explains the keenness of the competition. Today's college graduates can expect to earn $650,000 more during their working lives in today's dollars than nongraduates. That translates to a vastly better quality of life. Who wouldn't want that for one's child?

Parents tell us they worry even more about how they'll pay for their children's college education than they do about paying for their own retirement. And well they should. College costs are soaring, upward of 12 percent a year. To send a child through four years of private college today—tuition, fees, room, board, and books—costs between $60,000 and $80,000. State schools cost between $24,000 and $32,000. Are you ready? If costs of higher education continue to increase at this rate, ten years from now—when the children and grandchildren of many of you will set off for the school of their choice—the average cost of a four year education at a public institution will be $120,000. The cost for four years at a private college will be $250,000. Many experts consider these estimates conservative.

What's pushing the costs up so swiftly? As the overhead at institutions of higher learning continues to climb, enrollment drops, so the cost must be spread among fewer and fewer students.

Who can afford such expenditures for a single child, let alone two children, or three or four? Only the very wealthiest among us. The rest of us are going to need help. Even at today's tuition and cost-of-living levels, eight out of ten college students depend on some sort of financial aid.

There are three basic ways to put a child through college: with savings, with grants and scholarships, and with student loans. Of the three, grants

141

and scholarships are obviously the most desirable; you're spending someone else's money. Next comes savings. Loans are a distant but often unavoidable third. Given the tremendous cost of higher education, the answer for many of us may be a combination of all three—plus help from the child.

Each academic year, $29 billion in grants, scholarships, and student loans become available to students, and in such abundant variety that almost anyone can qualify for something. Of that $29 billion, an estimated $6 billion isn't even applied for. That's enough to give $20,000 in aid to 300,000 students, or $500 to every student enrolled in higher education.

This package of financial aid is divided evenly between grants and scholarships on the one hand, and the kind of aid you have to pay back with interest on the other. There are some 200,000 separate sources of financial aid, coming from Uncle Sam, the states, colleges and universities, business and industry, civic and religious groups, professional organizations, charities, and individuals. Corporations, especially, love to offer scholarship money, and for three reasons: it's usually a tax write-off for them, it's great public relations, and it's a proven recruiting device. If they can get you interested in their company now with a grant or a scholarship, they figure you'll consider working for them in the future.

Whatever the source of the educational assistance, it's not exactly easy money because you have to do a mountain of paperwork before you'll even be considered. But the aggravation and effort is more than worth it if it helps get John or Susan through college.

A little further on, we'll be looking thoroughly into how to apply for scholarships and grants, and where to search for the most advantageous loans. But we begin where preparations for a child's college education should begin: with a savings program initiated by parents long before it's time to apply for outside assistance.

HOW MUCH YOU WILL HAVE TO SAVE PER YEAR, PER MONTH, PER DAY TO PUT YOUR CHILD THROUGH COLLEGE

In January 1991, I lectured to a business group about personal finances, retirement, and college savings. Another well-known speaker on money matters had just told them not to bother saving for their children's college education because getting enough money together had become an insurmountable task. She had recommended that they focus instead on paying down their mortgages. The group wanted to know if I agreed with that advice. "Absolutely not," I said. But to judge by the record, most Americans do.

Parents may say that sending their children to college is their number one concern, even more important for most of them than saving for their retirement, but the shocking reality is that six out of seven parents do not have any savings program for their children's college education.

When I ask young people who stopped after high school why they didn't go on to college, their first response is usually, "I can't afford it." Their second response is, "My parents didn't save any money."

Why not? What's the problem? Often, it *is* lack of money. But far more often, it's lack of knowledge. As we saw in chapter 7, many people don't have a clear idea of why they should save, or how to set up a savings program. That kind of ignorance can be tolerated, perhaps, when it's only the parents who suffer. When children suffer, it's another matter.

If your child or grandchild is dependent on you for his or her college education, here's the bottom line: *You don't have to save the entire amount— but you have to save something.*

I'm not suggesting the impossible, that you alone should amass those incredible sums cited above to send a child or several children to college in the twenty-first century. The reality, in all likelihood, is that you're going to be able to save between a quarter and a half of what's needed. What you must understand, however, is that if you want your child to have a college education, you're going to be required to make a partial but vital contribution. That's why it's so important for you to begin at the earliest moment.

I don't care how much you save at the outset. It can be the pocket change you dump into a jar or a drawer at the end of the day. It can be a single dollar bill, placed in an envelope each morning. The important ingredient at this point isn't the amount, it's the habit.

Here are some recommendations:

For a newborn child: $2 a day, or $14 a week
For a five-year-old child: $10 a day, or $70 a week
For a ten-year-old child: $15 a day, or $105 a week

Once you get the habit, then you can set a goal.

How much you need to save per day, week, month, or year depends, first of all, on how much of the cost you intend to cover through savings. Of one thousand households with children polled by the International Association for Financial Planning, the median expectation was that 27 percent of college bills would be covered by savings. The rest would come from current earnings, financial aid, loans, and the *child's* savings and earnings.

A second major consideration is whether the child will go to a public or a private college or university. Based on recent estimates, for every dollar you need to save for a public school, you'll need $2.12 for a private school—more than double.

If you want your newborn to attend a public college or university, and you propose to pay the cost entirely out of savings, you should put away $185 a month; if you want him or her to attend a private college or university, you should save $390 a month. If your child is already 10 years old and you've yet to save a nickel, you'll need to put away $340 a month for public school and $725 a month for private school.

The absolute deadline for a college savings program should be when your child enters high school. If you've waited that long, it's going to be a struggle, because you'll need to sock away $600 a month to send him or her to a public university and $1,275 a month for a private school.

Let me emphasize that these are the amounts you'd need to save if you were going to pay the entire cost out of savings. As the survey cited above suggests, only one in four sets of parents does that.

There's one other reason why it's imperative for you to save enough to make a significant contribution to your child's college education: to set an example for the child. If you're cavalier about your responsibilities, your child may be as well. Across the country today, hundreds of thousands of young people are struggling under the handicap of bad credit records because they never paid off their student loans. Some defaults were legitimate hardship cases, but in thousands of instances the students didn't make good because it wasn't instilled in them by their parents that they had a moral obligation to pay back their loans with interest.

MAKING THOSE SAVINGS GROW

We've already seen that a dollar a day contributed from your child's birth for twenty years—a total of $7,300—and invested at 8 percent compound interest will grow to $17,361, assuming the interest is tax-deferred. (We'll talk about tax-deferred investments in the next chapter.) Now suppose that instead of one dollar you were to put *two* dollars into an envelope every morning from the day your child is born. At the end of the year, you'd have put $730 into your child's college fund. And suppose further that cash gifts to the child from grandparents or uncles and aunts or even friends are put into the college fund, so that each year the contributions average $1,000. If the money earns 8 percent compounded, at the end of twenty years you'd have $49,500, again assuming that the taxes are deferred. If the money earned 12 percent, you'd have $80,700.

Note that I've used twenty years in my calculation. You should, as well, because you don't need to have all the money ready by your child's freshman year. Young people may start college at eighteen, but they don't finish until they're twenty-one or twenty-two.

Just as your rate of savings is influenced by your child's academic plans, so is the return you try to achieve with his or her college fund. As we've seen, if the child has Harvard or Stanford or some other top private school in mind, the cost will be slightly more than twice what it would be for a good public university, compelling you to be somewhat more aggressive when you invest the funds.

Regardless of what your needs are going to be, when you're starting your savings program, you'll want to pool the money in a bank account until you have $5,000, then start moving some of it into higher yield investments, including stock mutual funds.

Wherever your child is headed, I believe that you should shoot for a minimum 10 percent return on his or her college fund. If you start the fund when your child is born, you can take some chances for the first ten years and try to do better than 10 percent. In the next ten years, however, you should become more conservative, and take fewer chances.

During the first ten years, for example, you could invest a regular monthly amount in several solid growth mutual funds. We'll examine mutual funds fully in chapter 12.

In the second ten-year period, you could buy zero coupon bonds, and place them in an educational trust. Zero coupon bonds are bonds that you can buy at a deep discount and receive the full face value when the bond matures. If you were to buy a $1,000 ten-year bond today, you would pay $400. Ten years from now, when you cash the bond in, you'll receive $1,000.

Tax-free U.S. savings bonds are available for educational purposes. The bonds must be bought in the parents' name only and the funds must be used to pay tuition. Also, there are income limitations for the parents to be eligible for this tax-free status.

Remember that up to $10,000 a year in cash and property can be given to each child without gift tax consequences. Under the Uniform Gift to Minors Act the money can't be touched by the children until they reach twenty-one, but then it's theirs to spend as they wish, so proceed with caution.

A number of states now offer some form of prepaid tuition plan that allows parents to fund tomorrow's education costs with today's dollars. In these programs, you can make either a lump-sum payment or yearly payments to a state-administered trust for a specified time. In return, the state guarantees to provide the student with tuition, room, and board when he or she is ready for college, regardless of how much the costs may have risen.

Prepaid tuition programs are excellent protection against inflation, but they do have some drawbacks. First, the youngster has to meet all the ordinary qualifications for admission; there is no preferential treatment for those enrolled in the advance payment program. If the youngster doesn't qualify, or chooses not to attend college, you get back what you've contributed plus only a nominal rate of interest. Second, your child is limited to schools that are part of the state's university program. Third, if you move out of state, there is currently no way to take your prepaid tuition with you; for your child to benefit, he or she will have to enroll in a school in the state in which you lived.

Recently a few insurance companies have started similar prepaid tuition plans, using an annuity as the funding vehicle. These plans are bound to become more popular, since they have the portability feature not found in state programs, but they will also cost more to cover commissions paid to the agent or broker selling the plan. Although the returns are higher with private plans, there may be tax consequences. Check with your CPA or financial adviser before entering any type of prepaid program.

For all the caveats, a prepaid tuition plan can be an excellent, cost-effective method of providing for a child's college education. Your child's high-school guidance counselor or the financial aid officer at the college your child plans to attend will be able to give you the details.

Whatever method you choose, and however slim your resources, the imperative is to start. If you've done no preplanning, hindsight won't help you pay those college bills when they come due next fall.

That preplanning, incidentally, should include a consultation with a CPA or tax adviser about ways to minimize or eliminate taxes on the college fund. Only the first $500 of your child's income is tax-free each year. A tax return must be filed for anything beyond this amount. The next $500 is taxed at the child's rate, typically 15 percent; anything beyond that is taxed at the parents' top marginal rate, which is normally much higher. If you don't pay attention to taxes through the child's first thirteen years, you'll slow the growth of his or her college fund. Once the child turns fourteen, he or she is entitled to a separate tax status, which should lower the tax bite considerably. At this point, the money can be put into the child's account or a special trust set up for his or her education.

SCHOLARSHIPS AND GRANTS: SOMETHING FOR EVERYONE

Most people believe that you have to have high grades to qualify for a scholarship. Not true. Today, only 3 percent of scholarships are based solely on grades.

Most people believe that you must be needy to qualify. Again, not true. Your parents could be millionaires, and you could still apply for and receive a scholarship.

Most people believe that you have to be a teenager to get a scholarship for college. Once again, not true. You can apply for a scholarship at any time, even well into your college career. If you're a junior in college, you can apply for a scholarship for your senior year. And you can apply for a graduate studies scholarship at any time, either during your undergraduate days or after you've received your bachelor's degree. Few scholarships place restrictions on age, and there are even cases of senior citizens winning scholarships to complete higher studies.

Time is of the essence in applying for a scholarship. As the early bird gets the worm, so the early applicant gets the endowment. There are thousands and thousands of scholarships out there, every one of them with a deadline for applications. If you wait, you may miss the deadline for the very scholarship you could win. In some cases, you might be the only application with the right qualifications. I'll say it again: Every year, $6 billion in scholarship money goes unclaimed.

Today, there are more special-interest scholarships than ever before.

• If you're interested in international study, opportunities abound. For example, if you are a writer between the ages of twenty-two and thirty-five, dedicated to pursuing a literary career, and have never been a Communist, you could apply for the University of Vienna's Woursell Creative Writing Grant.

• If your grandparents were American Indians, you qualify for special grants.

• If you're in the top 25 percent of your class, and have caddied at a golf course for the last two years, the Western Golf Association offers full tuition for all areas of study. Write to

Western Golf Association
1 Briar Road
Golf, IL 60029
(312) 724-4600

• If you excel in comedy or pantomime or both, the Laurel and Hardy Scholarship Fund may offer you $1,500, on the condition that you attend college in San Diego County, California.

• If you're a C student and want to attend Ball State, David Letterman may assist you.

• If you're an outstanding student cartoonist at a college newspaper or magazine, you may qualify for a $2,000 Charles M. Schulz award offered by the Scripps Howard Foundation.

These and thousands of other scholarships and grants are listed in The Scholarship Book, by Dan Cassidy (Prentice Hall, 1990). The book can be found in libraries, or is available at bookstores. Cassidy also compiled The Graduate Scholarship Book, and the International Scholarship Book. Listed scholarships range from $100 to $60,000 and average $5,000 for undergraduates and $10,000 for graduate students. If you would like to tap into this comprehensive scholarship, grant, and loan database, call the

National Scholarship Research Service
A Division of Cassidy Research Corporation
Santa Rosa, CA 95403
(707) 546-6777

Another source of scholarship information is

College Planning Associates
200 South Hadley Road
Suite 1102
Clayton, MO 63105
(314) 889-0585

CPA has a monthly newletter, *UPDATE*, which lists all new scholarships and grants as they become available.

During your junior and senior years in high school your mailbox will begin to overflow with college brochures and solicitations for scholarship research services. These are companies that profess to put you in touch with scholarship money tailored to your personal and academic profile. Of course this service isn't free—it ranges from $25 to $65. Usually you'll be asked to fill out a complete personal inventory, then you'll receive a computer print-out listing possible sources of financial aid. Many of these services are reputable, but be skeptical. Ask questions, get a guarantee they will find you several unusual sources of aid and check with your local Better Business Bureau.

Remember, the money is out there. It has to be claimed. A search of old newspaper articles about recipients of unusual scholarships might lead you to an award you can win because you uncovered it and no one else applied.

HOW TO APPLY FOR A SCHOLARSHIP

I'm not going to kid you. Applying for a college scholarship is an arduous business, involving a great deal of research and an incredible amount of paperwork. But the success rate is very high. Your chances of winning the scholarship you apply for are about one in four. If you apply for a number of scholarships, the chances are excellent that you'll win one or more.

You should begin to apply for a scholarship in your junior year in high school. You might even start to familiarize yourself with the opportunities as early as your sophomore year. The majority of high-school students wait until their senior year to start looking for scholarships. If you get a head start on them, you're that much better off. As Dan Cassidy says, "Every single day you procrastinate on filing an application is another day of deadlines passed and opportunities lost."

In setting up your scholarship campaign, it's extremely helpful if you can ask yourself, and answer, these two questions:

• Based on my current interests, what career do I want to choose?
• What colleges would I like to attend?

Write to every college on your list and ask for their financial aid application and list of scholarships. Then write to the society or organization that covers the profession you're thinking about pursing. For example, the public relations field is covered by the Public Relations Society of America, the physical education field is overseen by the National Industrial Recreation Association, and the computer programming field is covered by the American Federation of Information Processing Societies, Inc. You could even go one step further and write to particular companies to see if they sponsor a scholarship.

Applying for financial assistance entails filling out a lot of forms, but unless they're properly completed your petition won't get a hearing. Athletes excepted, no one has ever received a dime in scholarship money who hasn't made his or her case on paper.

The time to start is now, before you even have an acceptance letter. First, get a copy of the official student financial aid form, or FAF. It's available at high-school guidance offices starting in December of every academic year. Or forms can be obtained from

College Scholarship Service
P.O. Box 6300
Princeton NJ 08541
(800) 772-3537

You can mail applications starting January 1. Here again, promptness pays; some institutions use a first-come, first-served basis for doling out their financial aid.

Parents will have to fill out the form, because it asks all sorts of questions about income, assets, loans, credit card debt, and so forth. And you have to answer all the questions, because incomplete forms don't get processed and this document is the passport to financial aid.

When the form is completed, return it along with the required fee. (Fees are based on the number of schools you've selected to receive the financial information.) Then and only then will you be able to work with the financial-aid officer at the school to which your child has applied. Many federal, state, and private grant and loan programs will require additional paperwork, but once the FAF is behind you the hardest part is over.

Both the high-school guidance officer and the financial-aid officer at the college of your child's choice will be able to help you if you get stuck with the forms. And if you get discouraged, remember that three out of four entering college freshmen receive some form of financial assistance.

Some of that money is in the form of federal grants. Assistance under the Pell Grant program is based on outright need and tends to go to families with incomes below $32,500 a year. Grants range from $200 to $2,300. Even if you don't think you qualify, it's a good idea to apply anyway. It's a necessary step in getting other financial aid. It's also a prerequisite for qualifying for a guaranteed student loan.

FINDING THE BEST POSSIBLE LOAN

As good as your child's chances are of finding some sort of scholarship, assuming he or she searches diligently and applies early enough, scholarship plus savings may still not be enough to cover the cost of a college education. At that point, the only solution is to borrow. You have a number of options.

Although the federal government has cut back student loans in recent years, Uncle Sam is still the biggest benefactor, with $13.2 billion in subsidized loans and $6.5 billion in grants in the 1990–91 school year. Under the Stafford Loan Program, formerly known as the Guaranteed Student Loan Program, freshmen and sophomores who demonstrate financial need can currently borrow up to $2,625 a year, juniors and seniors up to $4,000 a year. You won't have to begin to repay the money until six months after graduation or departure from school, and you have five to ten years to pay it off. The interest rate is 8 percent for the first four years and 10 percent thereafter, low compared to 11 percent and up for standard bank loans. Unfortunately only 35 percent of private college students and 14 percent of students attending public schools qualify for these advantageous rates.

In the category of federal assistance, we can't overlook ROTC programs, which pick up most of the tab for students willing to commit to up to eight years of service in the armed forces, either on active duty or in the reserve, following college. These programs, available at some 530 colleges and universities, are open to young men and women.

If you earn too much money to qualify for financial aid, but aren't rich enough to pay college bills out of savings or current earnings, you have a variety of options.

The first of these options is to borrow money from the college or university your child has chosen to attend. An estimated 80 percent of the nation's 3600 colleges and universities and 9000 vocational-technical schools have some sort of loan program. Many such programs are established through a local bank, so you'll need good credit to qualify. The best source of information on such loans is the financial-aid office at the school.

If you don't qualify for federal assistance, and no funds are available from your child's chosen school, the next place to look is to your own assets.

All permanent life insurance policies have cash value in them, which can be borrowed without question or fuss. The best part of this loan is that it never has to be repaid; just pay the interest, and the loan principal will remain on the books as an offset to the surrender value.

If you have securities, you can use them as collateral to borrow money from the brokerage handling your account, or from most banks. Broker loans against your securities carry somewhat lower interest rates than other forms of personal notes, but here again there are no tax deductions.

As a last resort, you can consider a home equity loan. As previously stated, I'm not in love with home equity loans because I don't like to see your basic savings compromised. But a home equity loan for tuition payments can be obtained quickly, and the interest can be deducted from your income tax because technically it's a real estate loan.

If you have neither securities nor insurance policies, can't or won't take out a home equity loan, don't qualify for financial assistance, and can't cover the costs of college with savings and scholarships, there is still one avenue open. It's a relatively new form of borrowing for education called the "private supplemental loan," and it's made possible by six institutions, most of them not-for-profit, all with a large base of capital. Essentially, these private organizations provide the collateral needed to qualify for the loan. A bank, savings and loan, or other lending institution actually loans the money. Private supplemental loans allow students and their parents, or both, to borrow up to $20,000 a year and repay the money over a ten- to twenty-year period with the option of making interest-only payments while still in school.

Advantages: The loans are very flexible and anyone in need of financial aid can apply. Unlike federal and state loans, private supplemental loans are based on your ability to pay back the loan, not on income. These loans work best for middle- and upper-income families with good credit, who often get shut out of federal and state programs.

Disadvantages: Private supplemental loans charge from 11 to 13 percent interest, compared to 8 percent on government loans. You'll also be charged up-front fees, from 1 to 4 percent of the loan amount. This goes to the company guaranteeing your loan. The bigger the loan, the higher the interest and fees.

Whatever its drawbacks, the private supplemental loan has become increasingly popular in recent years as the cost of higher education mounts and the federal government tightens its restrictions. The Education Resources Institute (TERI), one of the seven groups nationwide currently guaranteeing private student loans, reports that its loan volume has more than doubled in the past year.

I recommend private supplemental loans only after you have exhausted all other sources of financial aid.

Here is a list of the leading loan institutions:

Sponsor	Name of Loan	Phone
U.S. Department of Education	Plus	(800) 562-6872
Student Loan Marketing Association	Family Ed	(800) 831-5626
ConSern Loans for Education	ConSern	(800) 767-5626
The Education Resources Institute	TERI	(800) 255-8374
The New England Education Loan Marketing Corp.	Excel and Share	(800) 634-9308
Knight Tuition Payment Plans	Knight Extended Repayment Plans and ABLE	(800) 225-6783

For more information on student loans consult:

The National Education Lending Center
824 Market Street
Wilmington, DE 19801

This agency supplies publications listing private and government lending sources.

I highly recommend, as well, *The Student Guide*, a free booklet put out by the U.S. Department of Education. You can obtain this booklet by writing

Federal Student Aid Program
P.O. Box 84
Washington, DC 20044

Or call the Federal Student Aid Information Center, (800) 333-INFO. The center is open from 9 A.M. to 5:30 P.M. EST Monday through Friday.

The projected future cost of college for today's newborn babies only *seems* insurmountable. Remember: You'll need to finance only a third of it from savings and investments earmarked for this purpose. Start saving as soon as possible, diversify your investments, and assemble as much information as you can about scholarships, grants, and loans. No gift you could ever give your child could be more valuable than a college education.

11

Pyramid Investing: The Magic Number Is 12

PYRAMID investing, like the structure for which it's named, rests on a wide and solid base and tapers gradually to a point. At the base are a multitude of low-risk investments. The higher up on the pyramid, the greater the risk of the investment, but the smaller its size. The investments of greatest risk at the very peak are but a fraction of the whole.

Stop building a pyramid after completing the base, and you haven't got a pyramid. Place all your money in low- or nonrisk investments and you haven't got an investment program. Like the pyramid, the program must build layer upon layer, each higher layer smaller than the one on which it rests.

While the pyramid is, or should be, the model for every investment program, exactly what goes into each layer, and in what amount, will vary with each individual. The pyramid you build should not be identical to the one I build because our circumstances are different. Pyramids change, based on your age, your personality, how much risk you can stand, how much money you have, how big your commitments are, what plans you have, and the state of the economy. When we talk to financial advisers we always ask them how much money they have in the stock market. And they always give an answer: 20 percent, 50 percent, 75 percent. But the answer is that day's answer. It could be different a week later or even a day later.

THE FIVE LAYERS OF AN INVESTMENT PYRAMID

With the above-mentioned qualifications in mind, let's construct a basic investment pyramid layer by layer, from the bottom up.

First Layer

All federally insured bank accounts, including certificates of deposit (CDs), checking, savings, and money market accounts; all U.S. Treasury investments: T-bills, T-notes, T-bonds; Series Double E savings bonds; taxable and tax-free money market mutual funds; and tax-sheltered annuities.

One or more of these items should be the foundation of every pyramid, no matter how large it is. Whichever one you choose, you should be certain that you're getting the highest possible interest rate because over time even a quarter of a point on a sizable quantity of money can make a considerable difference.

Remembering, once again, that the answer will be different for everyone, these investment items should constitute between 25 and 75 percent of your investment pyramid. The 25 percent would be for a young person just starting a career, with few cash reserves. The richer you are and the older you are, the more of your money you're going to want to put into the bottom of the pyramid. At the same time, however, you must recognize that investing too safely, as we've seen, exposes you to a risk of a special kind: falling behind inflation. Let's say that during 1990 you kept all your savings, amounting to $10,000, in bank CDs averaging 7.5 percent, and that you had a high enough income so that your top federal income tax rate was 28 percent. The $750 you earn in interest gets hit, first of all, with $210 in federal tax, giving you an after-tax return of $540—even lower if you pay a state income tax as well. For this exercise, we'll assume that you've now got $10,540 in the bank. But in 1990 the official inflation rate was 6.1 percent. To find out what the spending power of your $10,540 is, you multiply the $10,540 by .061, then subtract the result, $641, from $10,540. The bottom line: you've got $9,897 in total spending power. Taxes and inflation have made you slightly less well off than you were a year ago, even though you invested your savings at 7.5 percent. Your real rate of return was minus 1 percent.

Early in 1991 I was on a live talk show in Pittsburgh with two other money experts. One young member of the audience asked us what we thought of bank CDs as investments. We replied, almost in unison, "They're not investments." Technically, of course, they are, but practically, the best they can do is keep you from losing ground. For this reason, you should think of the first layer of your investment pyramid as a safe place to "park" your cash while you're trying to find something better to do with it.

Second Layer

Bonds and bond income mutual funds.

When corporations want to raise money but don't want to dilute their ownership, they sell bonds, which they agree to redeem in a specific number of years. Corporate bonds range from the supersafe, conservative, low-rate bonds of the strongest companies, paying in the range of 7 to 10 percent, to the now infamous junk bonds, which pay 12 percent or more and carry considerable risk. Obviously the less well established a company is, the higher rate it has to pay to attract investors. Junk bonds don't belong this low on the pyramid. We'll deal with them later; here we'll confine ourselves to the more conservative bonds.

Corporate bonds carry a slightly higher rate than banks pay, but carry more risk than bank accounts. The bonds will always pay interest, but their value will rise or fall, depending on the market. And the market, in turn, depends on what happens to interest rates. As interest rates drop, bond prices go up. As interest rates climb, bond prices go down. Suppose you and I invest $10,000 in 9 percent corporate bonds, and shortly thereafter interest rates rise substantially. Soon, 11 percent bonds are on the market, and then 12 percent bonds. With these opportunities available what investor would want to buy our 9 percent bonds? As with any commodity, when demand drops, prices fall. Conversely, if interest rates go down, the value of our higher-paying bonds will go up. Bonds are constantly seeking their own natural and stable level. Those paying above-market rates sell at a premium and those paying below-market rates sell at a discount, and these prices are quoted daily. A change in a bond's rating for better or worse will affect its price as well.

The most important lesson to learn about bonds and bond funds is that *yield*—the number you always see in the advertisements—isn't what you make; it's just the quoted number that the fund is paying in interest. The only number you care about is your *total return*, which is the yield, plus or minus the value of the investment at the time you want to sell it. If the value is more than you paid, you win. If it's less, you lose.

Most people tend to think of the bond market as very stable. The truth is that the swings in the bond market can be so frequent and severe that bonds should be bought only as long-term investments. Look at bond prices in the eighties. In 1980, with interest rates rising, bond prices were in a freefall. That year, total returns for investment-grade corporate bonds was 0.9 percent—terrible. The next year, 1981, wasn't much better: a 2.9 percent return. But in 1982 the return on bonds was 36.6 percent. The years 1984, 1985, and 1986 were also bonanza years, with total returns of 16, 25.3, and 16.9 percent, respectively. All in all, the eighties gave corporate bondholders a total return of 12.4 percent. (Junk bonds, incidentally, averaged only a slightly higher total return, 13.1 percent, during the eighties—and then came the crash. So taking on all that extra risk just wasn't worth it.)

Unless you have millions of dollars, the best way to get the proper amount of diversification is to invest in a corporate bond mutual fund. In this manner, you'll be investing in dozens of investment-grade corporate bonds at once, and won't be badly hurt if two or three lose some or all of their value. Corporate bond mutual funds also go by the name of income mutual funds; many are no-load or low-load.

If you're one of those people who feels strongly and emotionally about not paying income taxes on your investments, and you're already in the highest tax bracket, you should consider tax-free municipal bonds, many of which earn the equivalent of 9 or 10 percent taxable interest.

Bonds and income mutual funds should comprise 20 to 40 percent of your investment pyramid—20 percent if your cash reserves are limited, 40 percent if they're more substantial.

Third Layer

Common and preferred stocks, and stock mutual funds, also known as equity mutual funds.

Over the years, I've met a number of individuals in nonfinancial professions who had demonstrated a real aptitude—a gift, even—for investing in securities. A few years ago, we produced a TV feature about a fireman, Glenn Gilley, whose hobby was researching and investing in stocks. Glenn absolutely delighted in recalling how he had started when he was in the fifth grade and how he read the *Wall Street Journal* every day. He also delighted in watching his picks climb in value every day. Chuck Allmon, one of the top stock market advisers and money managers in the world today spent 30 years as a photographer with the *National Geographic* before turning full time to the stock market. It was while he was roaming the world that he honed his investing skills.

If you are similarly inclined, and have shown your skill at picking equity investments, by all means continue. I also recommend that you use "dollar cost averaging" when purchasing the stocks and funds you select. Suppose you want to invest $1,000 in a certain stock, but don't have enough to put the whole amount in today. Instead, you determine to invest $200 every other month until your total investment is $1,000. By purchasing with a fixed amount of money each time, you'll buy fewer shares when prices are high and more shares when prices are low. Let's review an example:

Price/Share	Number of Shares	Total Price
$10.00	20.00	$200.00
$13.75	14.55	$200.00
$12.50	16.00	$200.00
$13.50	14.82	$200.00
$15.00	13.33	$200.00

The average price per share on the five purchase dates was $12.95. If you were to divide $1,000 by $12.95, you'd get 77.22 shares plus a small fraction. Using dollar cost averaging, however, you've bought 78.70 shares—ending up with 1.5 shares free. Looked at another way, you paid $12.71 rather than $12.95 average over the period. Over many years and price swings, the tiny difference here can amount to a considerable sum of money.

It may be, however, that the time and effort you have to put into doing the research and making your own stock purchases would be better spent in another cause. If that's the case, you should consider investing in mutual funds.

Over the last decade stock mutual funds, in particular, have proven that you can double your money every four or five years before taxes. Remember, a doubling in five years is roughly a 15 percent return per year. There are all sorts of mutual funds with varying objectives and degrees of risk; as we'll see in chapter 12, there is no need to agonize over which ones to choose when we can readily identify those with the best records. Past success is no guarantee of future success, but it does indicate competence.

What portion of the pyramid should the third layer be? If you're young, aggressive, and willing to pay attention, and even learn to pick some winners yourself, you can make this layer a big part of the whole, as much as 80 percent. If you're at or close to retirement, and you have no stomach for risk, the layer should be a skinny one, no more than 20 percent of the whole.

Fourth Layer

Higher-risk common stocks and mutual funds, and higher-yield corporate bonds.

In the old days, many traditional investors wouldn't buy a stock that was selling for more than seven times earnings. (If a stock selling at $10 a share earns $1 a share during a fiscal year, the stock is said to be selling at ten times earnings.) Today, it's increasingly difficult to find a good investment selling at that low a multiple; on the New York Stock Exchange, stocks sell at an average of twelve times earnings; the stocks that make up the Standard and Poor's 500 index sold recently at fifteen times earnings. Similarly, traditional investors looked for stocks selling at or below their book value. (The book value is the theoretical worth per share of a company's stock if it were to liquidate its assets and distribute the proceeds to the shareholders.) Time has eroded this standard as well, even though 28 percent of all NYSE stocks and 45 percent of American Stock Exchange stocks trade at prices below their company's book value. Remember this: A company and its stock have separate lives. Supply and demand drive the price of the stock; just because a company trades below book value doesn't mean its stock price will go up.

Higher-risk securities in today's markets are those selling at eighteen times earnings or more, and way above book value. These securities are generally listed on the American and NASDAQ, or over-the-counter, exchanges. Once again, if you're adept at picking equities, well and good; if you're not, let someone who is good at this do the picking for you. One way to do this is to invest in growth stock mutual funds, which feature a higher degree of risk than those you'd put in the third layer of your investment pyramid. These funds tend to be more volatile as well, featuring higher highs and lower lows. These options, too, will be explored in chapter 12.

High-yielding corporate bonds would be those offering a 9 to 11 percent return. Although this is a high yield for bonds, it's still well below the junk bond yield, and these are definitely not junk bonds.

The fourth layer of your pyramid should contain 5 to 15 percent of your invested savings.

Fifth Layer

Riskier over-the-counter (OTC) stocks, stocks selling for less than $5 a share, junk bonds and junk bond mutual funds, gold, other precious metals, and collectibles.

At the peak of the pyramid, we're taking significant risks in exchange for the possibility of substantial rewards, but we're doing so with small amounts of money relative to our overall investment. Stocks selling for less than $5 a share, which are usually referred to as "penny stocks," are a popular form of high-risk investment. Generally, you lose more often than you win on these investments, but when you win you usually win big, and one big win will usually make up for four or five losses. Some people do make incredible sums of money investing in penny stocks, but they work very hard at it, and know what they're getting into. You can't invest in penny stocks unless you're willing to spend time researching each investment.

Many Fortune 1,000 company stocks were first offered as penny stocks. There's nothing wrong with investing in penny stocks as long as the securities are legitimate, diversified, and carefully selected. But be warned that this area of the securities market attracts an undue proportion of con artists who solicit investments over the phone, promising that you'll double your money in a year or two by putting it into far-out investments. If these investments were such a sure thing, the people selling them would hold onto them. I am constantly astounded by the number of otherwise conservative investors whose greed conquers their fear and who wind up getting fleeced by these schemers. To help keep yourself from getting taken, stick to those lower-priced stocks quoted on the NASDAQ system. They've had to meet strict requirements to get into the "club."

Into this layer of the pyramid, you can place stocks you buy on the tip of someone knowledgeable, or those you buy out of your own knowledge or conviction. Most of us have special knowledge of the industry in which we work. That knowledge can often be the spur to an excellent investment. About half the time special knowledge comes from the company where you work. You know when sales are strong, or when an exciting new product is about to be introduced. Sometimes knowledge comes from personal experience. You encounter a product you like, or are impressed with a new restaurant franchise—think of how rich you'd be if you'd bought shares years ago in Polaroid or McDonald's—or notice an unusual number of cars on the road made by a certain manufacturer. The stock of Subaru's American company has split so many times since the car was first introduced into the United States that it's difficult to calculate just how much it's worth today.

As for junk bonds—or high-income bonds, as the brokers who talked so many retired people into buying them called them—the one good thing to be said for them was that they provided the investment lesson of the eighties. The lesson of that deplorable fiasco was that they may well return 14 percent interest, as promised, but they may also lose their value. Bond funds, especially, rise and fall with the economy and the fortunes of the companies whose bonds they've bought. No one selling junk bonds explained this lesson to the customers; no one told them that a bond mutual fund was not like a bank account, that when they sent in their $100,000 there was no guarantee that their investment would always be worth at least $100,000. Today millions of Americans are still getting 14 percent on their original investment, but they're sitting with junk bonds worth 60 to 70 percent of what they paid for them. They're in a quandary. Sell the bonds, and they take a real loss. Moreover, their income drops. If they invested $100,000 in junk bonds returning 14 percent, they're getting $14,000 in interest income. If they sell the bonds for $60,000 and reinvest the proceeds, they'll be lucky to get 8 percent—or $4,800. On the surface, it would seem that they're better off to hold the bonds. But what if the bonds lose even more value, or become worthless? For those in this predicament, there is no simple or general answer; it should be decided case by case.

For those not in this predicament, ironically, junk bonds today might deserve a careful look. The price of many of the bonds has sunk so low that they might represent extraordinary bargains. Suppose you bought a 14 percent bond for seventy cents on the dollar. Based on your purchase price, the eventual yield could be staggeringly high. Caution: Even discounted junk bonds, no matter how high their return, are good investments only if the prospects of the company that issued the bonds are sound. If the company goes belly-up, you've made a terrible investment.

At the lofty tip of the pyramid are gold, rare coins, and other collectibles.

Investment-grade rare coins, in particular, have been the number one investment over the past twenty years, but that's no guarantee what they'll do in the next twenty. The rare coin portfolios that appreciated the most were, for the most part, selected by experts, not by casual collectors. If you want to try your luck, there are three principles to remember: First, the rarest coins tend to appreciate the fastest, so I'd buy one very rare coin for, say, $850 in preference to ten coins at an average price of $85. Second, rare coins are typically bought at retail and sold at dealer wholesale (unless you can find another collector who really wants a coin), so there's a price spread to consider. Third, if you expect to experience serious appreciation, on the order of 12 to 20 percent a year, you should expect to hold on to a coin for five to twenty years.

Many people feel strongly about owning at least a small amount of gold. If you want to buy a few American Eagle Gold Bullion coins every year and stash them in your safe deposit box, you're probably not going to hurt yourself. But I wouldn't put my life savings, or anything close to it, in gold. True, it has been an inflation fighter for 5,000 years—but not, unfortunately, for the past ten years, as the supply of gold has grown, thanks to new high tech mining techniques, and the demand has weakened. Will gold regain its luster? Only time will tell. In the interim, it won't pay interest or dividends.

As to silver, I'd avoid it like the plague. I don't believe there's any serious chance that it will appreciate greatly in price.

Whatever investment or investments you place into this fifth layer, their cost should not exceed 5 percent of your overall commitment.

Now the investment pyramid's built. What do we expect from it? At the outset, I cautioned that each pyramid will differ, depending on the circumstances of the individual. There is one exception: Every investment pyramid should be constructed to reap an average 12 percent annual return over time.

WHY 12 IS THE MAGIC NUMBER

Let's suppose that like most people you pay a combined federal and state income tax of about 25 percent on gross income. If you're earning 7.5 percent interest at the bank, and you deduct 20 percent for taxes, you're earning 6 percent—the same percentage by which inflation diminished the value of money in 1990. The most you've accomplished with a 6 percent return after taxes is to stay even with or just ahead of inflation—*provided you don't touch the earnings.* Use the money, and you fall behind. If you don't use the money, you don't fall behind, but you're not gaining any ground. Your life isn't going to improve because your money isn't growing, as much as you may delude yourself into thinking that it is.

Let's suppose further that, while the inflation rate nationally were to remain at the 6 percent figure it reached in 1990, your inflation rate will rise to more like 8 percent, reflecting the fact that you're financing a house and a car at higher rates and spending money on goods and services such as college tuition and medical bills whose costs are increasing much faster than 6 percent a year. Now, instead of staying even with inflation with your 7.5 percent return, you're actually losing money—or, more accurately, spending power.

Earn 12 percent on your money, and it's a different picture altogether. Subtracting 6 percent inflation from a 12 percent return still gives you a real return of 6 percent before taxes—a very positive number. And if you can manage to defer the taxes on the earnings, you would double your spending power in twelve years even after inflation.

Good financial planners zoom in on two factors right away: your life expectancy and your future spending power. If you're fifty years old today, there's every likelihood that you'll be alive twenty-five years from now. If you're comfortable living on $50,000 a year today, you're going to need roughly four times that much in twenty-five years, or $200,000, in order to maintain the same standard of living. (If you still find this too hard to believe, just remember that Chevrolet I bought twenty-five years ago for $2,850 that would cost me more than $12,000 today. Should there be another such increase in prices over the next twenty-five years, an equivalent automobile could cost $48,000.) That $200,000 will probably consist of three elements: Social Security benefits, pension benefits, and income from investments.

Now let's make some assumptions: that both Social Security and pension benefits will increase along with inflation; that together they will account for $80,000 a year in income; and that the remainder, $120,000, will have to come from investment income. To get that kind of income, even at 10 percent, you'll need $1.2 million in capital, without considering taxes.

A final assumption: that you have $125,000 to invest today.

The rule of 72 tells us that if you invest the money at 8 percent, tax-deferred, your money will double every nine years. After nine years, you'll have $250,000, after eighteen years, you'll have $500,000, after 27 years, you'll have $1 million. Not quite enough.

If, however, you invest the $125,000 so as to get a 12 percent return, tax-deferred, your money will double every six years. You'll have $250,000 after six years, $500,000 after 12 years, $1 million after eighteen years, and $2 million after 24 years. More than enough!

Twelve percent is a very achievable return, well positioned between safety and risk. In designing your investment pyramid, you should do so with the objective of an *overall* 12 percent yield. Some investments will make less than 12 percent. Others will make more.

I'm not suggesting that you should make 12 percent each and every year.

During any given year, or even a two- or three-year period, you may not earn 12 percent. But as you approach the five-year mark, if you're not earning 12 percent overall, you're doing something wrong. In all likelihood, you're not investing a sufficient share of your savings in American and worldwide business and the profits and growth they produce. Said another way, you're *loaning* your money (receiving interest) instead of *owning* your money (receiving a piece of the action). Someone else is reaping the reward when you loan your money—it's clearly not you. I repeat: You can't make 12 percent, on average, over five, ten, and twenty years if you shy away from common stocks, corporate bonds, and the mutual funds that invest in them.

One problem—a chronic one among small investors—may be timing: You make an investment at the top of the market that almost immediately loses value. At this point, most small investors have a tendency to panic, dump their investment program, and take a "true" loss as against a paper loss. They've been hit by the double whammy: buy high, sell low.

A second mistake is to make a poor investment and then hold on to it because you don't want to acknowledge the poor choice, even to yourself. You may even put more money into the investment as its value drops. That's a good idea when you have hard knowledge that the investment will turn around; it's a bad idea when you're trying to kid yourself.

A third problem associated with investment programs that fail to yield 12 percent is that of undue timidity. It may be the biggest problem of all. There is a very large group of investors, particularly among the elderly, I call the "Frightened Hoarders." They have plenty of money, but for the most part they keep it in passbook accounts, where it loses real value every year. They don't understand that a deposit in a bank is not an investment but a loan to the bank—which the bank lends to someone else for twice the interest it's paying.

Until the rash of bank failures in recent years, millions of Americans believed that the safest thing they could do with their money was to put it in the bank. I'm not antibank by any means; as I've emphasized over and over again, three to six months worth of money should be in a bank, where you can get at it quickly in case of emergency. But anything more than that does not belong in the bank. As demonstrated earlier when we built the first layer of your investment pyramid, by not taking risks with your money, you're safe in the short term, but you've bought into a second kind of risk, that of losing out to inflation.

Some people with 10 million dollars want all that money to be in the bank; they'll accept the lower yield, even knowing they're losing ground to inflation, in exchange for the ability to sleep soundly at night. Men and women in their sixties and seventies call me all the time to ask me if they've done the right thing by putting all their money in the bank at 7 percent. I'll ask them how much money we're talking about, and they'll give me a very respectable figure. Then I'll ask them how their health is, and they'll say it's never been better. Finally, I'll ask how long their parents lived, and they'll say that their father lived into his eighties and their mother is still alive. So I'll say, "Why have you closed down shop and become so conservative that you're acting like a person who is broke and a day away from death's door?"

When you are seventy years old and have amassed a sizable fortune, you should be adding at least a small increment of risk to at least 25 percent of your investments. If you don't, the spending power of your fortune in real dollars could be halved in a period of ten to twelve years, and halved again in another ten to twelve years. In twenty to twenty-five years time, your net worth is a quarter of what it was in terms of what it can buy.

Given the prospects of longer life and less generous pensions, that's just not going to work. In order to maintain your living standard, and perhaps even survive, you're going to have to take some risks. In this regard, investment counselors like to talk about the "cow and bucket of milk" theory. Save your money until you've got enough to buy a cow. Sell the buckets of milk the cow produces, and use the money in venturesome ways. But never risk the cow. Translation: Don't risk the basic capital on which your security is built. Do risk whatever income that capital produces.

Suppose you have $50,000 in the bank—your stash against emergencies. The money's earning 8 percent, or $4,000, in some kind of CD. Leave the stash where it is. But put the $4,000 into more challenging investments, and when next year's interest rolls around, invest it in the same way.

What sort of challenging investments? My choice, by far, is equities.

THE CASE FOR EQUITY INVESTMENTS

It's a given in our society that the stock market is no place for the small investor. In that spirit, Woody Allen once defined a stockbroker as someone who keeps investing your money until it's all gone. It's a memorable one-liner, and it gets a lot of laughs, but it happens to perpetuate one of the costliest and most erroneous myths ever disseminated. The truth is that anyone who had maintained a soundly administered equity investment program since the end of World War II would have made a fortune.

In that interval, a period of more than 45 years, the Dow-Jones averages have maintained a relentless upward march, interrupted only briefly by periods of consolidation and retreat. When you chart this rise, even the crash of October 1987 looks like a small dip. In almost every single two-year period the market was considerably higher at the end of the period than it had been at the beginning. One exception was the bear market of 1973–74, but by 1978 the total return of the market was way up above 1973.

Consider the decade just concluded. At the beginning of the 1980s, the news was bleak: interest rates were high, inflation was just beginning to descend from astronomical heights, real estate was down, and the stock market was down, as were the spirits of individual investors. At that point, the wise contrarians bought all the stock they could. And well they should have, because as so often happens, everything turned around, and throughout the eighties we had the greatest run-up of stock prices in the history of the market. Over the past decade people who invested wisely in stocks made 15 to 20 percent a year on their money compounded. If you had invested in mutual funds you would have made 12 to 18 percent a year. Unfortunately, millions of Americans who might have participated in this bonanza remained on the sidelines, believing that the market was no place for them.

Why? Where did this notion come from that is so completely contrary to the facts? To a great extent from the media, and within the media, mostly from young television news producers who have little if any experience in dealing with the everyday economics of married or family life. Most of them have never been married, don't have children, have never bought a home, and, if they live in New York or Washington, may not even own a car. What's more, they have never made an investment, bought a stock, or a mutual fund. The reason they haven't is because they have little if any money, and all of their perceptions are influenced by their lack of money.

Not all the blame can be placed on the media. To a certain extent, it's the small investors who perpetuate the myth by making the mistakes we referred to a few pages earlier: bad timing, stubbornness, and timidity. One small investor who does poorly can sour a lot of other small investors on investing in securities. But, barring a calamity of such magnitude that all investments are wiped out, a well-counseled and patient small investor will do just as well in the long run as the professionals, and perhaps even better. The small investor doesn't have the same pressures that are on the big investor, pressures that often require the professionals to make decisions that aren't in their best interests. Professional money managers need to perform before an audience. They are constantly worrying about their jobs. They are subject at all times to informational overload, to the point that they can lose sight of basic long-term objectives. And at year end, they are often forced to make sales they shouldn't make in order to get depressed stocks off their books—even if there's an excellent chance the stock will rebound in the new year.

History has proved that the only way to get into the 12 percent range and beyond is to invest in equities and real estate. A few years ago, I had the pleasure of interviewing John Templeton, founder of the Templeton Funds and one of the most successful investors in the history of Wall Street. He put the case very simply. "If you want to beat inflation over a long period of time, there are only two places to invest your money: stocks and real estate. And if you want to be eaten up by inflation and taxes, put your money in the bank or a low-rate investment."

There have been periods when real estate has appreciated faster, but they have been brief periods, and we certainly aren't anticipating one today. That leaves only equity investments: common stocks, bonds, or stock and bond mutual funds.

The biggest mistake most Americans have made in the past, and are continuing to make today, is not having an appropriate portion of their retirement nest egg invested in securities or stock mutual funds.

If you are young and aggressive, you should have at least 75 percent of your money in equities. Forget about what the Dow-Jones did today or this week or this month or even this year. What you really care about is how your stocks or stock mutual fund will perform over a five-, ten- or even twenty-year period.

Even if you're middle-aged, you should invest a good percentage of your savings in equities. If you're forty-five years old, your earnings are good, your health is good, you're optimistic about the economy, and you believe that the world is poised for a major economic takeoff, then you might want to have 50 percent of your retirement nest egg in equities. If you're nervous about conditions and feel the country is headed for a deep recession, then you might want to reduce your position to 25 percent. But some portion of your savings should always be in equities, and over a five-year period you should try for 50 percent or better.

Earlier, I said that the richer you are and the older you are, the more of your money you're going to want to put into safe investments at the bottom of the pyramid. But we've seen what happens when you invest *all* of your money to yield an 8 percent return. To make a 12 percent return, even the richest and oldest among us must invest in higher-risk equities to some degree.

The time to jump into the stock market is when the news is bad. The time to get out of the stock market—to cash in a few chips—is when the news is good. If the market takes a tumble, and the value of your securities diminishes on paper even by 20 to 30 percent, it's not going to change your life, provided you've diversified.

Most people are still foolish enough to put their money into one or two little baskets. Money is like manure; it must be spread around to do the most good.

DEFERRING TAXES ON PROFITABLE INVESTMENTS

Whenever we make a profit, it's diminished by two factors: inflation and taxes. We can't do a great deal to control the impact of inflation, but taxes are another matter.

All profits are taxable, but most taxes can be deferred. If you make these investments the right way, you will not have to include interest or dividends or even capital gains on your Form 1040 for the year in which the money was earned. This year's tax can be deferred to next year, and next year's tax to the year after that, and so on. While the tax owed must theoretically be paid at some future date, the truth is that a tax dollar not paid today is a tax dollar not paid. Instead of going to Uncle Sam, the money remains with you for years, continuing to earn more money.

Put $2,000 into a savings account paying 8 percent interest, and you'll have $160 at the end of the year. If you're in the 28 percent bracket, your $160 will diminish to $115. Put the same $2,000 into an Investment Retirement Account (IRA), and invest it in the same bank at the same rate, and you'll keep the entire $160. The $45 in taxes you've deferred is yours to invest for as long as it remains in the IRA. Only when you use the money will you pay the tax.

What we want to achieve is a mix that will give us a 12 percent return over a certain period of time—a "clean" 12 percent, before taxes but with the taxes deferred. There are several ways to do that.

The first, just mentioned, is to put money into an IRA. The obvious limitation is that you can add only $2,000 to the account each year. But the income is fully sheltered.

The second is to put money into a 401K or SEP plan set up by your employer. As we saw in chapter 7, both plans permit you to invest up to 15 percent of your total income, with an annual limitation of just over $8,000, both plans require an employer contribution, and both plans enable you to defer taxes. Not only do you pay no tax on the portion of your salary you invest, you pay no tax on the amounts your investment earns until you take the money out.

If you're self-employed, there's a third way open to you, provided you have incorporated: a corporate pension plan. Once again, you pay no tax on the earnings or on what your investment earns until such time as you withdraw the money from the pension plan. The drawback to this program is that you must make contributions for all your vested employees.

A fourth way to defer taxes on investment profits is to buy high-quality tax-sheltered annuities.

Fixed and variable annuities are contracts, made with a major insurance company. In this case, the insurance company acts as a bank, and your annuity as an investment savings program. Annuities are good for long-term savings, where you want your taxes to be zero. If you want to lock in your return, you can purchase a fixed rate annuity, but the rate will be a lower one. I recommend a variable annuity, in which you have the opportunity to achieve at least a 12 percent return. Variable means that you can put the money into different investments pockets within the annuity, including stock and bond mutual funds. You decide where your money should be invested. You can create an investment pyramid, the only difference being that all profits will be sheltered from tax for as long as the annuity exists or rolls over.

When you purchase an annuity you should make certain that it's "flexible" as well as variable, permitting you to make additional contributions if you wish to. The major drawback to an annuity is the often hefty surrender charge you must pay if you decide to withdraw your money within a few years of investing it. Only after six or seven years can you do so without paying any penalty with most good annuities.

As with IRAs, the magic age is 59½. You certainly shouldn't make the purchase if you suspect you might need to withdraw the money in three or four years; not only would you pay the penalty and taxes on the earnings, you'd more than likely have to pay a surrender charge to the insurance company for cashing out early.

As you get older and your annuity prospers, you will undoubtedly come under a lot of pressure from the insurance company to "annuitize the annuity." What this means is that in exchange for giving up the lump sum, you will be given a fixed payment every month either for a fixed term or the rest of your life. As appealing as it may sound to have a steady check coming in, it's normally not a good idea to annuitize the annuity. In the first place, that check the insurance company sends you will look half as big ten years from now as it does today, and half again as big in another ten years. In the second place, you lose control of a meaningful asset. You no longer have the opportunity to invest the asset as you wish, nor do your heirs benefit as much when you die. Most certified financial planners tell clients that annuitizing the annuity is not a good idea, and I agree with that.

With this one qualification in mind, you should think of fixed or variable, flexible annuities as valuable investment devices that will defer taxes on your profits. To find out which annuities are the safest and best, I recommend advisory services put out by the A. M. Best Company, Standard and Poor's, and Moody's. These services are available in most major libraries.

It's been said that the next major financial crisis in this country, after the banking crisis, is the crisis of shaky insurance companies, and we're already starting to see many insurance companies fail or receive very low ratings by the aforementioned services. In today's economic climate, it's extremely important that you scrutinize the financial condition and stability of any insurance company from which you intend to buy a product. Make sure the company you do business with has the highest possible rating—up in the A-plus or triple-A category.

In seeking ways to defer taxes, keep in mind that you're not limited to one vehicle. All four—IRAs, 401K and SEP plans, corporate pension plans, and annuities—should be considered.

REAL ESTATE INVESTMENTS: YES OR NO?

I'm often asked about investments in real estate, particularly by those people fortunate enough to have bought their homes before the inflation in real estate set in. For many of them it's far and away the best investment they ever made, and they are tempted, as a consequence, to invest their savings in other real estate ventures.

It's my belief that you want to own only real estate you can control. If you own a small business, and you have the money, then by all means try to own the building your office is in because that will give you ownership and control. If your house has appreciated dramatically in value, and the house next door comes on the market, and the owner needs to unload it so badly he's offering it at a sensational price, I'd have nothing against that, provided you have the money to pay for it.

But I don't recommend investments in shopping centers and office buildings unless you're someone who is very familiar with that game. The vehicle for such investment is usually a limited partnership; how I feel about limited real estate partnerships is summed up by the following saying: At the beginning of the contract, the limited partners have all of the money and none of the knowledge; at the end of the partnership, the limited partners have all of the knowledge and none of the money. As a limited partner, you have absolutely no control. Only the general partners have that, as well as the privilege of extracting fees for themselves before any of the limited partners are paid. They can't lose, but you can—sometimes your entire investment.

If you want to buy a rental house or apartment building, I recommend buying property you can drive to in no more than a day's time. The closer you are, the more closely you can watch it. If the air-conditioning breaks down, you're there to fix it, or you get someone who can. Rental properties can be a terrible headache, especially for those who aren't accustomed to managing them.

Bear in mind that Congress has taken many of the benefits out of rental real estate. It used to be that you could depreciate any rental property over less than twenty years, which meant a considerable savings on your income tax during that time. Today, the depreciation schedule is stretched out over $27\frac{1}{2}$ to $31\frac{1}{2}$ years, giving you less tax relief per year. In addition, Uncle Sam says you have to have "active participation" in rental real estate in order to reap the benefits. This means that you have to make significant and bona fide management decisions as well as owning at least 10 percent of the property. A few benefits remain, however; for example, if your adjusted gross income is less than $150,000, and your property is generating a tax loss due to expenses and depreciation, you may be able to deduct all or part of these losses, up to $25,000.

If you do buy a property, remember to ask the seller to give you a mortgage for the balance. As we've seen, it's far better that way than through a bank. Finally, be as certain as you can that the rent you're going to be able to charge for the dwelling will cover the mortgage and all other expenses, so you have a positive or break-even cash flow.

But before you buy into these headaches, you might wish to consider the virtues of an investment that won't make demands on your time and may make you far more money.

12

Running the Mutual Fund Maze

THE myth that the stock market is beyond the means or risk level of the average investor gets its most effective debunking when we look at an investment vehicle specifically designed for that person: the mutual fund. Over the last ten years, more than 30 million Americans, the overwhelming number of them with modest sums to invest, have been having a love affair with mutual funds, which seem to have built a permanent bridge between Wall Street and Main Street. Three out of four mutual fund investors choose low-risk, interest-paying funds, and one in four choose stock funds with bigger potential for rewards as well as higher risks.

A mutual fund is a large pool of money used to buy and sell securities on behalf of individual investors. When you buy into a fund you get shares representing part-ownership of that fund's securities. By pooling your cash with money from other shareholders, you become part-owner of a multi-million dollar investment, and you share in any profits produced and absorb your share of any losses.

Like almost every other investment, equity funds—those that invest in stocks and bonds—tend to rise and fall with the markets. What makes them ideal for the average investor is that they are managed by professionals whose livelihoods depend on their ability to maximize the upside and minimize the downside.

A second advantage, if you're a small investor, is that you're buying diversification with the first dollar you invest. Most mutual funds invest in hundreds of different securities, your insurance that one or even a few big losers aren't going to hurt you badly. If you're investing for yourself with limited funds and can buy only a few different stocks, one big loser *can* hurt you badly.

A third advantage, if you're an average investor, is that you can buy into many funds for $500, sometimes even less, and make modest periodic investments as well. Most funds reinvest your profits and dividends automatically; this makes your money grow all the faster. And if you buy into a family of funds, you'll be able to switch your money from one fund to another at little or no charge as the need arises.

None of these advantages is of much consequence if the shares you buy don't appreciate. What has been the record? While some mutual funds have not done as well as others, the performance of mutual funds as a group over the last decade has been nothing short of spectacular. With the exception of the bear market of 1982–83, increases of 15 percent a year or more were not uncommon. And progress over longer periods was even more impressive. To take one recent two and a half-year period as an example, from December 3, 1987 through July 26, 1990, capital appreciation mutual funds rose an aggregate 60 percent, growth funds 65 percent, growth and income funds 57 percent, health and biotechnology funds 120 percent, and science and technology funds 70 percent. Not bad!

What small investor wouldn't have wished to participate in this growth? There was nothing to stop him or her. All it took was a few hours of homework to select the proper funds.

REDUCING THOUSANDS OF CHOICES TO TEN: FIVE CRITICAL CRITERIA

Mutual funds now represent over a trillion dollars of investment, come in more than 20 varieties and are sold under some 3,000 labels. Choosing from among them would seem like an impossible task. It's not.

They say that all the marketing theory in the world can be written on a matchbook cover, and I tend to agree. You don't have to read a 200-page book about mutual funds to be able to make an intelligent choice. There are five basic criteria to examine when you're comparing mutual funds, and there's no magic or mysticism to it. With so many funds to choose from, why not choose one that scores high marks in all categories?

My five criteria are presented here in order of importance.

Track Record

Does the fund have an outstanding record of profits for the last year, five years, and ten years? On average, 12 to 15 percent a year is the minimum acceptable return for stock funds. Why settle for less?

While it's important to know what a mutual fund has done over the short-term, I won't invest in a fund that doesn't have a wonderful 10-year track record, as well. Even if a fund has been going great guns since it came out six years ago, I would tend to shy away from it. If it's still going great guns in another four years, I may buy some shares at that time. In the meantime, I'm going to put my money with the best of the best, those funds that have shown over a ten-year period not only that they can make excellent profits, but that they're here to stay.

I can't emphasize too strongly that past performance is no guarantee of good results in coming years—that's where the risk comes in—but it *is* indicative of intelligent and consistent management.

How do you get the information you need to determine which mutual funds are the best of the best? One trip to your local library, or a bookstore or newsstand that sells financial magazines and newspapers, will give you all the information you need. Almost all of them carry charts and graphs listing the performance of dozens upon dozens of mutual funds. Among the publications you might try are *U.S. News and World Report, Fortune, Money, Changing Times, Forbes,* and *Business Week.* There are even publications devoted exclusively to mutual funds, such as *The Mutual Fund Forecaster,* which rates the funds according to their level of risk and predicts which funds will do well in the future. Another, *The Morningstar Mutual Fund Values,* offers one of the most complete analyses of mutual funds available.

The *Mutual Fund Forecaster* is masterminded by Norman Fosback at The Institute for Econometric Research in Fort Lauderdale, not far from my office. Norman is extremely talented at picking out equity mutual fund winners from a very large assortment, which is one reason why I've featured him in my TV reports on mutual funds. To subscribe to his newsletter, or inquire about it, call toll-free 1-800-327-6720. Rates are $100 per year, $10 for a single copy. Ask for a free copy to see if you like it. If you have more than $5,000 to invest, I recommend it. I also recommend the Morningstar *Mutual Fund Values* if the size of your investment justifies its $395 a year price tag. What ranks as one of the best values in the business, however, is the $55 introductory service, which includes a set of materials, plus three months of biweekly updates. Don Phillips is the editor of this service, which ranks all funds on a wide array of criteria that includes historical performance, consistency of management, fees, loads and expenses, and turnover of investments. Funds are ranked on a one-star to five-star basis, five being best. Why invest in a three- or four-star fund when there are plenty of five-star funds to choose from? Their toll-free number is 1-800-876-5005.

Once you've identified at least ten funds—and I do mean ten—call each fund and ask for its prospectus and sales literature. All of the funds have 800 numbers, which are usually carried in the charts. If not, call 1-800-555-1212 to get the toll-free number.

Consistency of Management

Are the same people managing the fund today who racked up those good records? Fidelity Magellan is one of the finest mutual funds in the country, but recently Peter Lynch, the man who managed it for many years, went on to other projects. This is a very important consideration. A lot of people have been burned because they bought in just as the old management was leaving and the new management was coming in. This is not to say that the new management won't do as well, but you have no way of knowing that, whereas old management has a track record available for your inspection.

How do you get this information? By calling up the funds in which you're interested—again, using that 800 number—and asking point-blank who the fund manager is and how long he or she has been there.

The Cost of Buying Shares

The sales charge or fee, if any, on a mutual fund is called a sales load. For some funds that load can be heavy, as much as 9.3 percent of the money we invest. Another load to watch out for is the redemption fee, commonly called the "back-end load," which can run 5 percent or more. Yet another is the "hidden load," a charge of up to 1 percent made by the fund for marketing more shares to customers.

What you're looking for is a "no-load" or "low-load" fund, one that charges either nothing or very little when you buy and when you sell. A mutual fund that charges nothing to buy its shares but doesn't perform well over time is no bargain; conversely, if the cost of buying into a mutual fund that has been increasing in value by 15 percent a year for ten years is 3 percent of your investment, it may be money well spent.

I normally avoid all funds that have a total commission higher than 4 percent on the front end. When I buy a mutual fund, I generally do so from the fund itself rather than through a stockbroker, because stockbrokers will collect their commission on the sale too. Usually, the personnel of the fund are extremely helpful when you buy direct.

Why do investors agree to pay higher sales charges through brokers? Many people would rather deal one-on-one with a stockbroker or agent. They like the convenience and personal service, and are willing to pay for it. And they want help in choosing their investments. When you go the no-load route, you're basically on your own. You do the picking. But this shouldn't scare you. You have access to the same information the broker does; there's nothing he or she has that you can't gather yourself—particularly if you're reading all the magazines, tracking performances of various funds, and subscribing to such special services as *Mutual Fund Forecaster* and Morningstar's *Mutual Fund Values*. You can compare numbers just as well as a broker can.

If you have serious money to invest and want professional help, I would not go to a stockbroker. I'd go to a certified financial planner (CFP) or chartered financial consultant (ChFC). One way to determine if such people are qualified to advise you is to ask if they use the *Morningstar* or other research service in picking investments. Such professionals, however, may not handle accounts of less than $100,000, and they may even charge a consultation fee of several hundred dollars.

The Fund's Objectives

There are four broad types of funds. A combination of funds from each type should match your investment objectives:

- Stock mutual funds
- Bond and income mutual funds
- Tax-free mutual funds
- Money market mutual funds

Stock and income (bond and tax-free) funds fluctuate in price per share, and money market funds don't. They just pay interest; their share price is always one dollar.

Many people buy an income fund because it will yield them 12 percent, without realizing that their per-share price can fall. They invest $10,000, let's say, and they get a $1,200 annual return, but when they decide to liquidate, they learn that their $10,000 is now worth only $8,500. The principal in this so-called "Savers'" account went down 15 percent.

Bond, tax-free, and money market funds all pay interest. Stock mutual funds do not, but they're the ones that offer the biggest opportunity for capital appreciation—as well as the most risk. Some eight million people are investors in stock mutual funds.

In terms of their objectives, all stock mutual funds fall into one of four basic categories:

- *Aggressive growth.* Translation: high risk.

- *Long-term growth.* This describes the bulk of American industry.

- *Growth and income.* Mutual funds in this category emphasize safety and yield—the yield in this case being mainly dividends.

- *Equity high income.* The stocks in these funds pay higher dividends and have modest growth potential as well.

If you're young and aggressive, choose funds that take chances in the hope of big rewards. If you're older and concerned about preserving your capital, choose a conservative fund that promises to try to increase its value by a modest 10 to 12 percent a year without taking undue risk.

In addition to their differing objectives, mutual funds can be categorized by the investment areas they choose to achieve those objectives.

International funds invest in companies outside the United States.

Global funds invest in companies throughout the world, including U.S. companies.

Sector funds invest in individual industries such as computers or electronics. If you want to invest in the entertainment business, there's a fund for that. If you want to invest in leisure-time activities, there's a fund for that. Utilities have always been popular in tough times; if you want to invest in a wide array of utilities from Maine to California, you could do so by buying shares in utilities funds. Socially conscious funds exclude investments in such industries as alcohol, tobacco, firearms, weapons, nuclear power, and gambling. Some of the better known socially conscious funds are Calvert Social Investment or Ariel Growth Fund (1-800-368-2750) and Parnassus Fund (1-415-362-3505).

Index funds invest in the stocks that make up stock averages such as the Dow-Jones index. If the Dow goes up, or down, your shares do too.

Balanced funds build an investment pyramid that includes everything you might put into your own pyramid: money market instruments, bonds, low- and high-risk stocks in both United States and foreign markets, and precious metals. Some of these funds, which are also known as *asset allocation funds*, also invest in real estate. If you're in these funds, you don't have to worry about moving your money around to catch all the highs or avoid all the lows. Some of the asset allocation funds, like the USAA Investment Trust Balanced Portfolio and the USAA Cornerstone Fund (1-800-531-8000), keep a fixed amount of money in several different areas. Others, like the Blanchard Strategic Growth Fund (1-800-922-7771) move the money in the fund around to concentrate on the best-performing areas of the economy at any time. One criticism of some asset allocation funds is that they have managers for each investment sector, which might increase their overhead.

Fund funds invest in other mutual funds. These funds are usually found in big groups of mutual funds; by investing in the fund fund, you're buying shares in all the group's mutual funds at once.

The Expense Ratio of the Fund

Some funds have no sales load, but have such high operating expenses, including the salaries of the people who run them, that they're almost artificially no-load. They emphasize the no-load feature in their sales pitch, but don't ever forget that a mutual fund has a checking account attached to it, as well as a management writing checks to itself and others. It's your money that's paying for salaries, rent, telephones, paper clips, trading commissions, travel and entertainment, and all other expenses of managing and operating the fund. The expenses of the fund should be on the conservative side; you don't want a fund that's taking out 2 percent or more of your money every year to run its operation, in addition to whatever it's charging you in fees.

The average annual expense ratio is around 1 percent, and I like funds that charge even less.

You'll find total expenses and management fees listed in the prospectus. Regard them with a miserly eye.

THE THREE MOST IMPORTANT WORDS IN AN INVESTMENT PROGRAM: DIVERSIFY, DIVERSIFY, DIVERSIFY

Spread your risk! Diversify—even when buying mutual funds. Because a mutual fund invests in many securities, you get a measure of diversification just by purchasing shares in the fund. Even so, I recommend that you carry diversification a step further and eventually put your money into at least five, ideally ten, different funds. In this manner, if one of your funds does poorly, there are many others to pick up the slack.

If you have $50,000 to invest in mutual funds, you should put $10,000 in each of five funds, or $5,000 into ten different funds, or even $2,500 into twenty different funds.

What kinds of funds? At the outset, I would concentrate on the broad objective, or general purpose, funds, as distinguished from the special purpose funds.

It would be irresponsible of me to recommend that you purchase one specific fund, or even five specific funds. Just as my investment pyramid will differ from yours, my choice of mutual funds may not accord with your investment objectives. Any fund I might recommend, moreover, might do poorly in the interim, or change its management or the character of its operations. So the funds listed on page 176 are offered more as a homework assignment than a recommendation to buy. Although a few of the funds lost value during the 1990 stock market decline, all had excellent five- and ten-year track records—one, the Japan Fund, appreciating 459 percent in ten years. All but one have moderate sales loads, or none at all, and the one exception, Putnam, has enough additional pluses to make it, too, worthy of study.

Mutual fund managers make mistakes, just like the rest of us. When they get nervous, they sometimes liquidate stock holdings and keep more assets in cash. If the market moves up and they're still in cash, they've lost their position. On the other hand, if they stay invested when the market goes down, they get caught as well. But most mutual fund managers have been in the business for many years, and hold the jobs they do because they've performed so well for such a long period of time. The best thing you can do once you've thrown in with them is to give them a chance to show their stuff—at least for three to five years.

Name	Minimum Investment	Sales Load
CGM Mutual 800-345-4048	$1,000	None
Fidelity Magellan 800-544-8888	$2,500	3.1%
Fidelity Puritan 800-544-8888	$2,500	2.0%
Janus 800-525-3713	$1,000	None
Pax World 800-767-1729	$ 250	None
Putnam Growth & Income 800-225-1581	$ 500	6.1%
20th Century Select 800-345-2021	None	None
Vanguard-Wellington 800-662-7447	$3,000	None
Japan Fund 800-535-2726	$1,000	None
Scudder International 800-225-2470	$1,000	None

The greatest handicap small investors have is their emotional response to price swings. They'll buy into a fund at $11.50 a share and sell it if it drops to $10.75, not stopping to think that a month or two from now it might be $12.25. The whole purpose of making your own investigation is to satisfy yourself that you've chosen your investments for good, solid reasons. Once you've made the effort, give yourself a chance to be proven right.

One exception: When you buy a mutual fund—or any security for that matter—it's a good idea to set a mental stop-loss point, at which point you'll sell your shares. That point shouldn't normally be less than 20 percent below the price you paid for the shares. If you bought the shares at 10, your stop-loss point could be 8; if at 20, your stop-loss point could be 16. Setting your mind to the possibility of a loss at the outset, but protecting yourself against a more serious loss, will do much to take the emotion out of investing, and permit reason to prevail. It's always a tough decision to sell any "loser," because it's never a loss until you do sell it. If you get firm, positive information about the fund's prospects as the price edges closer to your stop-loss point, you can always change your mind.

13

Constructing a Tax-Deductible Life-Style

THERE is nothing sillier than to live a life you don't want to live just to avoid paying taxes.

I have known Californians who loved living in California but moved to Nevada, where they really didn't want to live, because California has a state income tax and Nevada doesn't.

I have known men who discouraged their wives from returning to work after their children had left home on the grounds that "we'll just have to pay more taxes." That's the most foolish statement imaginable; there is no situation where the tax would ever be higher than the money an individual earns. To deprive anyone of the gratification of earning money while doing something she enjoyed because she'd be paying taxes is just short of lunacy.

If, however, it matches up with your professional and personal objectives, you can develop a tax-deductible life-style that will cut your tax bill dramatically—and that I approve of wholeheartedly. We're talking about completely legitimate and fully legal deductions. The best way to accomplish this goal is to build a career or business around the life-style you enjoy.

The key to a tax-deductible life-style is self-employment—either part- or full-time.

There are two separate tax systems in the United States: The first is a tax system for individuals; the second is a tax system for businesses.

People who own businesses, no matter how small, operate in an entirely separate realm from those who don't, as far as taxes are concerned. It's not enough that they own a business; their business must produce income. But once it does, they gain access to deductions that are inaccessible to individual taxpayers.

Build a business around something you love to do, and any money you spend in support of that business may become a deductible expense: your car, your travel, your telephone, your entertainment, and a host of other items.

Try to depreciate an automobile on a personal return, as well as deduct gas, oil, repairs, and taxes, and there's an excellent chance you'll get flagged by the IRS computer. On a corporate return, the flag will scarcely flutter.

Run your business travel expenses through your personal return and you've increased the likelihood of being audited. Run them through your corporate return, and you will have less explaining to do.

On a personal return, a home office can set off alarms. If you own a business that earns money, and deduct legitimate home office expenses on your corporate return, fewer alarms will sound.

Tax returns of small corporations aren't audited with nearly the frequency that personal returns are. The IRS, with limited manpower, turns its attention to the big and medium-sized corporations, as well as individuals who earn vast amounts of money, on the practical assumption that violations, if any, will involve much larger sums of tax-due interest, and penalties, accordingly, will be vastly greater. A partner at one big accounting firm told me recently that he couldn't remember the last time a small corporation handled by his firm had been audited.

Audits are emotionally, financially, and physically draining. Preparing for them can take weeks, and no one pays you for that downtime. In the process, you may need to consult with your accountant, and while you're not required to take him or her to the showdown with an IRS agent in which most audits culminate, it may be a good idea to do so. That's two to three hours of your accountant's time, at least, in addition to whatever time he or she spent in helping you prepare. At $100 an hour, an audit could easily cost you $500 or more, an expense made only marginally more palatable because it might be deductible. In addition, there's the cost of the penalties and interest you might incur. Some audits result in no change, but many more result in a tax liability. As to the psychological cost, it's incalculable. At the third successive audit of his personal return some years ago, a self-employed friend of mine discovered that he'd almost certainly overpaid on his taxes by several hundred dollars. When the auditor offered to authorize a refund if he could dig up further proof, my friend, whose two previous audits had resulted in no penalty, replied, "It will cost me more in lost time than it's worth. Just do me a favor, okay? You see that I'm honest. Won't you please leave me alone?" He's never been audited since.

The golden rule for claiming tax deductions is the same for businesses as it is for individuals: Take every single dollar you're entitled to and not a dollar more. If a deduction doesn't "feel" right, it probably isn't right. Morality does count here. If you flew to Hawaii for a vacation and took some job interviews just for the partial tax deduction, you know you're trying to beat the system, and you'd be mighty uncomfortable explaining to an auditor why you didn't take the job. It's absolutely critical that you be fair and honest in separating personal expenses from business expenses. Even the automobile you use for business runs up some personal mileage; an IRS examiner auditing your return will be favorably impressed if you've attempted to separate the two fairly.

In describing the advantages of a tax-deductible life-style, I'm not suggesting or implying that you do anything illegal or even cut corners. All I *am* saying is that the legal tax advantages available to the self-employed are yet another inducement to pursue the dream of independence. If you have such a dream and set up a business but don't incorporate that business, you'll be passing up an opportunity to put yourself into a favored category when it comes to claiming deductions.

As a self-employed person, you are entitled to take full advantage of the tax laws by setting up an "S" corporation. Once you do, you can run your major deductions through your corporate return, and purge your personal return of the kind of items that will invite an audit.

To keep matters simple at the outset, it *may* be more convenient for you to attach a "Schedule C" to your personal return. At some point, though, you should incorporate, separating yourself as a person from the business entity.

At the time of incorporation, you'll need to address these key issues:

• Since all income and expenses will now flow through the corporation, who will keep the books?

• How much salary should you draw?

• How will this affect your personal returns?

• What benefits will you and other employees take?

• What assets will the corporation own?

• What liabilities will the corporation assume?

• How much of the corporate equity side will be classified as stock, and how much will be loans repayable to you within IRS guidelines?

• Do you need an "S" corporation or a taxable corporation?

• How will your insurance requirements change?

• What will be the extra cost of operating as a corporate business entity?

Warning: In setting up any corporation and establishing its tax status, you'll need the help of an attorney and a CPA. Don't try to do this yourself.

CHOOSING A TAX HAVEN

Having said at the outset that living where you don't want to live just to avoid paying taxes is the height of folly, let me suggest that choosing a place to live that accords with your dreams and also taxes reasonably is the height of wisdom.

As bad as federal income taxes are, the income, property, and sales taxes charged by state and local governments can be more burdensome. Look for this trend to increase sharply. As Uncle Sam pushes more of society's burden onto the states, the states will continue to devise more ways to tax, and tax more aggressively with the means already at hand. In some states, property taxes are increasing 10 and 20 percent a year because the states can't support public works and schools on current revenues, even where those revenues are augmented by proceeds from state lotteries. Several states now include automobiles as well as homes and land in calculating property taxes. And for the dubious privilege of continuing to live in the Big Apple, New Yorkers must also pay a city income tax.

When it comes to state taxes, as opposed to federal taxes, the United States can be divided into three categories:

Tax hell states: Hawaii, Idaho, Maine, Maryland, Minnesota, New York, Oregon, Utah, Wisconsin, and the District of Columbia.

Tax haven states: Alaska, Connecticut, Florida, Nevada, New Hampshire, South Dakota, Tennessee, Washington, and Wyoming. Alaska not only operates with a balanced budget, it pays rebates to its residents in years when revenues exceed expenses.

Tax neutral states: All the rest.

The above list offers at least a partial explanation as to why so many people from the Boston area choose to live in nearby New Hampshire, and so many retired people move to Florida. When I moved to Florida from Rhode Island, I eliminated the burden of Rhode Island state income taxes. Florida has neither a state income tax nor a state inheritance tax, one reason why so many financial planning firms in the "Sunshine State" teach people how to become legal residents. But even with its successful state lottery, Florida is experiencing fiscal problems, and many experts are saying that a state income tax is no longer a question of whether but of when.

In identifying, pricing, and chasing your dream, it makes all the sense in the world for you to investigate the tax haven states to find out whether one of them fits your desires. But finding the right locale to live and work is far more important than the tax you'll be required to pay; taxes are a consideration only when you're satisfied on all other counts. Nor are taxes the only consideration when you're pricing your dream. That $50,000 or $100,000 you save by choosing a state in which housing costs are low can pay a lot of tax bills.

Here's the priority: first, life-style considerations; second, business and career ramifications; third, tax implications.

RETIREMENT PLANS FOR THE SELF-EMPLOYED:
THE BIGGEST TAX BREAK OF ALL

Ten years ago, a former colleague of mine, a television reporter, quit his job to become a freelance writer. Freelance writing is one of the most hazardous and least well remunerated of all professions. Only a very small percentage of those who pursue it manage to support themselves and their families on fees and royalties; all the rest have to work part- or even full-time at another job. But my former colleague was determined to give it a shot, because he'd always dreamed of writing books and screenplays. So he moved to Los Angeles where, following my advice, he filed papers of incorporation with the state of California, a perfectly legal move even though he would be the corporation's sole employee. He'd been reluctant to incorporate because of the costs and paperwork involved—costs, incidentally, that continue year after year—but he did so at my urging not only because a corporate tax return would enable him to write off his expenses but also because his corporation could set up a pension program. Under this program, he could contribute a portion of his earnings each year without paying taxes on them.

For the first two years, he wondered whether he'd made a terrible mistake. His earnings were barely enough to keep his family going, yet he continued to make annual contributions to his pension program. Happily, in his third year of freelancing, his earnings improved, and his fourth year was even better. That year, for the first time, he was able to make the maximum contribution to his pension trust, and he did the same the following year. By this point, his contributions totaled nearly $90,000, but the pension trust was worth nearly double that because of some excellent investments. For the last several years, my friend has continued to make contributions to his pension trust, but on a much more modest level. The value of the trust, however, has doubled again, to the point that it is now worth $4 for every dollar he has invested.

Today, my friend is living the life he dreamed about, secure in the knowledge that when he retires in fifteen years it will be with a better pension by far than he would have had if he'd remained with his employer.

The story I've just recounted illustrates the power of the best of all the tax benefits available to the self-employed: the opportunity to salt away a tremendous chunk of money every year. We've talked about this benefit in earlier chapters, but it's in the context of the tax-deductible life-style that it most clearly demonstrates the advantage of striking out on your own.

The opportunity to fund their own pension saves the self-employed up to thirty-three cents, in federal tax alone, on every dollar they contribute; that's the amount they would have paid in taxes had they not made the contribution. In prior years, when tax rates were higher, the savings were even greater. All that money that might have gone to Uncle Sam remains, instead, in pension trust funds, earning even more tax-deferred income each year.

IF YOU ARE NOT SELF-EMPLOYED . . .

There are three ways to shelter your income for retirement if you're not in business for yourself. We've dealt with all three in other contexts; let's review them here to see how they stack up against opportunities for the self-employed.

Individual Retirement Accounts (IRAs)

An IRA is the next place to put savings dollars after you've put away that sum to cover three to six months worth of expenses in the event of an emergency, but in any case no less than $5,000.

IRA deductions are the single best deal for small investors. Couple the deduction to the tax-deferred buildup on the income and you've got a return on investment that's unbeatable. Yet millions of Americans don't make IRA contributions because of a mistaken belief that they can't deduct them on their tax return. As previously stated, an individual can shelter $2,000 a year in an IRA account, a couple, $4,000. If you are single and make less than $35,000 a year, or if you're married and make less than $50,000, all or part of your IRA is going to be deductible. Limits on deductibility apply only if you or your spouse are covered by some form of retirement plan at work. If neither of you is covered, you may deduct your entire IRA contribution even if you make a million dollars a year. If you've deposited $2,000, you've just saved $560 in tax, an instantaneous 28 percent return on your money, and that $560 will earn more money, tax-deferred, if you add it to next year's IRA, up to age 70½. (If you pay state income tax, you save even more tax, making your return even greater.)

Even if your earnings exceed the limits and you can't deduct your contribution, you still get wonderful tax-deferral benefits. How good are these benefits? If you decide to put $2,000 a year into a bank savings account paying 8 percent, at the end of twenty years you'll have contributed $40,000, and you'll have $71,700 in the account. But if you put the same amount of money into a nondeductible IRA account at the same 8 percent, you'll have $77,100, an extra $5,400. If you contribute $2,000 for another ten years, the bank savings account will have $151,600, but the IRA will have $179,900, a difference of $28,300.

Most people who hesitate to set up an IRA fear they might need the money they're putting away and know that early withdrawal before age 59½ will cost them a 10 percent penalty. What they don't realize is that they are entitled to withdraw the money once a year, so long as they put it back within 60 days. If for some reason they're unable to do so, they pay the 10 percent penalty, as well as the tax on the income. Given the benefits of the IRA, and the unlikelihood of having to use the money if emergency funds are in place, that is a tolerable risk.

Another misunderstanding is that you have to contribute $2,000 every year, once you set up your IRA. Not true. Each year's contribution is a new IRA; contribute for 15 years and you've set up 15 separate IRAs. And to each IRA you are permitted to contribute what you can up to $2,000. If all you can manage in a given year is $500, then that's your contribution. The only restriction is an indirect one; banks that administer IRAs won't usually accept one under $200.

401K

As I hope I've made clear by this point, if you're not self-employed, the 401K plan is the best tax shelter you can have other than owning your own home. In 1991 you could put $8,475 into the plan; this figure is adjusted upward each year. It's not a tax deduction, but it's just like one, because the money comes right off the top of your salary and your taxes on it are deferred as well. In effect, twenty-eight cents or more of every dollar put in the 401K plan is put there by Uncle Sam, just as it is with the IRA. In addition, many employers make matching contributions: 25 cents on the dollar, 50 cents on the dollar, or even dollar for dollar. As with the IRA, the money in the plan multiplies tax-deferred. In fact, the 401K is like a great big flexible IRA because you can not only sock money away tax-deferred, you can roll it over when you leave or retire.

Where do you put your 401K dollars? Typically, there are five investments employers will approve, and you can choose among them:

1. A money market account.
2. A stock mutual fund.
3. A bond income fund.
4. A guaranteed investment contract, or GIC. This is a glorified certificate of deposit issued by an insurance company, which pays a fixed rate of interest per year. In 1990, that rate was 8.5 percent, tax deferred—a rate that most people would jump at, which explains why 70 percent of all 401K money is sitting in GICs.
5. The company's stock.

Money invested in a 401K account is yours to withdraw at age 59½, not before. Why 59½? Because many people like airline pilots and accountants with major CPA firms face mandatory retirement at age sixty. Until that time, you can borrow the money for specific reasons: sending your children to college, buying your first home, or paying medical bills. The money, of course, must be paid back with interest—interest you're really paying to yourself.

If you're eligible for a 401K plan at work, and not using it, you're passing up the best combination of tax-deferral and forced savings plan available to all but the self-employed.

Simplified Employee Pension (SEP)

SEPs are much like IRAs but are sponsored by your employer, and money paid in per year can be greater. Basically, your employer pays into your SEP and takes a tax deduction. You, however, don't have to report this money as income. If the plan allows, you may make contributions as well, up to 15 percent of your total compensation, or about $8,000, whichever is less.

Once again: If your employer doesn't offer a pension plan, profit-sharing plan, 401K, or SEP, you'd be within your rights to ask for one.

YOU VERSUS UNCLE SAM

Tax laws, like the common law, are constantly evolving. They are set by the Congress, but interpreted by the Department of the Treasury. What comes to the department in four paragraphs can be exploded into four pages of tax regulations. These, in turn, are tested in Tax Court as the Internal Revenue Service challenges corporations and individual taxpayers.

My early years in CPA practice were filled with tax-sheltering loopholes like investment credits, income averaging, and super-accelerated depreciation on real estate. These are all dinosaurs now. I remember more lenient times. You could be out of work and your unemployment compensation really wouldn't be taxed. You could buy a car and not only deduct the sales tax, but all the interest on your installment loan, and if you used the car in business you could deduct the entire cost over time, even if it were a Rolls. Then there was the capital gains tax, a bonus for every citizen who sold stock, real estate, or other investment property. As long as you owned the property for at least one year, 60 percent of the gain was excluded from tax— a great incentive for long-term investment. No more.

Most incidental expenses relating to our jobs and investments were fully deductible on Schedule A as "miscellaneous expenses," and this list was a long one, from business mileage to union dues to safe-deposit box rental charges. There was no 2 percent threshold to climb over. It was worth keeping track of every nickel and dime.

Times and the tax laws have changed. Slowly and inexorably, deductions and loopholes are being taken away from Americans rich and poor under the banner of "simplification" and lower rates. Ronald Reagan promised both when he took office. Technically, we got the latter, but not the former. IRS Publication 17, the official instruction booklet for use in preparing individual tax returns and available free to every taxpayer, is as unwieldy in the 1991 edition as it's ever been—228 pages of technical jargon. Even tax professionals have to struggle with the details more often than they like to admit.

In the realm of taxes, the question I'm asked more than any other is, "Should I prepare my own return?" The answer 80 percent of the time is no, yet almost 50 percent of taxpayers still prepare their own returns—most, I'm sure, to their disadvantage.

If your tax situation is ridiculously simple—meaning one job, one W2 form, and virtually no available reductions, deductions, or credits—then use form 1040EZ if you're single or Form 1040A if you're married. After you've prepared it, triple-check it.

Everyone else should get professional help.

Trying to address a complicated tax return by yourself is a classical case of being "penny wise and pound foolish." The cost of having a return prepared by a professional usually ranges between $25 and $250. Preparing a return yourself, you could overlook a tax break that would cost you far more than that.

I know very competent and highly paid CPAs who refuse to do their own returns because they don't specialize in the highly complex area of personal taxation. The kind of CPA they go to is the kind you want: a specialist in personal taxation who has passed the U.S. Treasury exam and is an "enrolled agent." This person will also be able to help you with your tax planning during the year.

Here's a list of money-saving strategies often overlooked by taxpayers but not by qualified professionals:

1. If you're in the process of buying a house, consider closing before year-end. The mortgage points you pay are fully deductible. Even if you can't take possession right away, often you can work out a short-term rental agreement with the seller. And if you're thinking of buying a house, make every effort to do so; it's the best deduction we have.

2. Whenever possible, defer income items until the following year. Ask your employer if he or she will defer any bonus or commissions until then. If you're self-employed, defer your billings until year's end, or tell your clients or tenants they're getting a Christmas gift by not having to pay you until after the New Year. (This works only when you use the "cash method" of accounting for tax purposes.)

3. If you're contemplating elective medical or dental procedures, and they add up to more than 7.5 percent of your adjusted gross income, you can pay for them in advance and take such deduction as the tax law allows, except for cosmetic surgery.

4. Miscellaneous deductions like unreimbursed business expenses, union dues, mandatory work clothing, and professional publications must

exceed 2 percent of your adjusted gross income. Here again, bunch them into one tax year if possible. Prepay dues and subscriptions.

5. Capital gains are now taxed as ordinary income; check your portfolio for losses you may have incurred. Remember, you're allowed to offset gains with losses dollar for dollar. If your losses exceed the gains, you can deduct up to $3,000 for any one year.

6. Gifts and charitable contributions of cash and property to approved organizations are deductible, provided you itemize.

7. Prepay any state or local income or property taxes. They're fully deductible.

8. If you're a parent, pay up all qualifying child care expenses, for a deduction or credit.

9. If you're divorced and paying alimony, it's a deduction. (If you're receiving alimony, it's income, which must be declared.)

10. If you've suffered an uninsured or underinsured casualty loss this year, you can take a deduction minus $100 for each loss.

This won't save you taxes, but it will save you money: If you have any consumer, credit card or personal loans, pay them off. The interest is no longer deductible.

TAX-FREE INVESTMENTS: YES OR NO?

One of the services your accountant can perform for you is to determine whether it's wise for you to put part of your savings into tax-free investments. Anyone in the 28 percent bracket or higher will do well to take a close look at tax-free investments that will yield the equivalent of a taxable 9 percent return or higher. But if you're not in the 28 percent bracket, even the best tax-free investments won't be worth it.

Some taxpayers with little or no earned income, senior citizens in particular, are so obsessed with saving money on taxes that they invest in low-yielding tax-free bonds without realizing that they would either be paying no tax or such a low tax that they would earn much more money with a taxable investment.

The formula for comparing a taxable investment to a tax-free investment is one you ought to know yourself, whether you use an accountant or not.

Step One. Calculate the reciprocal of your bracket by subtracting your tax rate from 100. In the case of a 28 percent tax rate, the reciprocal is 72 (100 − 28 = 72).

Step Two. Divide the rate on the tax-free investment by the reciprocal. Suppose the return is 6.5 percent; in decimal terms, that converts to .065.

Suppose the reciprocal is 72; in decimal terms, that converts to .72. Dividing .065 by .72 gives you 9 percent. In other words, you're as well off in your tax-free investment as you would be with a taxable investment earning 9 percent. If you can earn more than 9 percent with the taxable investment, you'd be better off doing so.

WARNING: CHECK YOUR FICA

Someone—either you or your accountant—should audit your FICA account.

FICA stands for Federal Insurance Contribution Act, the legislation that established Social Security during the Great Depression and the administration of Franklin Delano Roosevelt. At the time, Social Security was envisioned as the foundation upon which retirement planning could be built. Although most Americans today seem to labor under the delusion that Uncle Sam will take care of them when they get old, Social Security was never intended to pay for more than a third to a half of our living expenses during retirement. For many retired couples today, the $12,264 maximum benefit doesn't cover anything near these amounts, and as the federal government continues its desperate search for added revenues, the proportion of retirement expenses covered by Social Security benefits will in all likelihood decrease. As an example, if you want to keep on working after you begin to receive Social Security benefits, it's going to cost you. For 1991, workers under age 65 could earn only $7,080 without incurring a $1 reduction in benefits for every $2 above the limit. From age sixty-five to sixty-nine, the limit rises to $9,720, with a $1 drop for every $3 above the limit. Only when you're seventy can you work and earn what you wish without a reduction in Social Security benefits. IRS Publication 915 spells out how much, if any, of your benefit is taxable each year.

FICA taxes are the most insidious of all, because we never see this money even though we are paying income taxes on it. As if that weren't bad enough, there's a reasonable chance that we aren't being accurately credited for all our FICA contributions—the very credits we must build up in order to receive benefits at retirement. One young couple told me that they checked their FICA records for the eight years they'd been making contributions—and found errors in the entries for every single year.

Murphy's Law says that anything that can go wrong will go wrong. Your FICA account is vulnerable to an infinite variety of screwups. Companies move, merge, are sold, change their names or go out of business. Any or all of these can cause your records to be lost. Women who interrupt their careers to have children are particularly vulnerable to errors. The records of a part-time job may never make their way to the government's computer—another special problem for women, so many of whom work part-time during their childbearing years. Compounding the problem is the government's computer system itself, ancient by today's standards. The government has acknowledged problems and maintains it has fixed them, but that will be little solace to you if the errors on your FICA account were committed years ago, even if your records are 95 percent correct today.

To determine whether your account is accurate, you need only fill out a form SSA-7004, which you can obtain from your local Social Security Administration office. A few weeks after you mail the form in, you will receive a report from the SSA, detailing the credits on file for you. If you do find an error, report it. Be sure to have proof to back up your story.

Everyone should file a form every two years, but checking FICA records is especially critical for self-employed people, who must make FICA contributions as both employer and employee, and thus pay more FICA tax than anyone else.

And all of us should speak up when we feel we're being taxed unjustly, or at too burdensome a rate—a subject we'll address in the final chapter.

14

Protecting Yourself
and Your Family

ON the night of November 26, 1956, I awakened to the smell of smoke and the sound of fire trucks outside my bedroom window. I looked out the window and saw the worst sight I had ever seen: The greenhouse behind our house, built and owned by my grandparents, was burning to the ground. It was Thanksgiving night and I was nine years old.

Later, firemen would conclude that coal gas had built up in the greenhouse boiler room and collected inside the building. When my grandfather had opened the door that evening to check on the greenhouse temperature, the building had literally blown up in his face, burning all his hair and giving him the appearance of a man who had been wandering in the desert for a week.

For most of his life, my grandfather had earned a good living as a professional musician, but by 1956 arthritis had curtailed his playing, and the florist business, which he and my grandmother had run for most of their adult lives, accounted for 98 percent of their income. My grandfather didn't believe in insurance; on that one night, he lost everything he had. From that point on, he had to rely on his children for support, and he died nine years later, a destitute and broken man.

Events like that you never forget; I have been a believer in insurance of all kinds ever since.

Every insurance contract is a legal bet, made with the insurer, that something bad is going to happen to us in the near future. The insurer makes a lot of money betting that it won't, and it's one bet we don't mind losing.

For many years, I bought all of my life insurance policies from a big, strapping insurance agent of Irish, English, and Sioux Indian descent named Paul Shehan. Paul was an old-fashioned insurance salesman who maintained an office in his North Kingstown, Rhode Island, home, which overlooked Narragansett Bay, and came to your home or office to discuss your insurance needs with you. Although he understood every form of insurance, his passion was life insurance, which he sold in $10,000 to $250,000 face values, depending on the client. He truly believed that families, particularly families with young children, needed life insurance, and to make his case he would tell the story of a young serviceman, a father and husband, who bought a $10,000 policy from him with a cash deposit, and was killed in a car accident later that evening. The policy paid off, thanks to Paul's diligence.

I probably needed less convincing about the merits of life insurance than any client Paul ever had. Soon after I began work at Price Waterhouse, a friend and colleague at the firm dropped dead at the age of 24. He had been in perfect health, but for reasons no one could determine his heart had simply stopped. Some years later, I heard the story, a famous one among airline pilots, of the captain of an airliner who had reached over to awaken his young copilot and discovered that he was dead.

By the time I moved to Florida, Paul had sold me five $50,000 life insurance policies. In addition to selling me insurance, he was a friend, and I trusted him implicitly. In the fall of 1986 we had lunch together. It was the first time I'd seen him since leaving Rhode Island. Before we parted, he promised that he'd come to Florida to meet Fran and see our newborn son Sean. I never saw him again. Before six months had passed, he had developed terminal cancer. He passed away after fighting the disease for three months. He was fifty-one. I remember praying at the time that he'd had enough life insurance, because I knew that his wife, Shirley, and their children would need it. Happily, he did, and Shirley was not only able to provide for the children but to continue the family business.

I tell these stories not to be morbid, but because it would not be responsible of me, in writing about personal money matters, if I didn't make the point that we never know when we are going to leave the planet earth. Many of us have the well-known "denial of death" syndrome. We truly believe that death is too far down the road to worry about and that life insurance is a waste of money—something for others but not for us. For those who have no dependents, that could be true. For the rest of us, it's almost never true. The undeniable reality is that being underinsured or without insurance could ruin our loved ones' lives.

Today, unfortunately, another factor intrudes: a ground swell of anger among the American public against insurance companies. They are angry because some insurance companies charge such high prices for automobile insurance, while others have decided not to carry automobile insurance any longer. And they are angry at life insurance companies as well because recent disclosures have persuaded them that these companies and their salesmen have been selling them policies that historically have cost too much and provided too little protection.

To me, letting such feelings hinder one's judgments about the need for life insurance is a classic case of throwing the baby out with the bathwater.

I can no longer count the number of times I've sat in the homes of young and middle-aged couples, listening to them say that their children mean more to them than anything else in their lives, and then learning that they have little or no life insurance. I remember asking one man, an electrician, what would happen to his children and to his wife, who didn't work, if he were to be killed on the job. I'd already established that their savings wouldn't even cover his burial. "We don't like to think about death much," he replied. "Maybe you don't, but your wife sure better," I said. "She could be on the streets, or be forced into marrying a guy she doesn't love." The electrician was silent for a moment. "Well," he conceded, "maybe we *should* talk about it."

I'm not a fanatic about life insurance. To the contrary, as a CPA I did everything I could to discourage my clients from overinsuring. One of them—we'll call him Wilfred—was a true life insurance junkie. Thirty minutes after a life insurance salesman would appear at his door, poor Wilfred would be the proud owner of yet another $50,000 life insurance policy. He had his reasons. He was a workaholic and a chain smoker and had a bad temper to boot, and he was convinced that the combination would put him into an early grave. He loved his wife and children and wanted to protect them against this possibility, but the protection he acquired—$2.5 million in today's dollars—would have enabled them to live like they'd won the lottery rather than lost the family breadwinner. In the meanwhile, his premium bills were so large that neither he nor his family could enjoy their life together.

But if I'm not a fanatic about life insurance, I *am* a believer in dealing with the problem rationally. It's not that difficult. It doesn't take long. The solution isn't expensive. And once it's in place, you and your loved ones can enjoy the present without worrying about the future. Having been brought up in a family with modest resources, it's especially comforting to me to know that if I were to die tomorrow, my insurance benefits, when added to my assets, would provide for my children until they're independent adults and for my wife for the rest of her life.

LIFE INSURANCE: WHAT KIND? HOW MUCH? FOR HOW LONG?

Basically, there are two types of life insurance policies. The first is *permanent* life insurance, which pays a benefit to your designated beneficiary upon your death, and builds up cash values as you pay your premium each year. The second type of policy is *term* insurance, which pays a benefit to your designated beneficiary upon your death, but has no cash buildup provisions whatsoever. Of the two, permanent life insurance is far more costly at the outset, reflecting its growing surrender value. Over a lifetime, however, permanent policies end up costing a lot less because as we age term insurance becomes prohibitively expensive.

There are three types of permanent policies: whole life, which can be paid up in a few years; universal life, which is basically like term insurance but has an investment side pocket, a money mutual fund, that lets you build up cash value; and variable life, which is like universal life except that it offers a variety of side pockets, such as stock mutual funds and bond funds.

I estimate that nine out of ten people who buy permanent life insurance policies believe that on the death of the person covered, the beneficiary will receive the cash value of the policy as well as the face value of the policy. If the cash value is $60,000, and the face value is $100,000, they expect the beneficiary to receive $160,000. They are wrong. The beneficiary receives only $100,000—the $60,000 cash value and an additional $40,000 in insurance payouts. Can you blame those to whom this has happened for being angry? On the advice of the insurance company and their agent, they'd invested all that money over the years and gotten a miserable return and wound up with an inadequate insurance benefit worth less than their investment. Had they known the truth, many of them would never have bought this type of insurance or paid so much into it.

Since my own protection includes half a million dollars in permanent life insurance policies, I'd be a hypocrite to say that I'm against all permanent life insurance. But I bought those policies so long ago that they're no longer costing me anything. Their cash surrender value is paying the premiums. When premium time rolls around, I simply borrow the money available in the policy to pay it. It's done automatically. I could probably find a way to insure myself more economically, but I keep the present policies in force because I bought them from agents who became my friends.

Were I starting over, however, I would not buy as much permanent life insurance. And I would buy even more term insurance. A term insurance policy for nonsmoking male age twenty-five should cost about $125 a year for each $100,000, a bargain given the peace of mind it offers. Your insurance agent will probably try to sell you a more expensive whole life or universal life policy, either one of which would produce a bigger commission than a term policy. At this point in your life, however, such policies in large denominations don't make a lot of sense, no matter what your life insurance salesman tells you. It usually makes more sense to separate your insurance coverage from your investments.

If you're young and have a family, you'll want to buy at least $200,000 of the cheapest term life insurance, and $500,000 ideally, particularly if you're striking out on your own. An ideal ratio would be $4 in term insurance for every dollar of permanent insurance. If you wanted $500,000 in face value coverage, you'd buy $100,000 in whole life coverage and $400,000 in inexpensive term coverage.

Some insurance experts recommend that the insurance coverage be divided between husband and wife, rather than concentrated on just one parent. If both are working, I would agree; if only one is working, the bulk of the coverage, I feel, should be on the wage earner.

Is there a point in life when you no longer need life insurance? Absolutely.

If you're sixty, own your home free and clear, have adequate savings and a vested interest in a generous pension plan, why pay a considerable premium to maintain a policy whose death benefit won't be necessary? The one clear exception is when you're rich and you need the proceeds from insurance to cover your estate taxes. For most of the rest of us, a retirement nest egg should be adequate for our senior years. Answering this question shouldn't be done on the fly, however; you need to be certain that your spouse's future spending power will be enough even if he or she survives you by forty years.

At seminars, many single men and women without dependents ask me if there's a reason to buy life insurance when there's nobody to leave the money to. I give them two answers: no and maybe. If they're absolutely certain that they'll never marry or have children, the answer's no. If they even think they would like to marry and have a family at some later date, then they ought to consider buying a small permanent life insurance policy while they're still young enough to qualify for lower premiums.

My closest friend and business associate, Ernie Baptista, is a top life insurance agent in New England. Ernie sells policies to people who really need them: small business owners who need to protect the family and the family business, as well as business executives with lots of assets, responsibilities, and dependents. Ernie believes, and I agree, that the top ten mistakes we make in regard to life insurance, in order of importance, are:

1. Having no life insurance at all
2. Waiting until we have health problems before buying insurance
3. Buying the wrong policies
4. Changing policies too often
5. Having too little coverage
6. Having the wrong agent
7. Not investigating the financial health of the company issuing the insurance
8. Not reviewing coverage periodically
9. Not understanding our policies
10. Not using cash values properly

By learning to avoid these mistakes, we can better protect our loved ones.

DISABILITY INSURANCE: CAN WE AFFORD IT?
CAN WE AFFORD NOT TO HAVE IT?

Whether employed by others or self-employed, you need disability insurance if the sudden cessation of your normal earnings would put you in a bind.

Insurance company statistics suggest that we're four or five times more likely to be disabled than we are to die an untimely death. At some point during our working lives, we could have an injury or an illness that will dramatically curtail our earning power, or eliminate it altogether, for an extended period.

Benevolent employers used to keep you on the payroll indefinitely if you were a valued and loyal employee who got sidelined due to injury or illness. That doesn't happen much any more.

When we're disabled, we get hit from two sides. Not only are our earnings curtailed or stopped, our expenses increase enormously. Even the best medical insurance has a deductible portion for which you're responsible, which can be significant when treating a disabling accident or illness. At such times, you'll get a lot of sympathy from family, friends, and colleagues, but none from the bill collectors. Disability or not, they'll take your house away from you if you fall too far behind on your payments.

The higher your earning power, the more your need for disability insurance.

The less money you've saved up, the more your need for disability insurance.

How much?

It's almost impossible to secure a disability policy for more than 60 percent of your total earning power. Assuming you could find such a policy, the cost would be so prohibitive as to be unworkable. You'd be spending so much money against the *possibility* that you might be disabled that you wouldn't have adequate funds to enjoy normal life.

But thanks to Uncle Sam, you may not need more disability coverage. Because the payout on a disability policy is tax-free, it would be approximately equal to your net pay, after taxes.

The real problem with a disability policy isn't so much the amount you receive as it is the delay in receiving it. Most benefits don't kick in until a month, three months, or even six months after you've become disabled. Such policies deserve careful consideration, nonetheless, because they may be the only disability policies most of us can afford. The longer the waiting period, the less expensive the premium. While it's true that you're far more likely to become disabled at some point in your life than you are to die an untimely death, the odds are quite good that you'll never become seriously disabled at all. If you do become disabled, and if you've done as you should and set that three- to six-month emergency stash aside, you can use the stash to cover your expenses until the benefits kick in.

When shopping for disability coverage, be sure to get quotes from at least four or five good insurance companies. To give you an idea of how dramatic benefits and premiums can vary from company to company, here's what happened when I went shopping for a new insurance policy for my airplane not long ago. My previous policy had $1 million in liability coverage and a $3,500 deductible for damage. It cost $9,150 a year. My new policy costs $4,305 with a zero damage deductibility and ten times the liability coverage. How did I get such a good deal? By asking everyone I knew in aviation for the name of a good insurance broker who would search for the best deal. I found him in Columbia, South Carolina. I'm not promising that disability premiums and benefits will vary as greatly, but I hope I've convinced you to shop 'til you drop.

A warning for the squeamish: Before any life insurance company sells you a disability policy with benefits of more than $1,000 a month, or a life insurance policy at face value of $100,000 or more—$50,000 in New York, Florida, and California—you'll be required to take a physical examination, part of which is a blood test. Welcome to the age of AIDS.

Fair warning: Don't lie on your application about medical problems, smoking, or drinking. And don't try to obtain disability policies from two or more companies. Insurance companies have a way of checking up on such things.

WILLS: THE WONDER OF LIVING TRUSTS

If you're like most Americans, you don't have a will. You need one. It won't benefit you, of course, but it will make all the difference in the world to your loved ones, and it will keep your memory shining. Without a will, your estate will be settled in a time-consuming and expensive fashion. Your survivors will be buried in paperwork and besieged by lawyers. You may feel that your estate doesn't warrant the bother, but that could change dramatically in the years ahead, even if all you do is buy a proper amount of life insurance.

Actually, you need two documents. The first is a simple will. The second is a revocable living trust. A friend of mine, Renno Peterson, an expert in such documents, calls them "loving trusts." He's the author of a terrific book of the same name. The will is tangential to the trust; it's the trust in which all your dreams, wishes, and aspirations are spelled out.

During your life, you control everything you put into the trust, which, effectively, is everything you own. The trust has a checkbook, which you are free to use. When you die, everything in the trust—your business, your home, your vacation home, your car, your investments—can continue as before. A revocable living trust gives you control and continuity. It serves you in life and gives you reasonable assurance that your assets will end up where you want them to go.

Revocable living trusts are not income tax shelters, in that the assets in the trust will be included in your estate for IRS purposes. When you have a complete and correctly executed trust document, however, your heirs will be spared the grief of going through probate. When you have a will alone, it guarantees that your family will have to go through probate. A living trust, therefore, guarantees that more money will go into your family's pocket and less into your lawyer's pocket.

There are attorneys in your area who specialize in setting up revocable living trusts. The cost to you should be no more than a few thousand dollars.

Do bear in mind that you and your spouse can each give a gift, up to $10,000 a year, without tax consequences to yourself or your beneficiary. You are also entitled to a one-time unified tax credit, in which you can give a larger gift without tax consequences. That amount is currently $192,800. If you do not use it in your lifetime, it is applicable to your estate tax, if any. The credit wipes out any tax owed on assets up to $600,000.

If your assets are greater than $600,000, you should do some serious estate planning with both a lawyer and a CPA, each of whom should be an expert in the field. Not just any lawyer or CPA will do. At the outset, you'll have to do most of the work, because they can't write out a word until you've spelled out your intentions and desires. The more you can write out for them, the less it's going to cost you.

It always puzzles me that so many Americans worry about how heavily their estates will be taxed when the truth is that 95 percent of all estates aren't taxed at all by the Federal government.

THE BEST INSURANCE OF ALL: STAYING HEALTHY AND FIT

Experts on health and fitness tell us that as we age, our biological variable increases, up to a maximum of thirty years. At sixty, we can look seventy-five and act and feel it, or look forty-five and act and feel it. To an extent, the outcome depends on our biological givens, but most of us have it within our power to determine the outcome to a considerable degree. That power comes from the extent to which we live a healthy life and maintain our fitness.

The principles by which we maintain health and fitness are well known: a proper diet, plenty of rest and relaxation, no smoking, no more than two alcoholic drinks a day for men and one drink a day for women, and a regular and thorough exercise program. What must be said is that it's every bit as important to develop physical fitness as it is to develop financial fitness, especially if we are to enjoy those extra years of life medical science seems to be providing us. I can't think of an insurance policy as valuable as the longevity insurance you can provide yourself and your loved ones by taking good care of yourself.

15

Retiring Early and Worry-Free

MAYBE it's our increasing disenchantment with the rat race and the urban environment in which it's run. Maybe it's our growing conviction that time really is more valuable than money. Maybe it's finally sinking in that those extra years on earth we're being promised by medical advances give us the time to live a leisure-rich second life. Whatever the reason, the idea of retiring early—as early, in some cases, as fifty-five, but no later than sixty-two—is catching on across the land.

There are more people in their fifties crisscrossing the United States in RVs today than ever before. By the thousands, couples in their fifties are moving out of high-priced urban homes in tax hell states and into low-priced dwellings on lakes and lagoons and along golf courses in tax haven states. At an airport in Boca Raton not too long ago, I ran into a retired couple in their fifties who were about as happy as any two people I'd ever met. I first noticed them as they hopped out of a beautiful, brand-new Mooney, a very fast single-engine airplane. They appeared to radiate well-being, and I could almost feel their energy. When I asked where they were from, they both laughed. "We're not from anywhere anymore," the husband said. "We sold our house and bought this plane and now we just fly all over the country. I wake up every morning and say to my wife, 'Honey, where would you like to go today?' Maine? St. Louis? The Pacific Cascades? We're having the time of our lives."

THE COST OF EARLY RETIREMENT

How much would it cost you to live if you were to retire today? The answer is different for everyone, but experience has shown that the amount would be between 70 and 80 percent of what you lived on before retiring. Why that much less? Principally because most people don't retire until and unless they've gotten rid of high-interest burdens such as mortgages, equity loans, and credit card balances that can account for 20 to 30 percent of their yearly budget. Another reason might be a move to a less expensive dwelling. A third reason is that in retirement, with earnings from work diminished or eliminated, most people are that much more cautious about their living expenses.

While the specific amounts needed will also vary from case to case, we find that in "spending dollars"—the amount of money left after income taxes are paid—most retired people do quite well on $30,000 to $50,000 a year.

Where does all that money come from? When you retire at sixty-five, you expect about a third of it to come from Social Security, a third from a pension plan—either yours or your employer's—and a third from savings. (At the high end, only a quarter of the amount would come from Social Security.) Early retirement is a different matter. You can't claim Social Security benefits until you're at least sixty-two, and if you take money from your retirement plan before age 59½ you'll incur a 10 percent penalty in addition to the tax. The penalty, created by Congress years ago, seems outmoded in terms of today's early retirement realities, but unless the law is changed, we'll all have to live with it.

Despite these restrictions, retiring early is very feasible when you plan ahead.

SAVING FOR RETIREMENT: HOW MUCH? HOW SOON?

The question I'm most frequently asked, perhaps, is, "When do I have to start saving for retirement?" My answer never changes. The earlier you start, the less you'll have to save per day, per week, or per year. Age twenty-five, when retirement is the last thing on your mind, and when suggestions that you actually save for that far-off day would probably be greeted with derisive laughter, wouldn't be too soon. If you wait until your forties, you'll be in trouble, and if you wait any longer than that you'll have to save so much that you'll have no funds left to enjoy your preretirement years. One working couple without a dollar in savings came to me after calculating that to meet their retirement savings target they'd have to bank $2,000 a month. "Steve," the husband complained, "we'd have to close down our lives." I recalculated their needs and showed them how they could meet their goals by putting away $1,200 a month. Even this figure seemed impossible to them until I showed them how to do it.

Knowing that most people find it easier to save weekly rather than monthly, I suggested that they write a check to themselves every Friday night, and deposit it in a bank account. Because there are 4.35 weeks in a month, I calculated that they could reach their $1,200-a-month goal by saving $275 a week. But where would the money come from? When we analyzed their budget, we found that they were spending a small fortune on minivacations and clothing. By setting a limit on both categories rather than eliminating them altogether, we were able to squeeze out the money without completely depriving them. Today, they're writing a lot more checks to names like Fidelity, Scudder, and Twentieth Century, and a lot fewer checks to Saks, Bloomingdale's, and American Express, and they consider their added peace of mind a more than adequate trade-off for the few pleasures they've given up.

The late thirties, forties, and early fifties are a particularly difficult age to save for couples with children as well as parents who are no longer working. Not for nothing is this age group known as the "Squeeze Generation." They're squeezed from one end by the children, who need to be put through college—we've seen what a horrendous expense that can be—and at the other by one and perhaps two sets of parents who waited too long to save for *their* retirement and now need their children's help. Under these conditions, it's virtually impossible to put away the kinds of sums you'd have to save to fund a retirement program—and yet the longer you wait the tougher it gets. Advance your retirement schedule by five or ten years and without an early start on a retirement savings program, the burden becomes unbearable.

Here's a typical comparison of how much you'd have to save each year to retire with $500,000 in ten, fifteen, twenty, and thirty years. Although your overall goal should be my "magic number," 12 percent, we'll be conservative and use an overall 9 percent return in a tax-deferred account. All amounts have been rounded off for the sake of simplicity.

Years	Annual Savings	Total Saved	Total Appreciation	Grand Total
10	$32,900	$329,000	$171,000	$500,000
15	$17,000	$255,000	$245,000	$500,000
20	$ 9,800	$196,000	$304,000	$500,000
30	$ 3,700	$111,000	$389,000	$500,000

It should be obvious from the above table why it's so important to get started early enough to let the magic of compound interest work in your behalf. Not too many of us could find a way to put away $32,900 a year for ten years.

But in determining how much we need to save for retirement, and when we need to begin, our calculations don't stop here. We need to know, as well, how much the $500,000 will be worth in terms of future spending power.

Years	Amount	Projected Future Spending Power
10	$500,000	$307,000
15	$500,000	$241,000
20	$500,000	$201,000
30	$500,000	$120,000

To keep pace with inflation and maintain your future spending power at current levels, you would need to increase your annual contributions by 5 or 6 percent. If you start your retirement savings program at thirty, for example, you'd pay in $3,700 the first year, $3,900 the second year, $4,150 the third year, and so on.

If you want to retire in your fifties, it generally means that you're going to have to save 20 to 30 percent more than you would if you planned to retire at sixty-five. I've seen at close range what an impact on daily life that level of savings can have. One of my great uncles and his wife were Rhode Island plant growers with one consuming dream, to retire to Florida in their fifties. Everything they did was done with that dream in mind, down to the kind of food they put on their table. Some people considered them parsimonious, but most everyone who knew them admired them for their single-minded effort to create the nest egg they would need to retire early and spend the rest of their lives traveling. They ended up doing precisely that, selling their Rhode Island business and buying a motel in Hollywood, Florida, which, together with their nest egg, gave them the income to live the good life.

HOW TO CALCULATE YOUR RETIREMENT NEEDS

To calculate how much money you'll need when you retire, you need three numbers. The first is how much you would require if you were to retire today. The second is your personal inflation rate—which ought to be fairly close to the national rate, since at retirement you've supposedly gotten rid of those high-interest costs and are watching your spending. The third is the number of years until your retirement date.

Let's suppose you've decided that you could live comfortably on $45,000 gross in today's dollars, and that you plan to retire in fifteen years. Assuming your personal inflation rate is 6 percent, you would need $108,000 gross in fifteen years to live as you're living today.

A personal inflation rate of 6 percent is probably an optimistic figure. It's true that our debts diminish as we age, but that's about the only good part of growing older. The one thing we can virtually count on in later years is an increased need for medical care; as we've seen already, the cost of such care in this country is skyrocketing. In a 1990 study, A. Foster Higgins & Company, a New York employee benefits consulting firm, found that the cost of health care plans for 2,000 employers it surveyed had increased an average 46 percent over two years. Should this shocking trend continue, the cost of providing medical benefits would reach $22,000 per employee by the year 2000. A national health care program may be the only answer, and we're told that one is coming, but I'm not counting on it in my retirement plans. If and when it does come, you and I as taxpayers will be footing the bill in any case—further adding to our cost of living.

One other benefit I'm not counting on very heavily in my retirement planning is Social Security. I'm sure it will still be around, but the benefits may pay for little more than groceries and utilities. Nonetheless, it's helpful to know how much your Social Security benefits will be when you retire. To find out, call the Social Security Administration at 1-800-937-2000 and ask for the pamphlet called "PEBES," *Personal Earnings and Benefits Estimate Statement*. When it arrives, fill it out and send it back to Social Security. You'll get it back with a calculation of how much money you'll receive, adjusted for inflation, when you reach retirement. There is no charge for this service.

The other number you'll need is how much money you can anticipate from your pension. This is a tricky number, especially if you're job-hopping as so many people are these days, which means that you're not hanging around long enough to get vested in any corporate pension program. Or you could be working for a corporation that's attempting to squeeze pension benefits or cut its pension program out altogether. There are those who say that pensions will eventually go the way of the buggy whip. A federal court has already ruled that a corporation doesn't have to pay your health benefits once you retire, even though it had once agreed to do so. No one can predict what will happen, but you can't rule out the possibility that when it comes to a pension you'll be on your own. It's for this reason that I urge you yet again to contribute as much as you possibly can to any pension or 401K plan at work, if your employer has one, to urge him to set one up if he doesn't have one, and to find a job with an employer who does have one if your current employer won't budge. The 401K plan is the pension of the future: it's your money, and it's tax-deferred.

If you're self-employed, of course, you'll want to have a Keogh Plan. Either way, Keogh or 401K, the money should be in an investment program compounding at an average of 9 to 12 percent a year.

Pension, profit-sharing, 401Ks, and SEPs should be the principal means by which you save retirement dollars. Personal savings and investments would be next. Social Security would be third. Fourth is your home or a business, either or both of which you might wish to sell on retirement.

Retirement ought to be a time in your life when you're paying interest to no one and are receiving interest payments instead. If you're serious about retiring early, you should cut back on luxuries so that you'll have the money to pay off most or all of your debts—mortgages, home equity loans, car loans, credit cards—by making extra payments. As we've seen, the savings in interest, particularly on home loans, can be tremendous. Call your lender to make sure that prepayment is okay under your contract and doesn't involve a penalty. If you're contemplating early retirement, but are currently buying a house, negotiate a mortgage with as brief a time span as possible. A fifteen-year fixed rate mortgage is a great idea at any time if you can afford the slightly higher payment, but a virtual necessity after age forty-five; thirty-year loans are for the young and financially strapped. And don't take out an equity loan unless you absolutely have to.

Here are eight simple rules to live by if you want to prepare for an early and worry-free retirement:

1. Start saving today, not tomorrow.

2. Use tax-deferred investments to stall off Uncle Sam.

3. Set your total return goal at 12 percent.

4. Calculate your own needs and what it will take to achieve them, using the methods outlined above.

5. Count on Social Security to pay for no more than 20 percent of your bills—and, if possible, only for your groceries and utilities.

6. Spread your money around. Never put all your eggs in one basket.

7. Even if you're in good health and have terrific genes, don't count on working until you're ninety-two. Assume the worst.

8. If you're fortunate enough to have a retirement plan, make sure you understand your rights, and how your plan operates. Call, write or visit your plan's administrator when you have a question or concern. And read a free government booklet called *Your Pension: Things You Should Know About Your Pension Plan*. You can get a copy by writing

Pension Benefit Guaranty Corporation
2020 K Street, N.W.
Washington, DC 20006-1806

BRIDGING THE GAPS

Retiring early, you or your spouse, or both, might well need a part-time job or a small business to supplement your income while waiting for Social Security and pension dollars to kick in—unless, that is, you're exceedingly rich. It should not be a full-time job or a business that requires full-time attention, because if you're working full-time you're not retired. On dozens of occasions, seniors have told me that they're retired but have a full-time job to make ends meet. All these people have done is to substitute a menial job for their lifetime work.

If you're self-employed and have the kind of business that permits you to work as little or as much as you want, you're that much better off. My goal at fifty-five will be to work very hard about half the year, and not nearly as hard the other half. Having changed careers once already, I'm so confident that I'll make changes again that I'm already adjusting my lifestyle, just as I did in planning my move from accounting to television and radio.

Your part-time job can be a few hours a day, a few days a week, a week or two each month, a few months a year. If you're living in a resort area, there will probably be peak seasons when employers will be thrilled to have someone they won't be required to employ throughout the year.

Many retired people today spend a few months a year in locales where they can get part-time work in order to pay their bills and avoid disturbing their nest egg. Most enjoy it as a means of staying mentally and physically active, but one of the most sobering stories I've ever worked on concerned former executives in their seventies and even their eighties who were working part-time at McDonald's not because they wanted to but because they had to. If ever there was an inducement to take a $5 bill out of your wallet every night and drop it into a kitty, this was it.

There's a difference between having enough money for security and enough money for enjoyment; you don't want to be thinking each time you spend a hundred dollars that you're jeopardizing your future and will wind up as a burden to your children.

Mark Twain once said that the perfect life is the one in which you die on the day your money runs out. The contemporary translation of that idea can be found on the stickers pasted to thousands of RV bumpers: "We're spending our children's inheritance." We all want to provide for our loved ones, but nest eggs are meant for those who worked so hard to create them. Nothing saddens me more than the sight of senior citizens running to the bank each week to get the interest in their accounts posted in their passbooks. They no longer understand—if they ever did—that money in and of itself is without value, that it becomes valuable only to the extent that it can help them enjoy life. Part of that enjoyment may come from helping others financially. But a good portion of it ought to come from rewarding themselves for all their years of hard work. They can't see that the end of their life is approaching and it's time to hop on a plane to Hawaii. Unless there's a balance between security and pleasure, retirement makes no sense.

Historically, three-quarters of all Americans stay right where they are when they retire. They want to remain in their homes, close to their children and friends. The desire to stay where you've set down your roots is an understandable one, but it doesn't always make the best economic sense. If—a big if—you can find a retirement setting that gives you the kind of life you want and is also more affordable than your current life, you're way ahead of the game. And if you had the foresight to buy a vacation home in that setting, as I recommended in chapter 8, you're ahead that much more.

RETIREMENT PLANNING FOR WOMEN

In an old comedy routine, Alan King would read a long list of obituaries, each of which invariably ended with the words, "Survived by his wife." It's true. Women outlive men by about six years on the average and the gap is widening. By the year 2000, most women will live to eighty and beyond, and be more active than women of that age were a generation before. The question is, how will they pay for their extended time? The question becomes even more complex when we consider the changes in modern women's life-styles. Many women are now opting for careers over marriage; some women even prefer parenthood without the sanction of marriage. Then of course there are those who are either widowed or divorced. No matter what the circumstances, women stand an 85 percent chance of living out their "golden years" alone and most don't and won't have enough income to live on comfortably. According to the U.S. Census Bureau, the average income for women over sixty-five is $6,300 a year. Could you live on $125 a week for the rest of your life?

Put this problem to women in their thirties and forties and many will reply, "My husband's providing for me." Perhaps, but marriage licenses don't include financial guarantees. Consider Alice, who married Joe at nineteen and hasn't worked since. When Joe died in 1989, Alice, then fifty-five, assumed she would collect Social Security survivor's benefits. Wrong. Alice doesn't become eligible until age sixty and even then she'll collect only 70 percent of such benefits; full benefits kick in only at age sixty-five.

And then there's Karen, whose husband Jim, an executive with a Fortune 500 company, retired at sixty-five. Their golden years together were wonderful but brief; Jim died at seventy. When Karen asked Jim's pension administrator to change the records and put her name on the checks, she got the shock of her life. No more checks. Years before, she learned, Jim had elected to accept a higher lifetime payout for himself by waiving his rights to survivor's benefits. Karen never knew what he'd done, because until 1984, no consent form was necessary.

In most cases, unfortunately, surviving spouses usually collect only half their husbands' pension benefits, which can be reduced still further by the amount they're being paid by Social Security.

When it comes to pensions, a woman must take the initiative well before the fact and find out exactly what rights and survivorship benefits are available to her in the likely event that her husband predeceases her. And then she must protect those benefits. Every woman who might depend on survivorship benefits has the right to request a summary pension plan description from her husband's employer. Divorcees may also have survivorship rights, but this is usually determined by the court. Whatever her status, a woman owes it to herself to get her rights in writing.

And what about single women? Staying single has now become a more acceptable life-style for women, but with independence comes a greater need for retirement planning. The rule of thumb is the same for the single person that it is for couples: In order to enjoy the same standard of living, retirees need 70 to 80 percent of what they spent during their working years. If you're used to $40,000 a year, you'll need $28,000 to $32,000 in retirement just to keep pace. Since Social Security will provide only a fraction of that, you can't start too soon to do some serious planning—and saving.

As virtually automatic as my own planning has become, I know that I like to discuss the specifics with my wife before coming to any decisions. Single people don't always have the comfort of talking over their decisions with someone close to them. They should. The National Center for Women and Retirement Research offers a step-by-step program designed to help women identify and achieve their financial goals. Dubbed PREP, for Pre-Retirement Planning, the program was developed by Dr. Christopher Hayes of the Southampton campus of Long Island University and Dr. Jane Deren from the National Council on Aging. PREP seminars are held around the country. Workbooks containing detailed financial questionnaires accompany the program and when properly completed provide a complete analysis of your financial strengths and weaknesses as well as an assessment of your financial knowledge. To find out about a PREP program in your area, contact

PREP Project
Long Island University Southampton Campus
Southampton, NY 11968
(800) 426-7386

In addition to the seminars, PREP has several publications available.

No matter how well we take care of ourselves, none of us can fully control how long or how well we'll live. We can, however, control our finances to the point that we can be happy and secure until our final days. If we plan well and soon enough, and stick to our plan, we can also retire early and worry-free.

16

The Ultimate Makeover

I never had any formal education about how to manage money. Being a CPA doesn't automatically train you to do it. Everything I've learned has been self-taught. Anyone who follows the prescription laid out in the previous chapters can do what I did. An hour a week is all you need to stay on top of your financial affairs.

If you're too insecure to plan for yourself, it's imperative that you get help. There are thousands of Certified Financial Planners (CFPs) and Chartered Financial Consultants (ChFCs) out there, eager to help you. Your job, if you go this route, is to pick a good one. That's not difficult to do; you'll know by the end of the first interview.

The best financial planners will explore your career and family and retirement objectives, and won't move on until they're absolutely certain that you and they understand what you want. The planners you'll want to avoid will attempt to sell you financial products from the outset—you need this annuity or that limited partnership—the sale of which will give them a commission of 4 to 8 percent.

When you're in the corporate world, it's often possible to arrange intensive financial planning seminars offered by organizations like the Kemper Insurance Company. I conduct "live" financial planning seminars for audiences of TV stations across the country, as well as organizations like the Soap and Detergent Association and the Mechanical Contractors Association of America. The leaders of these groups realize that their members are hungry for information about their money and financial security. But no sales pitch accompanies my seminars, and I recommend that you steer clear of those seminars whose organizers are trying only to sell investments. Financial seminars should be educational in nature and without obligation to buy. Many free seminars offered by brokers and planners do utilize a soft-sell approach, and I see no harm in those. The sponsors understand that in order to gain clients they have to educate them first. But there's no pressure, and no sales tactics are applied, and every seminar you attend will make you that much better informed.

But whether you get help, or do it by yourself, it all comes back to how you want to live your life, and to that single guiding principle I mentioned at the outset: that money is nothing more than a tool to help you achieve your dreams. Whatever decision confronts you, whether it involves earning or savings or spending or investing money, if you make each decision with this principle in mind, very little can go wrong. You may make a wrong turn or two, but eventually you'll wind up precisely where you've always wanted to be.

The soundest financial advice I ever received was also the most basic: "You make your plan, and you work your plan." As noted in chapter 1, it came from a Wall Street financier. Henry Stites was a multimillionaire who lost all his money in the crash of 1932. Tempered by that experience, he spent the rest of his life counseling others on how to avoid financial pitfalls.

The most basic advice I can give you is to decide how and where and with whom you want to spend your life, and then use money to fulfill those dreams. Life becomes exquisitely simple when you know exactly what you want and what it will take to get it.

As long as I've been in this business and as many people as I've met, it constantly amazes me how often people get away from the basics, or fail to act on what they know. They know what an IRA is, but they fail to set one up. They know they should set aside the equivalent of three to six months' income for emergencies, as well as a small amount each month toward their retirement, but they spend the money wastefully instead. They know they should arrange without delay for health and life insurance, but they put the matter off.

The time for such indecision is past.

THE PARTY'S OVER

There's almost no one in the field of economics who doesn't suspect that some big monster is lurking just over the horizon, a panic worse than the Great Depression. Whether that monster surfaces or doesn't, no one denies that we have boiling problems in our society that are going to spill over into all corners of American life.

When I was in school, a high-school dropout was virtually unheard of. Today, 30 percent of young Americans are not graduating from high school. In some states, as many as 45 percent fail to graduate. When 30 to 45 percent of the populace is on the street, without a high-school diploma, working for the minimum wage—if they're lucky enough to be working at all—turning to drugs out of frustration with life, and unable to afford medical care, you have a very unstable society.

Thirty years ago, we had indigents in our society, but no such thing as a homeless class. We have such a class today, and it's growing every year.

Inexorably, we are becoming a society of haves and have-nots, and the resentment of the have-nots deepens with every passing year. That's why an increasing number of homes in upper-class neighborhoods have "Armed Response" security signs on their front lawns. That's why some wealthy people, wary of kidnappers, won't permit pictures of themselves or members of their families to be displayed or published. That's why Jerry Dunphy, the popular Los Angeles TV anchorman, got shot through the side of his Rolls Royce and why he'll never drive a Rolls again. That's why the Los Angeles freeway shootings began. Such episodes are mere items on the evening news or in the morning newspaper until they involve someone you know. A business friend of mine, John Reisenbach, who syndicated my television show, returned to his Greenwich Village apartment with his wife at 11:30 P.M. one evening in 1990 to discover that his telephone was out of order. Needing to set up an appointment for the following morning, he went out to a pay telephone to call a colleague named Larry Schatz, another good friend of mine. As they were talking, Larry heard a voice say, "Gimme the money, man, gimme the money, man." And then he heard three shots. John's body was found not far from the phone booth.

I happen to be one of those who believes that the man who fired that gun, whoever he might have been, did not begin life with the desire to steal or kill people. A prosperous, humane society educates and creates opportunities for all of its citizens. Two hundred years after the ratification of the Constitution, all men and women are still not created with an equal chance to gain a decent life in the United States.

But the problems afflicting the country today are not confined to the underprivileged. The American middle class, as well, is in the throes of a shakeout period. When it's over, hundreds of thousands of astounded Americans who didn't save and who piled up debts they couldn't handle will have been cast to the side. In 1990 some 750,000 Americans filed for personal bankruptcy. By 1995 it's projected that one million persons will do so. That's about 1 percent of society's "taxable units," and a 1,000 percent increase over twenty-five years ago.

Recall that the average credit card debt of an individual declaring bankruptcy is $40,000. Most consumer credit counseling organizations are so busy these days that persons seeking help have to put their name on a waiting list. One counselor told me recently that a family whose circumstances she'd reviewed had $67 a month left over for discretionary spending and savings.

One of the symptoms of the widespread sense of economic frustration in society is the tremendous increase in gambling in recent years. Inexpensive air fares have enabled people to fly to Atlantic City or Las Vegas or even Deadwood, South Dakota, where they bet their savings on the dubious proposition that they will beat the odds. Those odds are nothing compared to the odds that confront the millions of people now playing the lottery in forty-four different states. In my home state, Florida, where the jackpot can reach $25,000,000 or $30,000,000, I've seen people invest a third of their weekly disposable income in lottery tickets. The odds of winning anything are one in thousands, and of winning the jackpot, one in millions. It's not for nothing that lotteries are known as "the tax on ignorance." One in thirty-three Americans today—3 percent of the populace—qualifies as an obsessive gambler.

WHAT WENT WRONG?

The problems of these people and others with similar, if less extreme, financial difficulties, can't all be ascribed to their own failings. To some degree, the difficulties stem from forces over which they have little or no control. One of these is surely discrimination, not as bad as it was before civil rights legislation made it illegal, but still a major impediment for blacks, Asians, Hispanics, and the foreign-born. Sex discrimination remains a problem, as well; although the gap is closing on many fronts, women are still paid far less than their male counterparts in many occupations.

Another complicating force is the inexorable advance of science, which produces benefits for all of us but has its downside as well. Robotics and computers, for example, are creating magnificent economies of production but diminishing opportunities for humans. When I was a young CPA at Price Waterhouse, the firm had a client named Pervel Industries, a manufacturer of plastic fabric for raincoats. In one year, Pervel's accounting department shrank from forty to six people, as a computer took up the slack. Multiply that example several hundred thousand times and you get some idea of the shakeout that is occurring in American enterprise.

Throughout the book, we've dealt with some of the other forces that are making life in the United States so uncertain for so many people: deflation, "downsizing," and loss of employer–employee loyalties, resulting in the replacement of older workers for younger ones. There are, without question, many causes of these various problems. But all of them share a common denominator: money. Money well spent solves problems and fulfills dreams. Money poorly spent destroys dreams and lives and, eventually, a society.

Naturally, the first obligation of any government is to defend the country it governs, and no sensible person can argue the need to maintain a vigilant and strong defense. But a case can be made that in seeking to defend our way of life on all fronts throughout the Cold War we have so badly neglected our internal needs as to make our society vulnerable to collapse from within.

Astronomer Carl Sagan points out that since World War II, America has spent roughly 10 *trillion* dollars on the Cold War, defense, and war itself. Ten trillion dollars is enough to buy the United States itself in *today's* dollars—

all of our assets and possessions excluding the land. Ten trillion dollars is ten thousand billion dollars, or ten million million dollars, or $50,000 for every one of the men, women, and children who have inhabited the United States since World War II ended in 1945.

Could this tremendous outlay of mostly nonproductive goods and services be part of the root cause of our growing deficit load and social decay? Of course it could. The same good sense that makes us acknowledge the need to defend ourselves must also acknowledge what the Cold War has cost the Soviet Union, which, as this is written, is in a process of disintegration. Nor can we fail to note that between 1945 and 1990, Germany and Japan, the two countries that didn't have to worry about the Cold War or Korea or Vietnam or the Middle East, have risen from the ashes of World War II to become the financial superpowers of the world.

But to blame the decay in our society entirely on the Cold War would be a cop-out. The problem goes deeper than that, to an economic fundamental that is violated only at tremendous cost.

THE HIGH COST OF HOCKING THE FUTURE

The most serious problem in the United States today is that we are living beyond our means. The symptoms of the sick society I've described above originate from a common germ: The determination of government, business, and individual Americans to spend for the present at the expense of the future.

The case against personal debt has been made many times and in many ways in these chapters. Let me turn briefly to the economic behavior of corporations and the government during the last ten to twenty years, and to the ways in which this behavior has jeopardized you and me.

All corporate America has seemed to care about in this interval is quarterly earnings. Too many corporations have put virtually nothing aside for the future, nothing into the development of products. Consider high definition television (HDTV), the coming thing in big screen TV. The definition is so clear it looks like a window. You almost want to reach out and touch what's there. When HDTV becomes available, Americans are going to throw their old TVs on the dump and spend billions of dollars to buy the new sets. Will American corporations get these billions? They should have, because HDTV was developed in the United States by American engineers and scientists. But once they'd developed it, they weren't willing to spend the money required to sell it, and so they sold their technology to—guess who?—the Japanese. Why wouldn't the Americans spend the money? Because they were more concerned about showing a quarterly return higher than the previous quarter, and expenses of any kind, even for research, diminish the size of current profits.

In 1955, 90 percent of all record players were made in the United States by

American workers. In 1991, 1 percent of all record or CD players are made in the United States. Same problem. In effect, the United States got out of the stereo electronics business.

In Japan, where most stereo and other electronic equipment is now made, the economic growth rate is three times what it is in the United States. With half the population of the United States, the Japanese have twice the number of engineers and scientists. Countless products, like the HDTV, are invented in the United States but manufactured in Japan. The Japanese sell to us three times what we sell to them.

In 1992, when the European Economic Community becomes a reality, it will be like three more Japans coming "on-line." Many of the 320 million people in the countries that make up the EEC already have a better standard of living than we do. If our corporations continue to emphasize short-term profits at the expense of long-term growth, our standard of living will continue to drop, we will become the world's employees, tenants, and servants, and the American dream of a better life for our children will be gone.

Nothing in recent American corporate history suggests that we will be able to turn the tide that has been running against us in recent years. To the contrary, just about everything points to the contrary, and no better example exists than the case of those infamous junk bonds sold by securities dealers throughout the United States to unsuspecting investors. Some were used by small, worthy companies with no access to traditional sources of capital to raise the money they needed to survive and prosper. Most junk bonds were used for takeovers. Takeovers almost never produce substantial economic good, except for the takeover artists who sell off the assets of their new acquisition and pocket the profits. In the process, however, they bankrupt the acquisition and destroy thousands of jobs as well as the capacity to produce products that could redress the trade imbalance and generate taxes that might help offset the deficit.

Recently American business has found a new means of expressing self-interest and shortsightedness, one that is potentially the most damaging of all. It has begun to sell off America, piece by piece, to the highest bidders: Japanese, British, Dutch, French, German, Canadian, and Arab interests. The Japanese alone are buying one thousand businesses a year at a total tab of $70 billion. They now own close to 4 percent of corporate America—one company out of twenty-five and 8,000 companies in all. One in ten American banks is Japanese-owned and -controlled; in California it's one in four.

The exact amount of United States property currently under foreign ownership is not known, but the best estimates put it at somewhere between 10 and 15 percent. That isn't an alarming level. In fact, the money paid for American assets by foreigners has actually helped our balance of payments. What *is* alarming is the rate at which such transactions are increasing: 50 percent a year, a double every two years. Should these transactions continue to occur at the same or even a similar rate, foreign interests will control a majority of the corporations, banks, and commercial buildings in the United States within ten to twenty years. In 1988 a team of Yale economists, projecting the rate of acquisitions by West Germans and Japanese, predicted that these two groups alone would own 35 percent of all American industries by 2008.

On the surface, that might not seem to be a problem. The industries will be functioning, people will be working, stockholders will receive dividends, and taxes will be paid. But when ownership and control of the assets in this country pass into foreign hands, all sorts of problems can result. Profits can be exported for investment in other countries, rather than reinvestment in the United States. Foreign owners can bring tremendous pressure to bear on Congress to pass measures that aren't in the long-range interest of the country as a whole. Even without direct pressure, film studios owned by Japanese might hesitate about making motion pictures dealing candidly with World War II. As not only our means of production and our financial institutions but our resorts and golf courses and even our clubs come increasingly into foreign hands, a serious loss of national pride could result.

WHAT BAD GOVERNMENT IS COSTING YOU

The same fiscal shortsightedness exhibited by America's corporations is reflected by the largest corporation in the world, the United States government, in which you and I have our greatest investment by far, and whose management of its affairs profoundly affects the quality of our lives.

When the government runs up a deficit, it's you and I who pay for it. When it prints money to pay its bills, the money in our savings accounts loses value.

No one ten years ago could have imagined a federal deficit as large as it is today, growing at such a stupendous rate. In 1975 the total public debt was $533 billion; in 1990 it was $3.2 trillion, about six times bigger in 16 years. During the eighties, the public debt increased an average 13 percent a year. Each person's share of the debt in 1975 was $2,500; by 1990, it was $12,800. In 1975 interest on the public debt was $32 billion; in 1990 it was $240 billion. After the outbreak of hostilities in the Middle East, some economists were predicting that the 1991 deficit alone would total $500 billion. That's half a trillion dollars—almost as much as the entire public debt accumulated during the country's first 200 years of existence.

The greater the government's debt and the more money it prints to service that debt, the more money you and I have to pour into Social Security to pay for those whose benefits must keep rising to meet inflated costs. When I first started working part-time for my uncle in the early 1960s the FICA tax deducted from my wages was in the neighborhood of 3 percent. In 1991, the FICA tax, the most burdensome we pay, was 7.65 percent on the first $53,400 of earnings—nearly $4,100 a year for many Americans, and growing. Our employer is required to match this amount. When we're self-employed we have to pay both halves as employer and employee, amounting to 15.3 percent of that $53,400—and Congress anticipates raising the base even higher. By the year 2000, it's estimated that the maximum FICA tax will rise from today's $8,170 combined employer–employee limit to $13,265 a year.

The graying of America isn't lessening the burden. In 1960 there were just over five workers to support one Social Security beneficiary. Today, it's just over three workers per beneficiary. By the year 2020, slightly more than two workers will support a single beneficiary and the system will be bankrupt or close to it. No wonder so many of us under fifty wonder if we'll ever collect a dime.

Currently, the most insidious part of this problem, as I suggested in chapter 13, is that all federal and state taxes are computed on the FICA dollars deducted—dollars we never even see. It's not for nothing that FICA is known as the most hidden tax we have.

If you are a successful self-employed person living in a high-tax state, you're paying 15.3 percent in FICA taxes, 28 percent on dollars earned in the top federal bracket, and as much as 11 percent in state taxes, an effective rate of nearly 46 percent on earnings.

Roughly 20 percent of our federal tax dollars today go toward paying the interest on the deficit alone, and next year it will be more. Indeed, the greater problem is not the size of the debt but the rate at which it's increasing.

Every year, the Tax Foundation in Washington, D.C. sets a "tax freedom day." That's the day on which we stop working to pay our taxes and begin to work for ourselves. Each year, that day falls later and later. In 1991 it was May 8. Think of it: For more than four months, we work to pay our taxes. Only then do we begin to work for ourselves.

It's important to realize that at least 80 percent and perhaps even 90 percent of our tax dollars are not only well directed and well spent, but flow back to us in the form of protection, sustenance, and benefits. We could not exist as a people without a government that makes the system function. But anyone who has ever run a business, no matter how small, or even attempted to balance a household budget knows that what turns profit to loss and comfort to privation is the 10 to 20 percent of our resources or revenues that don't get managed well.

You and I can live by the book, doing absolutely everything we should—saving money, avoiding debt, investing well, staying insured—and still be ruined because the corporation in which each of us is a shareholder is so poorly managed. If the system breaks down, the value of our homes and other investments will plummet because no one will be able to buy them.

It's absolutely imperative, therefore, that this corporation be run the way it should be. It's not being run that way now. If it didn't have the ability to print money, it would have already gone belly-up.

Our federal government has a wretched accounting system, perhaps the worst of any major organization in the United States. It was never properly set up in accordance with generally accepted accounting principles, and no one seems to care about the multitude of "on-budget" and "off-budget" items that make it virtually impossible to keep track of our tax dollars. In 1989 the American Institute of Certified Public Accountants recommended to the President and Congress that the federal government appoint a chief financial officer who would report clearly to the people where the nation's money was coming from and where it was being spent. To date, nothing seems to have come of this report, and the largest financial organization in the world is unable to give an audited accounting to its shareholders—you and me.

If this slipshod management of national assets and treasure continues, not only will the national debt continue to increase, and our taxes with it, it's entirely conceivable that the value of the dollar will fall so low that it will erode whatever wealth each of us has invested in savings accounts, real estate, and the financial markets.

If Congress doesn't deal effectively with a perennially swollen budget, if inflation and interest rates are allowed to climb out of sight, then the ranks of the jobless and the homeless will reach the proportions they did in the 1930s.

HOW WE CAN MAKE AMERICA OVER—AND WHAT WILL HAPPEN IF WE DON'T

Do I believe the scenario I've just described will transpire? I would say the odds are one in three that it will. Technically, that makes me an optimist, but considering what we're talking about, those are truly terrible odds.

I have absolutely no desire to be the next prophet of gloom and doom. I'm an optimist by nature. But I'm a realist by training, as well. I wouldn't bet on another Great Depression, but I wouldn't bet against it either—and I'd be a fool if I didn't prepare for the worst-case scenario.

In society, you're either well off or you're not. You either have economic freedom or you don't. Each of us has to decide on which side of the fence he or she wants to be. When we ignore the future and focus on the present we're tempting the fates. None of us can afford to be unprepared for the worst, because if it happens and we're not prepared, we could be joining the ranks of the homeless.

During the 1990s I urge you to invest up to one-quarter of your savings on the international level in order to spread your risk and not rely on one country and one currency.

I also urge you to get politically active, not only to encourage the candidacy of good people but to let your representatives in Congress know, in writing, that you won't give your vote to anyone who supports a growing federal deficit. During my seven years as an unpaid lobbyist in Washington,

D.C., I discovered that 200 letters on a Congressman's desk could move mountains. It saddens me immeasurably that the American voter doesn't understand this simple concept.

It's time we reach fiscal adulthood. We *will* have to bear the burden of new taxes if we are to keep our national deficit from becoming a mudslide that obliterates everything in its path. Higher income taxes won't do it. The revenues will have to come from national sales taxes or value added taxes or higher gasoline taxes. At the same time, spending will have to be brought under control, and we must offer incentives to "unemployables" to get back to work and off the government dole.

To me, the next five years are the most critical. We must watch financial events not on a monthly or weekly but a daily basis. It's critical, as well, that we stop thinking exclusively about ourselves and start thinking more about those around us and society as a whole. We should give as much of our spare time as possible, and money as well, to organizations attempting to help the less fortunate among us. And if we're disgusted with politicians, the government, and the system, we should stop complaining and act. As Ted Turner says: "Lead, follow, or get out of the way."

Recall John D. Rockefeller's answer when asked how much money was enough. He answered: "Just a little more." As humorous and revealing an answer as it is, it's also a prescription for misery.

The eighties—the "Me decade"—left us with homeless people, greater unemployment, a threatened environment, worthless junk bonds, thousands of bankrupt savings and loans, and hundreds of thousands of bankrupt families.

Everything I'm hearing suggests that Americans want no more of this. Money isn't everything, and winning isn't the only thing in a balanced and fruitful life. May the nineties be remembered as the decade when we got our priorities, our lives, and our country back on track.

Acknowledgments

My dream of publishing this book was made possible by creative, wise, and supportive friends and associates, including Randy Pace, Leonard Gross, Michael Bennahum, Dan Farrell, Sterling Lord, Paul Aron, Roger Lipton, and the trustees, faculty, and staff of Bryant College. Their contributions of wisdom have been immeasurable.

My career in television and radio was advanced and enhanced by the counsel, guidance, support, and friendship of Ernie Baptista, Jim Bagaloff, Glenn Graham, Mike Nicolella, Burt Kantor, Steve Caminis, Ellen Margaretten, Phil Beuth, Walt Gilbride, Paul Bartishevich, Steve Clements, Karen Cadle, Ed Busch, Tom Kennington, Ray Manzella, Jake Winebaum, Al Primo, Lois Brown, and scores of station general managers and news directors from coast to coast. Thanks a million!

My sincerest thanks to the many thousands of viewers and listeners who follow my work and write to me, cheering me on. Your support gives me the courage and strength to continue for many years to come. Helping you to improve your lifestyle, wealth, and happiness is my ultimate goal.

This book is dedicated to my darling wife Frances for all her love, support, and encouragement, and for making my dreams come true.

INDEX